Koko Ken

The Story Of A Spina-Bifida Baby Boomer
(w/a tad bit of fiction about non-fiction people)

By

Ken Martinez

Order this book online at www.trafford.com
or email orders@trafford.com

Most Trafford titles are also available at major online book retailers.

Printed in the United States of America.

ISBN: 978-1-4669-6197-5 (sc)
ISBN: 978-1-4669-6196-8 (e)

Trafford rev. 04/24/2013

www.trafford.com

North America & international
toll-free: 1 888 232 4444 (USA & Canada)
phone: 250 383 6864 ♦ fax: 812 355 4082

From the 'pen' of Mathew McKeegen:

Like the cover of the book 'Koko Ken' by Ken Martinez says, this is a story of a spina-bifida baby boomer w/a tad bit of fiction about non-fiction people. It tells about his first memory, a chicken foot on a downtown sidewalk, and his last in the book, Maryann and the skilled nursing facility where they both lived. It tells of early TV & other passions, street food, be-bop, and George. You'll meet Ron, Ken's best friend of over fifty years, and other friends.

Ken wasn't to live past six weeks. Now, Ken tells that he 'wants to see a hundred [years old] and to know that he is a hundred and wants to get to the punch and cake on his own at his centennial birthday party.' At sixty-one (as of this writing) he has plenty of time to write at least one sequel and maybe a book of poetry or two. I think that a lot of people would appreciate if he did just that.

I've included a few things that friends and people that have known Ken have said or written about him:

Ken Martinez is a very interesting and talented writer. He writes about being handicapped but you wouldn't know it until he tells you or when he walks. He's a very positive young man.

~Peggy King, The Oakland Tribune

Ken Martinez is a real renaissance man.

~Bakersfield Californian

Ken, after I read your stories, I was sad. I wish that there was more to read.

~Lisa,. Bella Vita Skilled Nursing, Activities.

I like your stories, ('TV And Other Passions' and 'Harold And Maude And Jr.') Ken. I didn't stop reading till the end. I recognize a couple of the people, I think. I think it will make a good children's book.

~Ruth Donahoe, Childhood Friend

Hi Ken

I really like these stories—I can't wait to read the rest! Here at Microsoft we do a lot of document reviews . . .

Early TV & Other Passions, it's amazing how they bring back my own memories of early TV (since I used to watch Romper Room, Captain Kangaroo, etc). Good job, Ken

The story 'Harold And Maude And Jr. was very delightful and at the same time it brought feelings and memories of my own childhood and times long lost.

Was 'Poem Of A Poet' actually written in 1971? Your poem was very unique and insightful . . . . yet sad. It made me feel like there's something that the poet still needs to get out . . . because he is suppressing a need to be understood

'The First Story About Cory' had a darker and real-life feel than previous chapters. I found myself reading several passages a few times so that I could absorb it more. I then began to look at the actual page as it was formatted and then it dawned on me. Even if I could not read a word of English . . . just looking at the page as it is laid out is artwork in itself. If I seem to have a hint of understanding . . . it's because I am Avant Garde ☺

I really liked Coy's Poem.

Greg Cottingham

It's me again, Mathew. With all of this said and done, when you read Ken Martinez's 'Koko Ken', you'll be happy with him, sad with him, and certainly, you'll fall in love with him.

Mathew McKeegen

I am Kenneth Martinez's mother, and I would love to share with you a little of the life this outstanding man has lived.

Kenneth was born with spina bifida which meant, at that time, he would not live over 6 weeks. Our friends and relatives started praying for this baby and now Doctors say that it is because of a "higher power" that he is alive today, and is, without doubt the oldest person living with his severity of spina bifida. It has not been an easy life for Ken with many surgeries, at times not being able to walk, suffering lack of body controls. But he never let it get him down. He would say "this is the way I am, and I do what I can in the way I can do it."

Ken has many special talents:

1. He is a gifted musician—playing the piano, guitar, and other instruments, and composing many songs. While in college he was asked by many of the churches in the area to provide music for a service—playing the piano and singing. He developed a music ministry, earning money, canned goods, etc. for many churches and homeless missions.

2. He developed a love for cooking and worked in a number of restaurants as a chef. He wrote an article for a food magazine which was published. One of his favorite pastimes was to watch cooking shows on TV. He also enjoys the History and Discovery Channels. Because of his personal "taste" for foods, he sometimes has a little trouble enjoying foods prepared by other people—even in restaurants. Ken also has worked as a telemarketer, being good at it.

3. Ken has also had a talent for writing. While in college he was on the college newspaper staff and had his own satirical column.
Several newspapers asked him to write an article about living with spina bifida. One of his greatest goals was to write his life story.

4. Ken has read all 33 Steinbeck books and owns 32 of them—2 are first editions. Ken has traveled around the world and has been to 32 countries.

5. Ken has a great sense of humor and can be VERY funny and entertaining. His father has this talent.
Ken's life motto has been "I never fail—I just find my limits." We are proud to call him our son.

Vi Martinez

DEDICATION

Because of all your encouragement, love, and
tzddean (It's Gaelic), I dedicate this book to . . .
. . . well, you know who you are.

CONTENTS

TO MY READERS, A BRIEFING

*S**pina bifida** (Latin: "split spine") is a developmental congenital disorder caused by the incomplete closing of the embryonic neural tube. Some vertebrae overlying the spinal cord are not fully formed and remain unfused and open. If the opening is large enough, this allows a portion of the spinal cord to protrude through the opening in the bones. There may or may not be a fluid-filled sac surrounding the spinal cord. Other neural tube defects include anencephaly, a condition in which the portion of the neural tube that will become the cerebrum does not close, and encephalocele, which results when other parts of the brain remain unfused. This is Serious Business which, at this time in medical history, often caused death.*

In the early '80s, recovering from my divorce, I moved from Ketchum, ID to Palo Alto, CA to live temporarily with my sister, Sherri Martin and her family, the other Martin's until I found an apartment. My Brother-In-Law was and still is a pastor in the Nazarene church. Also attending the church were two college mates of mine and the Martin's, Jan and Doug Burgesen and their two children who (the two kids, Stevie & Cindy, not Doug & Jan ☺) could not pronounce 'Uncle Ken'. It came out 'Koko Ken'. Soon, very soon, I was known to the whole church (even to my niece Jennifer and my two Nephews, Todd & Gabe) as Koko Ken, which gave me the title of this book.

About five weeks after I completed most of these stories, I gave them, on a flash drive, to a friend, Rick Barnes to read. He liked some and his comments on the others were, 'They don't do anything for me.". I respect his opinion. Since then, I've added to the stories, but not for him. I came up with some dialog that I think adds to the characters and makes these stories more interesting.

Ken Martinez

You and I are about to play a game. It is easier than 'Where's Waldo'. In this briefing to the book, I mention different characters without naming what stories they appear in. It's up to you to find them. In the following paragraphs are clues.

These characters are my children. These characters are me—with some allowances. I've lived a very fortunate life, experienced things many people wouldn't. In 1950 my parents were told that I wouldn't live past six weeks because of a birth defect called Spina-Bifida, a spinal disease. As of this writing, I've lived sixty-one years.

My family and others have told and urged me to write my story. I've tried and I feel that I've failed. I felt that I was either boring the reader or bragging. I finally came upon this idea—write a series of stories, (or chapters), some in first person, highlighting different periods and adventures of my life.

I've added a bit of fiction to make the stories a tad more interesting. Let me explain. 'Porter St' actually happened two years before I wrote it. The dialog is, well, a lot of it is long forgotten. I had to reinvent some of it. Even the ladies, *Elaina* and *Miss Duck* (without the drugs but with the alcohol) in other stories are part me, to a point. George is my nephew's daughter's toy dog whom she talks to. George is also me in one of my stories.

I've put people's personalities that I've known into different setting. Joey is me during my drinking days and also a friend that I don't remember his name. Joey is mainly me with some Alan, a good friend from my past (Ty is 100% Alan except for his ministry).

The homeless shelter in Memphis is actually a nursing home in Phoenix that was probably the worst place that I have ever live. Because of my handicap, I now live in assistant living facilities. I had to leave one assistant living facility, at no fault of my own, and was placed at the nursing home for two months until they could place me into another home. Basically, I was homeless.

An overnight hitchhiking trip from Buhl (near Twin Falls, ID.) to Hayward, CA is written, in 'Travels With Chuck' as a weeklong hitchhiking trip from Memphis to Nevada and then, a bus ride into Idaho. The stops and sights are actually some adventures I had in these towns and cities over a forty year period

Another thing that I fudged about is my ex-wife and stepson. She wouldn't appreciate me using their real names. I know that he wouldn't care. He was four when I got married but I liked what I wrote about a 2½ year old so, I included it here. I purposely do not talk about a divorce. I tell people, in my real life that if

2

she was here to give her side of the story, only then will I talk about it. I still live up to that.

I mentioned about Ty/Alan. Well, my best friend of over fifty years is Ron. He is mentioned as Ron among other names in these stories. His characters are all respectable, just like he is.

While writing this, I let people read what I wrote. I've gotten comments from, "I liked 'The Porcupine; the rest didn't do anything for me." to, "When I finished reading this, I wished I had more to read." You decide. So, kick back and read & hopefully, enjoy.

~Koko Ken

EARLY TV & OTHER PASSIONS

As I'm typing this chapter / story, I am sprawled out in my recliner with my laptop braced on my thighs with my 60's and my Jazz music playing from my laptop. I have a glass of iced tea on a coaster from the old western town Hangtown, CA, sitting on my end table. My studio apartment is a mess but I'm happy. I'm in writing mode, working in a situation that suits me except for the dust storm outside. I'm enjoying the fork lightning when I look to see it. Usually I'm too late and I only hear the thunder. It's afternoon.

My life began in Bakersfield, Ca. and then, to Wasco, CA. in 1950. I was born in Mercy Hospital, a Catholic hospital. I wish I could say 'in a log cabin in the backwoods of Kentucky' but I wasn't. I was born with a birth defect — spinal-bifida. I wasn't expected to live past six weeks. A month later, I moved from the hospital to Wasco. As of this writing, I am sixty-one years old. Because I wasn't expected to live, I was baptized a Catholic by proxy. I have always been a Protestant, a member of the Nazarene church. Fourteen month later when my sister was born, the nurses, CNA's and other aides asked how long I had lived. If I hadn't been so young, I'd be impressed that they remembered me. "Oh, he's in the car with his Grandmother." Mommy answered. Daddy brought both of us in. I got quite a bit more attention than both my Mommy or my Grandma did.

Mommy and Daddy were the youth directors at our church plus Mommy taught piano almost eight hours a day, six days a week. Daddy had a full time job for Caterpillar Tractors. This pretty much amounted to two full time jobs for each of them. By the end of the Sunday service, they were both dreadfully worn-out. The people in the church knew this and would often take me to their home, calling my parents in the early afternoon, telling them where I was at. My parents never worried about me and were grateful for the rest. I was told that my 'babysitters' were grateful to have a happy baby who seldom fussed, for the afternoon. This was life in a small church town in the early fifties.

My main babysitters, and soon, my sister Sherrill's were Auntie Mayo and six-teen year old Vernice. Years later, in the 90's I found out that Auntie Mayo's name was Annie Mayo—but she was as good as an aunt. Mommy and Daddy and I had moved back to Bakersfield and Vernice went to our church even though she and her husband, M.A. lived in Shafter—20 miles away. I would joke with her saying that Mom, my ex-wife, and her were the only ones to see me naked. Vernice used to give me baths in Wasco.

The first time that I saw a TV set was when I was two or three. The TV antenna was very TALL. We went to some friends' house for dinner and to watch wrestling. On the screen was lots of 'snow'. Because of it, my parents had no idea what was going on. Our friends were used to it. At the age of two or three, I had no interest in wrestling.

I was walking with braces and crutches by the age of three.

In my third year, I rode in a parade on a small Caterpillar tractor on a flatbed truck with another boy on his tractor. I do remember the parade but I don't remember what it was for.

That year, my Daddy built a sandbox for my sister and I. We would pretend that we were on a desert island looking for buried treasure. I don't know how we knew about buried treasure—maybe from TV. My folks have a picture of me and Daddy and we're each reading a magazine. I was two or three. At the time, I considered myself a bright child and a TV picture is worth a thousand words but a thousand words can tell the truth.

For my third birthday, Daddy built me a slide. It had shelves for some of my 'curios' (toys). Mommy was worried on how to entertain my party guests but they spent almost more time on the slide than I did that day.

One Saturday morning, speaking of Daddy, we were downtown. I saw a chicken foot and leg on the sidewalk. I pulled my hand from Daddy's and started running down the street. Daddy soon caught up with me and asked where I was going. "I want to see the chicken with only one leg." I told him.

Later that year, we moved to the city of Sacramento in '53 when I was three. The next year, two very important events happened—Edna Odem, my neighbor and my first love (I was four) and secondly, Kindergarten. I have no idea how old Edna was when we moved next door but, not too much older than Sherrill or me, I think. Her Daddy owned the house that we rented and eventually bought. We also went to the same church. Their house had a circular driveway and a bay window in the breakfast nook. Because of these, I thought that they were rich.

Outside the city was the Raines' farm. Jessie Raines, a teen in Daddy and Mommy's church teen group was another one of my loves. I would day after day fantasize about her—well, as much as a four year old could fantasize. Sometimes, when Mommy and Daddy went out of town, Sherrill and I would stay at the Raines'. Jessie taught us how to churn butter in an old fashioned butter churn and how to slop the hogs. She gave or made me a cloth zebra that she had named Lucky Jeff. I kept Lucky Jeff until I lost him in '80. Until then, he sat on my bed with Zippy, a toy cloth monkey and another cloth monkey that I made out of two socks with nylon stocking stuffing. I still have the monkeys. In 2012 Zippy and his friend both turned fifty-three. Zippy is still my best friend. In another few pages, I'll tell you why.

In Sacramento and the SF Bay Area, Winky Dink aired on Saturday mornings at 8:30 a.m. My sister and I would lie on the floor, watching Winky Dink. Mommy bought the 50 cent 'magic drawing screen' which included crayons. The 'magic screen' was a large piece of vinyl plastic that stuck to the TV screen via static electricity. At a climactic scene in every show, Winky would arrive upon a scene that contained a connect-the-dots picture, a cliff, or other disasters. He would then prompt us kids in front of the set to complete the picture, and the finished drawing would help him continue the story. We would draw a bridge to cross, a river, an axe to chop down a tree, or a cage to trap a dangerous animal.

At the end of the show, we were told to draw a character with which Jack Barry (the host who would soon host many other game shows) would have a conversation.

Romper Room on San Francisco's KTVU was geared for preschoolers. I would watch it because my younger sister loved it and also, because it was TV. The show would start and end with a Mattel Jack-In-The-Box playing 'Pop Goes The Weasel'. When they had their cookies and milk, our Mom would bring us cookies and milk so that we could be a part of the show. Miss Nancy would look into her Magic Mirror. A kaleidoscope effect, almost a phantasmagoria, hallucinating, psychedelic effect would happen and poof! The glass and the back of the mirror had disappeared. Miss Nancy was looking right at each of us saying, 'Romper, bomper, stomper, boo. Tell me, tell me, tell me, do. Magic mirror, tell me today, did all my friends have fun at play?' And, then she'd say, 'I can see Sherrill and Maryann and Kenny and another Kenny.' Then, the Jack-In-The-Box would play 'Pop Goes The Weasel'. It was probably in 1980 that my niece, Jennifer was on Romper Room.

Other shows we enjoyed watching were Howdy Doody, Captain Kangaroo, American Bandstand, all while sitting on the living room carpet.

I remember watching wrestling with no snow on the screen. I think that the reason was that Haystacks Calhoun went to our church. His finisher he called 'The Big Splash' where he would drop his 600+ lb. body over his opponent. He dressed like a hillbilly, wearing bib overalls. I don't remember Haystacks Calhoun from church but Daddy told us that he loved kids and that he was a gentle man. He did like Sherrill and me, my Dad told us years later when we were old enough to understand. Wrestling wasn't as brutal or as cartoonish in those days as it is now. The only other wrestler that I knew by name was Gorgeous George.

On another note, I remember one Saturday when my folks were cleaning the church (one of their churchly duties), Daddy took both Sherrill and me out back of the church. There was a shack on fire. I was fascinated and watched it burn for what seemed like hours.

In '54 we moved to Hayward, CA. My family tried several churches like Hayward Nazarene and San Leandro 1st Nazarene church where Wayne and Wanda pastored. They pastored the Wasco church when we was there. We settled into the East Oakland Nazarene church where Daddy became their music director, Paul Miller was teen director. Paul became big in the church internationally. Because of the church, I knew many notable people. We lived at the end of a court, a two lane driveway full of duplexes. At the street was a huge oak tree. We only lived here for a year so I don't remember much about Hayward. Also, I don't remember watching TV there at all.

Mommy would walk me back and forth the two or three blocks to school. I can remember my Grandpa Martinez, when he and Grandma came to visit, walking me to school and walking my sister and me to a small neighborhood store around the corner, He would buy us popsicles, penny candy or candy bars for a nickel. My only memory of first grade was the big, round reading table. One day, after I read my paragraph, I fell asleep. I don't embarrass easily but, I was so embarrassed. The teacher let me sleep until it was my turn to read again.

The Martinez custom has always been to open Christmas gifts on Christmas Eve. After Mommy dressed us in our jammies, she found some excuse to keep us in our bedroom. Sherrill (In fifth grade she started going by Sherri.) and I shared a bedroom. Daddy stayed in the living room. When Mommy, Sherrill, and I went back into the living room, under the tree was full of presents. I figured it out. Looking at Daddy, I started to laugh. "You're Santa Clause, aren't you?" He only smiled. My sister wasn't too happy. I ruined it for her.

Sherrill and I would often go to the oak tree and would hunt and dig for buried treasure. When my cousin Joey came to visit, he would help us hunt, with the treasure maps I would draw. He never did take us serious. We would find nails and such but never any treasure. I don't know if I remembered the sandbox.

On the way to the East Oakland church was a huge two or three story house with a huge circular driveway. Whenever we passed by it, my sister and I would sing the hymn 'Mansion Over The Hilltop.'

It was at that church that I met Ron Geiss. He was really too young for me to notice. He was two years younger than I was. In a few years and from different churches we would meet again at children's summer camp in the Santa Cruz mountains. We would become lifelong friends.

I don't know why but one of the teens gave me a Jerry Mahoney dummy. Paul Winchell was a ventriloquist on TV and Jerry Mahoney was his dummy. Paul Winchell was also a Christian.

The summer of '55 my family moved to Richmond, CA. on Shane Dr. I started calling Mommy and Daddy Mom and Dad when I was in second grade. If I forgot and didn't remember to do this, the boys at school would tease me. To this day, My Dad, my two Uncles and my Aunt call my Grandma and Grandpa, Mother and Daddy.

My sister and I had a black and white terrier named Miss Midge and Davey Crocket hats. Dad got Miss Midge from the pound. Soon she had puppies and then, we had six dogs. One summer we went to Yosemite for a week. Dad took Miss Midge somewhere to stay. She never came back. I had three other dogs in my life — a toy dog that when I turned a switch, it would roll across the floor, an air dale, and a small puppy that would grow to over two feel tall at the shoulders. (See my story 'Harold and Maude and Jr.' and the picture at the end of 'Street

Food, Be-Bop, and Geo.') We also had a kitten named Snowball, a turtle, and two hamsters. The hamsters lived in a cage in the kitchen. In the cage was a box where they would move their wood shavings into to make their beds. On day, I put my hand into the cage and into the box. One of the girls bit me. It didn't hurt much but it sure surprised me.

Our neighbors had an Airedale. It was the biggest dog I had ever seen in my life. His name was Dugan. At first, my sister and I were afraid of it but soon Dugan would come to retaining wall separating our yard and put his paws on top of it and let us pet him. He never came into our yard and Dugan never let us go into his.

My sister and I were business entrepreneur wannabes. One Sunday after church, my folks had a guest pastor and his wife over for Sunday dinner. After dinner, Sherri and I decided that we'd form a charity and set out, door to door to collect money for the poor children who couldn't go to summer camp in Europe. A couple of hours later, we returned, bragging to our parents and their company. My parents were embarrassed and made us take the money back. An hour later, a lady brought us back home, insisting that she didn't give us any money. We insisted that she did. She was told to keep the money by my parents since it would be hard to find the donor.

My second grade love was Coleen. She sat next to me. One day a man and lady came to my classroom at school. My teacher, Miss Light introduced them to the class as Coleen's parents. She told us that he was in the Navy and that he was being transferred to Pearl Harbor in Hawaii and then she showed us where Hawaii was on the map. I felt sad that he was leaving his family to go overseas. Coleen kissed me on the lips and then she hugged me. I felt lightheaded and like I was going to faint. I was in ecstasy. I had never felt this that before. Then, she got up out of her chair, walked over to her family, took her Mother's hand and they walked out of the door. Then it hit me—I would never see her again. I felt like crying. It was very hard not to.

Third grade and September we moved from Shane Dr. to an apartment atop the church in downtown Richmond. The church was a good place to grow up, not only for the spiritual. The church had many alleyways and rooms and hiding places. It also had a bell tower with a room at the top of the stairs for many of our club houses. We formed and disbanded many, many clubs. Again, the church was a good—no, a great place to grow up in and play in.

North on the church property was the parsonage, across the street was the Alta, a supermarket where I bought eight oz. bottles of coke, candy, and pieces of sugarcane. The freeway runs behind the church. On the south side was MacDonald Ave., a busy main street. Across the street on MacDonald was a Blue Chip Stamp redemption store. In the window was a fuzzy cloth monkey with plastic ears, face, hands, and shoes. Even though I knew that I was too old for it, I fell in love with it. I even named it Zippy. Sometimes I would go in to the store and they would let me hold Zippy. I wanted Zippy for my next month's birthday. It was o.k. with my Mom but my Dad pretty much said 'No!' without saying 'No'. On my birthday, I got my favorite dinner, tuna casserole and Zippy.

Years later, I was looking at elementary school class pictures. Secretly, I was looking for Edna. She was sitting on the row below me, one person to my left. I noticed that she was black. I didn't know that in second grade.

During third grade, Sherrill and I entered a school talent show. All of her life, she was a magnificent singer. She sang 'Over The Rainbow' from the 'Wizard Of Oz' and I did a magic act with tricks I borrowed from a magician friend at church. My Dad was his assistant most of the times. Also on the bill was a boy from my class that was a terrific piano player named Perry. He announced that he had broken his arm (he was in a sling) and would have to play with only one hand. After he played, and. headed back to the stage wings, he took off the sling before he was off stage. People snickered. A girl did the Mash Potato dance to the song of the same name (I think!). I repeated my *Magic Career* in Sunday school one time.

A few months later I went to the hospital for observation. My sister and my folks came to see me every night and we'd play hearts. Even though I saw them every night, I was lonely. Zippy became my best friend.

About every one or two days a week I took arts and crafts at the hospital. The room was in the basement past the kitchen. I made a cloth monkey out of two socks with nylon stocking stuffing. I never knew if it was a boy or a girl and I never did name it. One day on the way to arts and crafts the head cook was out in the hall.

"What are we having for dinner tonight?" I asked.

"Turkey!" he said.

"Save me a leg, o.k.?" He didn't answer.

"I'll see you tomorrow." He said.

That night when I took the cover off of my plate, there was a huge turkey leg.

That same year, The Huckleberry Hound Show with Pixie and Dixie and Yogi Bear premiered and in '60, the Flintstones premiered, both in prime time TV. Other favorites were Saturday morning's Sky King, Bonanza, and the fifteen minute The Liberace Show co-staring his violinist brother George and his mother sitting in the front row from 1951 reruns. Liberace always had a candelabra on his Steinway piano. Another show in reruns was The Little Rascals. Their dog, Pete (Pētē) was an American Pit Bull.

Joanne Sullivan was the pastor's daughter. It was at her house that I first tried Grape Nuts, still my favorite cold cereal and watched The Beverly Hillbillies for the first time. On Joanne's birthday I was invited to her birthday party. I was the only boy she invited. I wasn't her boyfriend. I was her boy friend. One year, Montgomery Wards opened a new store on MacDonald. At their grand opening, they had games, pony rides. Hotdogs and quart sodas were a nickel a piece. We went together. Even though it was my treat, it wasn't a date. Cynthia Martin was my church love.

Cynthia would tease me and flirt with me. Her brother Jeff was in 'love' with my sister. Cynthia knew how I felt about her. On my twelve birthday, I finally asked her out for dinner. She lived about a half an hour away and it was raining hard. My Mom dropped us off at Kirby's restaurant. She ordered Chicken Fried Steak. I had never tried it but I ordered it. I loved it and still do. The restaurant was at a shopping center. After dinner we decided to walk around. The rain had stopped. At Woolworths we bought caramel corn and had our pictures taken together—a strip of four pictures for a quarter

Another boy in love with my sister was Mario. She was in third grade. Every day Mario would call her. After a while, she would lay the phone down and go to her room and read a comic book. When she came back, he was still talking. I don't know if he ever caught on.

Mario's Dad owned a pizza parlor. He invited my family, as his guest to the parlor for dinner. We had never eaten a pizza before and we didn't know what to order. Mario's Dad suggested peperoni pizza. When he brought it to the table, we had no idea how to eat it. There were no knives or forks. We were very green.

One Sunday night we had a special guest speaker from Japan. He was in the group of planes, possibly the leader who bombed Pearl Harbor. After the war, he became a Christian. He was there to give his testimony and tell his story. After the service, we went to the Parsonage for punch and cake. I talked to him some and he gave me his autograph. I can't remember his name or what I did with his autograph.

One 1958 day, my parents, still church youth directors but for all the church's youngsters and teens arranged to get tickets for the grade school kids to the King Norman Show, a local children's Saturday morning show. One of its attention grabber was to bring the loudest clapping and yelling youngsters up on the set to pick a letter from the words King Norman. Behind the letter was a cash prize. Before the show, I and probably everybody in the audience noticed that the letters weren't on the board yet, just the amounts. I memorized the highest number but I wasn't picked to go onto the set. The one who was picked chose a low dollar amount.

My bed was in the TV room. I would go to bed in my parent's room and before they went to bed, my Dad would walk me, half asleep to my bed. I never remember a thing. In 1961, my sister and I would ask our parents to wake us up if the Lennon Sisters sang Sad Movies (Make Me Cry) on the Lawrence Welk Show. They did but the song wasn't sung very often.

At the end of the long hallway by the TV room was the phone bench. Above it was an opened window with a shelf. On the shelf was a bowl of plaster fruit. One night while my Dad was walking me to bed, stopped, sat me on the bench, gave me a plaster banana and told me to eat it. Time after time I would slump down. Finally I had the banana at my lips. I dropped and broke it. The next morning I didn't remember a thing.

Granada Junior High School in Richmond lasted only about six weeks. I moved to West Pakistan that October. My passion was science. I was selected to read the barometer every day and it was there that I noticed my first pair of boy's black patented leather shoes. My favorite TV shows that year were:

After church, Ed Sullivan and Bonanza.

Mondays: To Tell The Truth and Pete and Gladys on CBS, ABC's at 8 pm The Rifleman, and at 9 pm, The Danny Thomas Show, again on CBS.

Tuesday nights: Dick Van Dyke and Dobie Gillis on CBS.

Wednesdays was church night. 8:30 pm was Top Cat and then Hawaiian Eye on ABC.

Thursdays: Ozzie and Harriett, Donna Reed, and The Real McCoy's, ABC.

Not much was on Fridays but Leave It To Beaver and Have Gun Will Travel. Sherrill and I had to compete with Mom and Dad to watch Have Gun since Lawrence Welk was on at the same time.

I have and have had other passions but these first twelve years were very dear to me.

HAROLD AND MAUDE AND JR

This story is about me, not a Harold. I just liked this title so, I'm Harold.

U p into the mid 70's, music was good. On the same station, I could hear Mike Post. Alice Cooper, jazz, and then, Waylon Jennings, That's when I started liking Waylon. I like the others, too. I didn't listen to the radio much back then, except in the car going to and from work. Years later, Amy Grant, a gospel folk singer and Alice Cooper would be golf partners many times in Pro/Am golf tournaments.

This story starts in '62. I just wanted to mention the people in the preceding paragraph. In 1962 Harold, his sister and his Mother left on Halloween day to join his Dad in West Pakistan, 60 miles south of Ralwapindi, 120 miles north of Lahore, to a construction colony named Baral, on the Jhelum River. The town was about a mile long and a mile wide with a brick wall around it's parameter. The construction project was a dam. It was to be the largest earth filled dam in the world. There were two companies on the project, American and British.

On the trip over, they spent two days each in Honolulu, Tokyo, and Hong Kong. Their first city to see in West Pakistan was Karachi (culture shock!) but soon, they learned to love the country as well as East Pakistan and India.

After a bloody civil war, East Pakistan won her independence and became the country of Bangladesh in 1971.

Harold and Maude and Jr. were all seventh graders. The company school was small and there was no cafeteria. The Protestant church met in the multi-purpose room, The three of them met eating lunch outside on the lawn.

"Hi! I'm Harold."

"And I'm Maude."

"That's an old lady's name!" said Jr.

"It is NOT! And what is your name, may I ask?" scolded Maude.

"Jr." answered Jr.

"Jr.?" Is there a Senior?"

"Yeah, my Dad."

"Do they call him Senior?"

"His name is Richard, Richard Dilborn."

"And you are Junior Dilborn?"

"You can just call me Junior for now, maybe for always."

It took a little while but soon, the trio became fast friends. At the weekly movie, both Harold and Jr. would hold Maude's hand. There was no jealousy. The movies were shown outdoors for free. It was a big decision whether to watch the movie or to watch the shooting stars overhead.

"We should form a club." said Jr.

"What kinda club?" they asked.

"An explorers club. We could explore the mountain (It was actually a big and long hill.) on the other side of town and there are some tunnels on this side. We could get some flashlights or candles. And, we could charge dues from *new* members for candles and snacks."

"That sounds fun!" cried out Maude, clapping with a big, broad smile.

Harold smiled, too. "Dues for the new members is fine. I'm glad that we don't have to pay."

"Don't you get an allowance? "asked Jr.

"Sure I do!"

"What do you spend it on?"

"It's none of your business but I spend it on my favorite foods. There's not much more to spend it on."

"Which are?"

"Packaged marshmallows, four boxes to a package, sixteen marshmallows to a box, a box of small bags of Fritos with toy dinosaurs in each box, and bowling alley French fries."

"What's your favorite dinosaur? Mines a Stegosaurus."

"I don't know the name of it. It has a long neck and tail and has four fins. I have two Stegosaurus that I'll sell you for a rupee (21 cents)."

"Deal!"

Maude stood up, "I have to get home."

"Me, too." said Harold. "Let's meet at the main gate Saturday at 10 a.m. and head up the mountain. We'll bring sack lunches." There was horse riding for a rupee an hour at the gate, too.

"We'll see each other at school tomorrow."

By 10:40 a.m. Saturday morning, everyone was there. Jr. had forgotten his lunch and had to go back home so that his Mom could make him one. He had never made a lunch in his life. As it turned out, he had the best one of the three

They named the 'mountain' Mount Barney, named after Barney Rubble — their favorite Fintstone. About a third of the way up Mount Barney they found their headquarters — a cave about three feet deep. A large rock inside formed a table.

I don't remember who but someone made the motion, "We need to name our club. Anyone have an idea?"

"Well," someone said. "if we can get Oliver or any other Brit to join, we could call it 'The International Explorers Society'." They all agreed.

"Is there any other business?" Maude asked. "We should elect a president. I nominate Harold."

Jr. frowned. "Oh, alright! I second it." The motion was passed.

"Anyone else have anything else to say?" asked Maude.

Harold continued. "Yeah! I was reminiscing about this all morning. October 14th was my 12th birthday. I took a girl out to a real nice restaurant, just the two of us for dinner. Well, my Mom drove us and picked us up two hours later. We both had chicken fried steak. It was my first date and it was my first chicken fried steak." smiled Harold.

Jr. gave Harold a surprised look. "Your first date? I've been on lots of dates. It's no big deal."

"You're full of crap, Jr.!" scolded Maude. Harold gave Maude a hard, surprised look. He was taught that 'crap' was a bad word.

Harold continued, "It was at a shopping center. I bought her caramel corn and we had our pictures taken together in a photo booth for a quarter. Her name was Cynthia. Her brother Jeff had a crush on my sister. We all went to the same church. I was going to order coffee to act grown-up but I thought that that would be pushing it—besides, I wouldn't know how much sugar or cream to put in it." Harold and Maude laughed.

Still laughing, "That's funny, Harold" said Maude, still laughing a little bit. "We do some fun things, don't we? They should make a movie about us, 'Harold and Maude and Junior', huh?"

"All that talk made me hungry. Let's eat!" said Jr.

The weeks passed. The explores explored. Christmas came. Harold's Mom and Dad took some palm and other branches and put them in a large brass vase. The family made some paper ornaments and strung popcorn for the 'Christmas tree'. (Their container of furniture and other things hadn't come yet.) The whole things looked like an upside down Christmas tree but they loved it. Harold's Dad hung a star from the ceiling. It was one of the nicest Christmas' that they ever had. Harold received a live monkey that one of his Dad's employees had given to his Dad. The employee was a Pakistani named Aaron Zeb. He looked just like Jerry Lewis and was just as funny. Harold named the monkey Zebby, after Aaron Zeb. When told this, Aaron told Harold's Dad that he was named after a Holy man and if word came out about the monkey's name, Harold, and maybe the whole family could be legally killed according to Muslim law. Harold quickly renamed Zebby to Jeri (The monkey was a female.)

The family also had a puppy named Rupee. Rupee used to slide around on the slick, waxed kitchen floor. One morning, Jeri was tied too her leash and the two were in the patio. Harold's Mom saw Jeri reach out with her hind foot (almost a hand) and pull Rupee's water bowl to her. Harold's Mom went outside and pulled the dish back were Rupee could reach it. Jeri reached out again and pulled the dish back to her. This happened two more times. The last time that Harold's Mom pulled the dish back, Jeri pulled it back to her, tipped it over, dumping the water out and then she sat on the dish with a 'So there!' look on her face.

The next year, a few weeks away a small mall, the new commissary and the ten lane bowling alley, and a movie theater were built. 'The International Explorers Society' membership hadn't grown a bit except a sixth grader that insisted we call him Sargent Swigged wanted to join. They decided that he was to weird so, he was turned down. Oliver did join and his one rupee membership dues was paid but the next day his Mother said that playing on Mount Barney was too dangerous, too many snakes and scorpion so, he had to quit the Society. (*Pakistan has a snake called a Krait. It can grow to a meter in length. It's bite feels more like an ant sting than a snake bite. They say that if you're bitten by one, just lie down and make yourself comfortable before you die. If you are bitten at night when asleep, you are dead before you wake up to feel the bite.*) Oliver was told that the society had already spent the dues that he had given them — for licorice but, the candy story was kept secret.

Two days later, Maude saw a scorpion on the headquarters table. It scared her so much that she said that she refused to go back there.

Their new headquarters was a grassy 8'x20' alley bordered on the right by the commissary and the back and left side by a tall brick wall. After this commissary was built, the Protestant church moved into the old commissary building on the other side of town. The Catholic church in the old mess hall where employees ate until their families arrived. Everything on the American side was red brick. The whole town was red brick. The Brit side was all gray stucco with high ceilings.

"Man, this is just like Top Cat's alley but with grass." said Harold. "I used to read Top Cat comics."

"I used to read the comics *and* watched the TV show." bragged Maude.

"Me, too." Harold said.

"Me, too." added Jr.

"We should have nicknames, too, like Spook or Choo Choo or Benny the Ball." smiled Maude. That idea was quickly voted down.

The society was put on hold for a while for no reason at all — it just was.

During the next few months, the movie 'The Great Escape' with Steve McQueen played (This became Harold's favorite movie of all time.), a new family with another seventh grader came from the States, and Harold found his second love, Georgia Post. She was the prettiest girl Harold had ever seen, blonde and, a *Ninth Grader*!

One Friday night, Harold went to a party and there was Georgia, more beautiful than he had ever seen her. It took him a long time but finally he mustard up enough courage to ask her to dance. While walking over to her, the song, 'Sea Cruise' finished. Harold asked her to dance and she smiled and accepted. The music started again—a slow song. Harold felt like he was going to faint. She took his left hand and put her right arm around his shoulder. After their dance, the impossible happened—she asked him for another dance, a slow song, 'Harbor Light's' by the Planters. Then, she asked him again! This time, it was Dion & the Belmont's 'The Wanderer'. Harold's dancing was awful. He looked like a cartoon character with its finger in a light socket. Harold was so embarrassed that he left the party. He couldn't face Georgia, and he didn't for several days. This 'romance' was over.

Harold made a new friend, another seventh grader at school—Jeff Di Gangi. Jeff had been living there as long as Harold but Harold was afraid of Jeff. Jeff looked like a hood. He had long hair with a duck tail. The two of them were in the International Boy Scouts together but like I said, Harold was afraid of him, so he avoided Jeff. Jeff's Dad, Skip worked in the same department as Harold's Dad.

One evening in late March, Harold's family was invited to the Di Gangi home. Harold, his sister, Jeff, and Jeff's brother, Mark spent the whole evening, except to come out for milk and cake, in Jeff's room.

"Hey, Jeff," asked Harold. "What do you miss about the States?"

"Real milk, not powdered."

In Jeff's room, Harold and his sister heard their first Beatles record, 'Please Please Me' sent over from England by Oliver's cousin. Jeff borrowed it to record on his Dad's reel-to-reel tape recorder. Jeff also taught Harold how to whistle with his thumb and middle finger.

That Spring, the 'The International Explorers Society' reconvened from their recess. Their new adventure was to explore the tunnels, the rain drain tunnels on the east end of the colony. The Summers brought, and still do, the monsoons, heavy winds and the winds bring heavy rains. The rain drains are quit necessary. Candles were bought and with the help of a flashlight, they were secured to the sides of the main and it's off shoot. They were secured every fifteen feet or so with candle wax. The expeditions were always exciting for the children. They met every Saturday morning. Jr. always remembered his lunch which seemed to be getting less fantastic as time went on.

One April Saturday morning, Maude let out a bloodcurdling scream from inside the tunnel. Harold and Jr. crawled as fast as they could to get to her. They found her looking out of an offshoot tunnel. On the other side of her, about ten feet away was a cobra, hood raised. The two boys took two of the lit candles and rolled then towards the cobra. Both were a direct hit and the cobra shuddered and slithered back down the other end of the tunnel. Despite the scorpion incident, they all decided to return to the cave on Mount Barney. No more snakes were seen but scorpions almost every day that they were on the mount. This, they took for granted. Maude didn't panic anymore.

In May, the rains and the winds came. School let out in late May for the summer. Each of the three's families took two week long vacations at different times. 'The International Explorers Society' took an unofficial summer recess until after school started — without a vote or discussion. In the three years that Harold lived in West Pakistan, he had seen the Taj Mahal three times, once inside, once, on it's backside, by train, and once by air. Other trips included Darjeeling in north eastern India where they saw Mt, K2, the second highest mountain in the world, and Kashmir, a region that is claimed by both West Pakistan and India. On trips to and from the Taj Mahal, they visited Bombay, Calcutta, and Dhaka, East Pakistan. On these trips, Harold's Dad would ask for chilled boiled water to be on the safe side. On one train trip in India from Darjeeling to New Delhi, the family had a sleeper compartment. From the compartment next door, they heard jazz. A jazz band had booked the two compartments next to Harold's.

Harold's Mom opened the thermos of water. It was boiling. "What to do?" they thought. A few minutes later, one of the band members knocked on their door and invited them over for tea and Cokes. A jam session began.

7 p.m., Friday Oct 11th, '63 Harold celebrated his thirteenth birthday a few days early. The 14th was on a school night. Thirteen eighth graders were invited — and came, one for each year. Harold's sister was there, too but she didn't count for a year. The night was filled with 21 questions, charades, and other games. Harold's Mother planned the evening. Their church, Nazarene, didn't approve of dancing but in spite of this, everybody had a fun time. Harold's Mom put the birthday cake on a chair while clearing a place for it on the dining room table. Rahana, a Pakistani eighth grade girl wasn't paying attention and she sat on the cake. Rahana was a clumsy girl with bad luck, but sweet. The students would talk and laugh about her behind her back. Harold's Mom had the foresight to bake two cakes. Harold

wanted and hinted that he wanted a book, 'The Complete Works of Edgar Allen Poe'. He received three copies plus the one from his folks. The party was over around ten. After everyone left, Harold's family each had another piece of cake before going to bed.

December was busier than last years. His parents both had birthdays that month. This year, the tree was aluminum with pink and powder blue Christmas tree balls and an angel on the top of the tree. The school and the church both had Christmas parties. On Christmas Eve, the church had a cantata (conducted by Harold's Dad), a short sermonette and communion. Christmas dinner was family and a visiting Nazarene missionary family. As a Christmas gift, they had brought a goose. Harold's Mom a turkey and Aaron Zeb gave the family a lamb. Harold loved the goose. The other family members didn't care for the lamb or goose that much. Harold and Sherrill refused to eat the lamb because of Bambi. Harold's sister's birthday was just a few days into January,

The society had its meetings every Saturday at ten a.m. at the cave without incident but, 'The International Explorers Society' was about to end, though. Jr. and Maude started seriously dating so Harold saw less of them. The two pretty much kept to themselves at lunch, usually going to either one's house. Jeff and Harold became closer friends. The next school semester, Maude was sent to a private school in Dublin, Ireland. Jr. talked his parents into letting him follow her. Harold missed the 'The International Explorers Society' very much.

Maude and Jr. both became cheerleaders in the tenth grade for the rest of their high school career. Jr. became known as J.R. As of this writing, the year is 2011, they just celebrated their 38th wedding anniversary. She has a PhD in archeology and teaches at some university back east. She's sometimes featured on different shows on the History Channel. Jr., or rather J.R. is on disability. He fell, climbing a rock near Yosemite.

So, now the adventures of Harold and Maude and Jr. come to a close.

Jr. was loosely portrayed by my good friend in West Pakistan, Andy, a cute, pimpled, and an always funny fella; Maude was portrayed by Cecilia, our first love. I don't remember their last names. Harold is still me. A movie titled 'Harold & Maude' was released by Paramount Pictures in 1971 staring Ruth Gordon & Bud Cort and has no similarity to this story except that I loved the movie and I love this story.

A Poem Of A Poet

By
Ken Martinez

The poet,
like all unknown poets
sat on top of a hill
        overlooking the city
(Known poets sit in their
 beach houses and write about mts.)

    This poet

would write about the city.

    This city
had a section called
      the Rider district.

    This poet
wrote poems and stories about
      the Rider district . . .
        making him
a writer & a poet.
He mostly wrote stories
but was called the poet
of
   the Rider.

   (triple space)

   AND before

Ken Martinez

The poet was the poet.

      (or the writer), he

played piano at a place

called HEDER'S, in the Rider-

             NOT

HEDER'S IN THE RIDER, but

              HEDER'S

located in the rider.

              -Ron played bass-
              -Kier   " "   guitar-
                 . . . and Bernie played traps-
              (they were paid $12.73
               a night)
               NOBODY knows why
                     73¢

And the poet became famous
as a piano player at

              HEDER'S

in the Rider.

              He was happy but poor
                    so
              he became the poet

                  of the Rider.
              He was still happy but poor
and the people left him alone-
not because he wanted them to
but because they wanted to.

While the poet of the Rider
sat on top of the hill (overlooking the city),
trying to think of something to write
                              (But he couldn't   ).
He saw a ladybug.

                         It was the same

                              ladybug
he saw the day before

                                   and

the day before that.

                              He knew
                              this
because the ladybug was caught in a spider's web

                                   and
was there the day before

                                   and
the day before that.

He set the ladybug free but
this act was useless because
the ladybug was already DEAD.
He gave the ladybug the name
                         Odessa
because she was lovely and he loved her
and she was a lady-
                              and, he
buried her.
He made a cross
                    out of two
                         sticks

which washed away
the first time it

                    rained.

It was all very silly
and stupid.

                He told ALL OF
                HIS FRIENDS about
                  the funeral'

He laughs at his stupidity
not knowing it is stupidity
he is laughing at
            BUT
everyone laughs
            So
he laughs with them
            So
as not to appear stupid.

                  Kier died

of a dirty needle. People say
it was an overdose, but
it was
of a dirty needle.
The group played as a trio

                  then.

            -Piano-
            -Ron played bass-
              . . . and Bernie played traps-
            (and they were paid $2.34
             a night more)
until the poet quit- because nobody want-
                ed to
hear just drums and a bass.

NOW the poet lives
In a beach house on the Pacific (ocean)
and writes about the mts.

     . . . mostly where
     Mt. Lassen is because
     he drove by there one
     day and that's the only
     mountains he knows about.

     The poet now is the
POET FOR THE AVANT GARDE because
they are the only ones who think that

          THEY

can understand him.

SOMETIMES

          HE
        WRITES THINGS
that don't make sense
       (EVEN TO HIM)
      just for them

      to read.
And that is about him.

     ~Finished~
(Well, sort of. This is all of the manuscript that I could find.)

THE TALE OF A GAELIC BARD

There were times that driving home from Pasadena College to Oakland (my freshman year) or to Redding (after then), I would have what they called driving drowsiness. I didn't feel like I had fallen asleep but it was scary. These bouts of drowsiness, which only lasted a few seconds, brought stories and memories to mind.

Once upon a time, a long, long time ago in the decade of our Lord, circa 1966, in a far off land in the Oakland, CA hills lived a young boy named Kenny Lee (his last name isn't important), a Spanish, Irish, Belgium, Swede. He was soon to receive the self-appointed title of 'The Gaelic Bard. (Bard is Gaelic for 'Poet'.). After this tale is over, in the mid 70's, Kenny Lee, for a short time would be a member of a 60's, 70's cover R&R band playing keyboards that musicians called 'Keys'. He could play Jerry Lee (Lewis) and Little Richard 'like a-ringing a bell' hence his stage name—Kenny Lee.

In the autumn of 1966, Kenny Lee entered Skyline High School. Kenny Lee was a loner and although he was born with a serious birth defect called spina-bifida, a spinal disease, he had many friends. Kenny Lee did have his share of teasing and insults from the way he walked—bent legged—but nevertheless, he was very popular and well liked at church and at school. Kenny Lee called the teasers, the Irritators. His school friends were either a group of students that hung out in the music/drama building or at the lockers at the end of building 'D'. Two favorite friends were Jody and Ross. They were very serious boyfriend/girlfriend. Ross was an excellent piano player with perfect pitch. He could play Dave Brubeck *like* Brubeck. Ross hung out in the band room, playing the piano in one of the practice rooms. Some days, Kenny Lee was in a practice room playing his Rock & Roll and some days Ross would stop in and encourage Kenny Lee and sometimes would show him some jazz chords to use.

Jody and Kenny Lee became special friends. Ross was never jealous. On May Day, he gave Jody two blue carnations with a poem entitled 'Blue Carnations'. He soon wrote a collection of poems called 'Blue Carnations' and that summer, gave it to Jody. Daphne Garner was a special friend too. In Kenny Lee's senior year, Kenny Lee would befriend a sophomore named Tom Hanks. Tom was a very funny, very brilliant drama student. Tom told the other kids that his goal was to own a comedy club, something that Kenny Lee had never heard of.

Room 30 at Skyline was where the handicapped (The word 'disabled' wasn't a politically correct catch phrase yet. Disabled meant incapacitated or immobilized – an insult. 'Handicapped' is a hardship.) students did all or some of their classes. Kenny Lee had study hall instead of gym in Rm. 30. The music of choice was Motown.

One day in '67, in his Junior year, it was announced that a reporter from the Oakland Tribune would be there the next day to interview the students. Kenny Lee didn't think much about it. In fact, he might have forgotten about it because he assumed that the reporter would be gone when he went to the room.

The next morning, Kenny Lee was told that he was excused from his German 1 class, which excited him very much. He was told to report to Rm. 30. Kenny Lee sat at a small desk by the window. The reporter, Peggy King was there, talking to Jan, a young lady with cerebral palsy. Soon, the teacher, Miss Helen DeSort called Kenny Lee over to a larger desk.

"Well, Kenny, can I call you Kenny or Ken?" Kenny Lee nodded 'yes'. "I hear that you're quite the poet." Kenny Lee was embarrassed. He smiled and blushed. Miss King continued. "Do you have one that I can read?" Kenny Lee handed her his notebook.

Most everyone has them…
Stilts, I mean.
They're used for walking.
Mine are bent…
Aching and hurting with pain.
See my world…
No one around.

> Stay away, people…
> You'll hurt yourselves.
> Everyone tries to fix them….
> The stilts, I mean
> They only make it worse.
> Look out, people…
> It's my life!
> Let me live….in peace.

"This one seems awful dark and bitter, Ken."

"It's how a lot of people feel . . ." Kenny Lee said, looking around the room. ", , , here and in a lot of places. It's a sad, rough life. This Christmas, I'm having surgery on my legs. I can walk now but if this works, well, I'll be as straight as an arrow." Kenny Lee gleamed. "I'm going to miss a few months of school but it will be worth it.

The two talked for the rest of the hour and then, even after the second bell rang for the next class. "Miss King, I really need to get to my next class."

"Miss DeSort will write you a late slip but I have two more questions. I was told that the other students are vanned here. Do you ride the van?"

"No, I ride the bus home. These kids don't live here in the hills. They live down in the city, mainly East Oakland. They're proud people but poor. "What was your second question?"

"Would you come back after school to help wheel the children to the van?"

"Yeah! I guess so."

Two weeks later - Wednesday, November 1, 1967: Kenny Lee's Mother woke him up about a half-hour early. "Paper's here, Kenny, with your article."

"It's not my article. It's Room 30's article."

"I think that you'd better read it."

After being silent for a while, Kenny Lee let out an, "Oh, no-o-o-o-? They're going to kill me at school today. Most of the article is about me. There were eight others interviewed."

"It's a nice picture of you wheeling Mike to the Van."

"The whole thing was scripted and staged. (Author's note: Like todays reality shows like the ones about pawn brokers and restaurant owners.)

One day, sitting in his Algebra 2 class in portable #9 and being bored, his mind wandered. He had some great thoughts there. They didn't make any sense but they were great thoughts. Kenny Lee turned to a clean sheet of paper in his binder and began writing these great thoughts down, thinking them faster than he could write them. In Kenny Lee's mind, he yelled out, 'Not So Fast! Geez!' Teacher and most of the students turned and stared at him. I guess that his complaint wasn't just in his mind. Kenny Lee was a little embarrassed but it was funny to him. By the end of the class period, he had a piece of work entitled, 'Water Dripping Everywhere'. It was a poem but he didn't know that it was a poem until his math teacher picked up from his desk and told him It was a poem. At that moment Kenny Lee became an author. His teacher, Mr. Wong encouraged him to show it to the creative writing teacher.

The next morning . . .
She was young and pretty and a very liberal, hippie in mind and spirit and young Kenny Lee was afraid to death of her—and he was in love with her. Her name was Miss (Miss! ☺) Lacy. Miss Lacy asked Kenny Lee if he would like to come to her creative writing classes the next day to read his poem. He nervously said 'yes'.

The next day in Miss Lacy's class was dreadful. Kenny Lee couldn't keep his eyes off of her and students kept asking him what the poem meant. He had no idea! He just kept asking, 'What does it say to you? That is what's important'. People gave their own elucidations (that's an intellectual poet's word for 'understanding'. The class had some self-appointed intellectuals—and maybe, some real ones.) Soon, Kenny Lee began to understand his 'Water Dripping Everywhere' but by that time, the school day was over and he didn't have a chance to explain the poem. It was just as well.

Also that summer, Kenny Lee wrote a fifteen page epic poem he called 'Tracy'. It had its very sad verses and people would cry when he read it. That year, he submitted it to the school literary magazine. They told Kenny Lee that if he would cut it to a third or a quarter of its length, they would include it in the magazine. He refused them. He learned that that was what writers do. This was the end of his high school publishing career but Kenny Lee kept on writing poems and one really bad story. Fame, except from Jody and Ross eluded him.

The last week in April of '69, the locker group, which consisted of three senior girls (Daphne Garner, Maggie, and Tracy—not of the poem fame) and Kenny Lee, were talking about the Senior Prom five weeks away. The three ladies seemed concerned if they would be asked to go. "Don't worry! If nobody asks you to the Prom, I'll take each of you." he joked.

The next month was a normal, almost boring month if it weren't for Kenny Lee's friends. Talk was about summer vacation plans. Year books were being signed. The first week of June came with warm weather and rain. Talk was about formals and hairdos being ruined if the rain continued into Friday—but, it didn't. The after party after the Senior Prom was to be held at Mel's Bowl in Alameda from midnight until 6 a.m. Kenny Lee, willy-nilly at 10:30 p.m. decided that he would go to the after party. He was known as a loner and he was sure that there would be other fella that didn't go to the Prom but would go stag to the after party.

Kenny Lee bowled alone and with friends. He ate. He played pinball with Tracy and Maggie. He ate. He looked around but he didn't find Daphne. Tracy and Maggie said that they didn't see her all night. He ate again. Part of the buffet was in the pool room. While he was finishing his shrimp cocktail, two acquaintances, not friends asked him to play pool with them.

"Oh, I'm not good at all. I'd rather not."

"Come on, guy! Play!" the egged him on. Finally, the talked Kenny Lee into a game.

Now, Kenny Lee really wasn't good at pool at all but that night, he was very lucky. He made shots that soon caught people's attention. On one shot, the three and five balls, his, and the cue ball were all in line with the side pockets. His thinking was that if he hit one ball, hopefully it would hit the other one into the side pocket *and*, if he was lucky, the second ball would follow in. Well, this didn't happen. What happened was that he hit underneath the cue ball, causing it to jump and hit the other ball into the pocket. The shot put backspin on the cue ball and it hit the three into the other side pocket. This set up the final, the eight ball for the win. After this, no one would play Kenny Lee who was now known as a hustler even though, no bets were made.

Monday morning at school, when he saw Daphne. She was furious when Kenny Lee came up to her to talk.

"Hey, mister, what happened to you Saturday night?"

"What do you mean? What's wrong?"

"You know darn well what's wrong! You stood me up!"

"I . . ." Suddenly, he realized what she was talking about. "I was joking. I told all of you girls that I'd take all of you to the prom but I didn't think you'd take me seriously."

"Well, I did. I bought a new formal and had my hair done. I spent a lot of money."

"I'm sorry! I really am."

It took most of the summer and many, many phone calls from Kenny Lee before Daphne forgave him.

It was a beautiful summer morning, not to hot, not to cold. It was just right. The birds were singing. The butterflies were doing whatever they do. To answer why Kenny Lee was in such a wonder mood, we need to jump back to four days ago.

It was ten a.m. and he sauntered out of my house (well, his parent's), turning left instead of his usual right. To go to his right was to go to his favorite bagel shop and left, to his favorite hot dog joint, which featured over forty sausage sandwiches with twelve types of mustards and horseradish to choose from. That night on the T.V. news, he was told that on that morning, ten-twenty o'clock to be exact, the Beagle's Bagel was robbed. A customer and the counter girl, to pretty for words, were shot but they were only grazed. The robber ordered lox and a bagel and a decaf. When he finished his breakfast, he gave the counter girl a note demanding all of the money in the register. He was caught a few hours later because his note was on the back of one of his bank deposit slips with his address.

The counter girl, Linda, lived in Castro Valley, thirty minutes away from Oakland. They went out every night since—for a while.

They were known as 'Coy & Sloan'. Kenny Lee was Coy and his best friend Ron was Sloan. He came up with these names at a bowling alley. He put those names on an electronic score sheet. We never advertised the names and probably, no one knew them except for him. I'm sure that Ron had forgotten our nom de plume by the end of the day. Diane and Linda, their girlfriends for a short time, thought that the names were cute. This was in the summertime before Kenny Lee went off to college, Pasadena (Nazarene) College, our church college. Ron was a high school senior.

Kenny Lee waited a year after high school before he registered as a Speech major. He felt that this was appropriate since part of his tuition was a small speech scholarship — the rest, student loans. Also, he's a poet, a non-published, non-performing poet but, this was about to change.

The school found Kenny Lee a small writer's (or NYC) size studio apartment made from a house's carport. It was quiet and he discovered writing better stories than the one he wrote in high school. His poetry took a turn. He was homesick and lonely and it reflected in his works.

P.C. was on the quarter system. Every quarter they had at least two variety shows. Kenny Lee did his Rod McKuen thing, poetry and song. McKuen was the 'Now' poet at the time. Kenny Lee's trademark (he didn't know that he had a trademark until a fellow student & writer, Richard Dyke told him that he did) was denims and flannel. Sometimes Kenny Lee 'd wear a long sleeved khaki shirt and slacks, vest and a brown corduroy Buster Brown cap.

The first variety show of the year was held in mid-October in the tennis courts. Eleven acts were billed — three poets (including himself), a reading from 'Death Of A Salesman', a bad want-a-be comic, and six singers or groups (including himself). The weather was nice but too cold for shirtsleeves. Kenny Lee wore the first of his denim and flannel. Bales of hay and a floor of hay provided the scenery. The lighting was provided by propane torches, hung on the fences — a bit risky with the hay.

Eight-thirty, it was show time. By ten, it was everyone on their own at the campus snack shop or to the Grinder, a local hangout for grinders (subs), real messy burgers and greasy fries.

The second variety show was in February. It was the same as the first but it was held indoors, because of the cold, with seventeen acts. Again, eight-thirty, it was show time. By ten, it was everyone on their own at the campus snack shop or to the Grinder, a local hangout for grinders (hoagies), real messy burgers and greasy fries. Oh, I didn't mention that the Grinder also sold cherry or vanilla Cokes or fifty-cent malts? The 1950's were relived.

The school year went on and on. Kenny Lee joined the Missionary Crusaders Club and was invited to rush Kappa Phi Kappa, an educational fraternity. He wrote humorous satire articles for the school paper, P'Cian. The students liked them but the faculty took note. At a regular college, not this church college, the pieces would be considered harmless. Kenny Lee was asked by the school paper, The P'Cian if he'd like to write a humorous satirical column about school life, each week. His publishing career was about to begin.

The school year ended, to Kenny Lee's delight and the summer came and then the new school year began again—to Kenny Lee's delight. It had been a slightly boring summer for him.

The next school year, Ron enrolled at P.C. as a ministerial major and as Kenny Lee's roommate. He was planning to become a Navy chaplain.

That year, Kenny Lee learned from a class mate from Adams, Minnesota (Population—under 700 on the border of Iowa.) that Minnesota still used dog sleds to ice fish in the winter, was elected Missionary Crusaders president. The cafeteria was closed Sunday nights so as a fund raiser, he suggested a coffee house in the student union once a month. The cafeteria would furnish different types of sandwiches, chips, and beverages. The price of admission was 10¢ a person and 25¢ a couple. They sat on the floor at folding tables folded down to the floor. At the chance of sounding redundant, student performers performed. Kenny Lee was too busy managing the events to be a performer. It was a huge success because much money was raised for the club.

The yearbook committee asked Kenny Lee to write the school's account of days gone by for the year book. They turned his efforts down because Kenny Lee wrote it in formal prose instead of his style, which was popular in his humorous satirical column.

Kenny Lee auditioned for the role of Schroeder in the schools production of the 1967's Broadway's musical comedy 'You're a Good Man, Charlie Brown'. He didn't get the part BUT he was asked to be the understudy for all four characters -Gary Burghof's character, Charlie Brown, and Linus, Snoopy, and Schroeder. Memorizing all four parts was quit a chore but he did it by hiding in his dorm room and missing a week and a half of classes. The musical was performed for four consecutive Friday and Saturday's with great triumph. Kenny Lee was able to perform all four parts, Linus twice. This was in 1971, a year to remember.

Kenny Lee had seen the musical, not the Broadway version with Burghof, in San Francisco in 1969 during his high school days, before graduation. (Gary Burghof went on to play Radar on the '70 M*A*S*H movie and T.V.—great accomplishments for the two men.)

Later that year, Kenny Lee auditioned for a student written melodrama as the 'The Handsome Hero'. He was told that he wasn't chosen to play the all American, handsome hero, 'The Handsome Hero'. He was gently told that although he was good looking enough, he didn't get the part because he was bent and weak in the legs, but he was asked to play the piano for the melodrama. He had so much fun doing this.

Each Friday evening, until the wee hours of the night, that dynamic duo, Kenny Lee & Ron would go to the Marriot coffee shop for hot buttered and salted tortillas, coffee and some talk and some studying. One evening at the coffee shop, across the aisle and one booth down:

"Lisa!'

"Maria, how are you? I haven't seen you since high school."

"Oh, Lisa! Hello! Oh, you know. I still work at the same store where I worked when we graduated from high school. And you?"

"I have a career as a dental assistant. I went from one dead end job to another. I didn't think that I'd be out on my own anytime soon until my Mother gave me the phone number to Grander College to train as a dental assistant and in nine easy months, they found me a job with benefits, vacation time, and flexible hours." Lisa began looking through her purse. "Here, I have their phone . . . . oh, here's their card."

"Thanks, Lisa but I'm very happy with my career. I've had three promotions. I'm the senior buyer for the woman's department. I travel to New York and Chicago's garment district. I'm just about to get a bite to eat. Would you be his guest?"

"I'd love to. It's the end of the month and I'm a little tight.

Ron laughed. "That sounded just like a T.V. commercial in reverse."

About three blocks from the college, on Washington Blvd was a bar and grill. One evening, Kenny Lee & Ron wondered in to see what the place had to eat. They two had the best and greasy chili that they had ever eaten. Kenny Lee saw an upright piano and asked if he could play it. They let him play for quite a long while. When he returned to the table, he saw a pitcher of beer on the table.

"What's this?" asked Kenny Lee.

Ron smiled. "It's payment for the entertainment. I told him that we weren't twenty-one and that we don't drink beer, never have but they left it anyways."

Kenny Lee & Ron finished their soft drinks and then returned to the college.

Their Friday evening hot buttered and salted tortillas and studying night came to a semi-end. Many Friday nights, Ron & Kenny Lee were doing church appearances—Kenny Lee's Rod McKuen thing, poetry and song, and Ron's sermonettes. While the idea was being formed and planned out, one night the two of them went to the chapel to pray about this. The night was quiet, perfect for prayer. The chapel was closed. On the door was a sign with the chapel hours, 6 am - 9 pm. Ron & Kenny Lee began their chapel prayer time before classes.

Ron & Kenny Lee first church was thirty miles away, a lot of gas money for college students. Gas was 39¢ a gallon. The audience was twelve people but the two boys didn't care because they knew what they were doing was what they felt the Lord wanted them to do. A young teenage girl found the Lord that evening. A love offering was taken the previous Sunday night for this Friday night—$72, a very, very generous amount. The two stopped on the way music was very good and the very nervous Kenny Lee's sermon went smooth. At the end of his sermon, he said, "We're going to go into a time of prayer now but first, I want to ask anybody if they need healing prayer, physically or spiritually to raise their hand. I want everyone to keep their eyes open to see who they are praying for." People lifted their hand but then, people started coming to the altar and then more people—without being asked to.

After the prayer time and when the people returned to their pews, Kenny Lee asked if anyone wanted to share why the raised their hands and/or came to the altar. One young lady (her name was Martha) stood. "A few months ago, my three year old daughter, you all know Sallie, suddenly went deaf. Doctors were baffled. Medicine and X-rays didn't solve anything. Please remember her in prayer." Others followed suit with their testimonies. Forty-five minutes later, the church pastor dismissed us in song, the 'Doxology' and 'Let There Be Pease on Earth'

Outside, Ron found Kenny Lee. "That was a good job you did preaching."

"Thanks! I was sure scared at first and then a calm came over me . . . well, for a while. This morning I was doing a little bit of plastering. I must not have cleaned off my hands good enough because while I was preaching, I reached down to scratch my leg and I snagged my polyester pants." Ron laughed. He really thought that that was really funny.

"Ron, in prayer when people say 'Lord or Jesus, words can't express our love or what you've done for me.' What do you think about that phrase?"

"I think that a lot of the New Testament and other books wouldn't have been written."

"Man, we do think alike."

The next morning, Ron preached a vibrant sermon on loving your neighbors and who your neighbors are. Afterwards, Martha asked if she could say something.

Ron smiled a yes. "Even though she can't hear me, I talk to Sallie a lot! This morning when I was getting Sallie dressed for church, she sneezed and she could hear me and she could hear the toilet flush in the next room and the cat outside." There was very much applauding, celebrating and praising the Lord after that.

The summer came. Kenny Lee's part-time job at the ASPCA turned full-time. Ron applied and got a campus security job during the six week summer school. When the summer session ended, they had to move out of their dorm room. They house sat for Kenny Lee's cousin and then, they went home. They decided that they had enough school for a while. Kenny Lee kept writing and added music and songs to his writing talents. Ron joined the Navy Reserves.

The story of Kenny Lee, the Gaelic Bard goes on and on and on but, this tale does not except that Kenny Lee is now a paid published Poet. One of these days I'll tell you my tale of The Gaelic Bard in his 60th plus years. He was born with a serious birth defect called spina-bifida, a spinal disease. He wasn't to live past six weeks.

MY FIRST STORY ABOUT CORY

There have been a lot of changes in the past twenty years. Now, in 1974, the Savoy Dance Hall charges $5 dollars for a ticket. That's $2.50 cents a dance. A person buys a ticket, or maybe six or seven, depending on how much money they have, then choose a girl of their choice and spend about two minutes dancing with her. I can remember hearing about when dances were only a dime. The locals call this the Rider district, the several square blocks before getting to Jack London Square, in Oakland, CA.

It used to be that at 3 a.m. the streets were full of people, especially Friday and Saturday nights, and a person could walk down the street without caution, feeling safe; but, not anymore. This is the Rider district—now the dumping grounds for the hopeless alcoholics and drug addicts. It's a haven for the lonely, the fugitives, ex-con, and the mentally ill.

Cory Davis woke up around eleven. He lit a cigarette and laid in bed, reading yesterday's newspaper. Soon, an announcement over a public address system told the people that it was time to eat lunch. Cory jumped out of bed and threw on his clothes and brushed his hair. He ran out the door and down three flights of stairs to the mess hall. It was full. The mess hall held seventy-five people. Two men patrolled the hall. Cory was directed to several benches to wait until there was room to sit and eat. This was not a prison but, a place for the homeless, a shelter.

When he saw an empty seat, Cory got in line to get his lunch. The menu for that day was spaghetti with sauce, cold beets, two slices of white bread and butter, a cup of warm milk, and peaches. Everything was eaten with a large soup spoon. There were no knives or forks,

Almost before Cory was finished with his lunch, one of the men patrolling the mess hall tapped him on the shoulder. "If you're done, get going,"

Cory got up from his seat and walked out of the room, through two corridors with rotting walls, past a toilet without a door, down a stairway that smell like vomit, until he reached the front door. On his way out, a social worker told him that if he wanted to stay there again that night, he'd have to be there by seven-thirty.

Outside, the sidewalks were piled with trash. As far as I know, the buildings are still unsafe and lice-ridden. Tuberculosis and syphilis are there. They called syphilis, the ral. Cory turned left and walked towards Broadway. Every half block or so, he would feel his back pocket, making sure that his wallet was still with him. In the Rider, there's no honor among men. Bum steals from bum, wino from wino, and addict from addict. About a block and an half from the shelter, a man in a torn T-shirt and a Salvation Army jacket stopped Cory and asked him for a quarter. Cory just laughed and walked on. About a block later, a man asked Cory for a cigarette for a quarter. They both leaned against a building and smoked. Finally, the bum took one last, long drag on his cigarette, threw it on the ground and walked away without a word — without a 'thank-you'.

On the streets are bars, coffee shops we'd call greasy spoons, old furniture stores, pawn shops, Chinese grocery stores and T&D Follies, a cheap porno movie house that isn't so cheap.

A few blocks later, Cory walked onto the onramp of Highway 17. He had a dinner engagement at six o'clock. He stuck out his thumb and within the next twenty minutes, he had a ride to San Francisco, some fifteen miles away across the Bay Bridge.

Cory got out of the car at Union Square and hitched a ride to a North Beach coffeehouse where he was to meet his friend. Back then, North Beach was folk and jazz clubs and coffee-houses. Now, it's mostly topless/bottomless strip clubs. I remember hanging out at the 'Hungry I' when it was a folk club with such acts as Peter, Paul, and Mary and The Kingston Trio. Lenny Bruce was big there, too before he died of a heroin overdose.

As soon as his eyes were adjusted to the dark, he found a table in the back. On stage, two young men about twenty years old were going over some material for that night's show. After a few minutes, the boys on stage said hello to Cory. "We're Coy and Sloan." One of them said. "Are you staying for tonight?"

Cory nodded yes. They continued practicing. Coy was a poet and a piano player and Sloan backed him up on drums. After about fifteen minutes, Cory spoke up again.

"Say, some of those poems are alright. How about if you write some of them out for me. I love poetry."

"I'll be selling a collection of them tonight, here but I'll give you an autograph copy before you leave."

"I would really like that, thanks!"

Coy moved over to the piano and Sloan, to a set of drums. A house sideman held his own on string bass. They jammed through a real bluesy 'Summertime' and then a tune that Coy wrote. Coy began speaking through the mike while they played:

> The lilacs are what I'm allergic to. My throat
> > clogs up and I sneeze a lot. I like sweet peas.
> > They're pretty. When I was in second grade,
> > My Mom had sweet peas and daisies growing
> > in the front yard. I used to pick my Mom's
> > flowers and sell them for a penny a piece. She
> > didn't like it much.
> When Jan and I went hiking in the hills, I'd sneeze
> > a little from the lilacs. She would laugh at me,
> > making fun of my misery, but I didn't mind
> > because I like to see her laugh. Then, she would
> > tickle me and I would end up chasing her until
> > we both would trip and fall. Then, she would
> > kiss me on the cheek.
> That was summer. Now that winter and rain are
> > Here, it's hot chocolate by the fire and television.
> > She still tickles me but I tickle her
> > back and she still kisses me on the cheek.

Cory clapped. "I like that. It sounded real good."

"Yeah, thanks!" Coy turned to Sloan. Was it any good? I just wrote it this afternoon. Is it good enough to do tonight?"

Sloan picked up the sports page of the paper and read it over. "It sounded better the way you read it than it reads on paper. Sure, it's good."

Cory spoke up again to Coy. Coy and Sloan were starting to get annoyed with Cory. "You play a good, mean piano. Have you ever heard of a cat named Cory Davis?"

"No, can't say that I have. What does he do, play guitar or keys?"

"Come what? Oh, yeah, uh, piano. Ten years ago, I played the circuits, jazz as good as Brubeck. Didn't do strictly union gigs like I was supposed to do. Got down to some heavy jamming." Coy expected Cory to ask if he could jam. "You don't stride, do you?" Cory asked.

"Say what, sir?"

"Stride the keys."

"No, I don't think so."

"It's where you alternate the bass between single notes on the first and the third beats of the measure and chord . . . here, let me show you." Cory did and Coy still didn't know what he was talking about.

"Your name's Coy?" Cory asked.

"Yeah, a nickname. Name's Ken,"

"Does my showing you help?"

"Yes sir!" he lied.

"Say, do you fellas hit the pipe?"

Coy and Sloan just looked at Cory.

"You know skee. Do you smoke?"

"Oh, no, neither one of us does," Sloan answered.

"Not cigarettes, you know, skee . . . a water pipe. Uh . . . weed—you know."

"No, we don't."

"Then I don't suppose neither of you would have a joint on you? All musicians carry joints."

"No! Say, look, we've got practicing to do."

"Oh, sure, go ahead. I'll just sit back here and not say a word. Yeah, go ahead and practice. Oh, but first, how do I get a drink around here?"

"It's closed until six." Cory sat back down in the back and didn't say a word for the rest of the afternoon. He just listened. "You know Ron (Sloan), I'm going to read 'Tracy', all two hundred and sixty-one lines, ten pages. Ron did a high five with Coy.

"I just got a job playing piano for tips and beer in San Leandro, two nights a week, Ron.

"That's great but, you don't drink beer."

"I drink root beer."

Around five o'clock, Coy and Sloan left the stage and went to a dressing room backstage. They ordered a pizza. Cory started outside to wait for his friend and he saw the collection of poems that Coy was talking about so, he picked one up.

Cory's friend's name was Bobby Andersen and he was twenty minutes late.

"Good evening, Cory." He said. He didn't speak like an old friend. He was too formal for that.

"Hey, Bobby, how ya been??

"It's been a long time, hasn't it, Cory?" He smiled a quick smile.

"Yeah, it has. Shall we go in and sit down?"

"Here? Well, if this is all that you can afford, I guess that it's alright with me."

"No! It's just that a couple of friends . . . Where would you like to go?"

"I was thinking about Alioto's,"

"Yeah, okay."

"Shall I drive, Cory, or would you like to?"

"No, go ahead. I'll pick up my car later." he lied. "I'd like to come back anyways to see my friends perform."

Cory and Bobby walked about a half a block to Bobby's car, a '57 cherry red T-Bird (the one with the portholes) and drove the few blocks to the wharf and Alioto's. "Bobby, Did I ever tell you about my Dad? His name is Pres. My Mother's name is Bess. She was a waitress; My Dad was a Taxi dispatcher. He left us before I was born and married a woman named Bessie. They had a son fifteen months after I was born and get this—this is freaky—he insisted that their son be named Cory, like me. Some-thing else that was freaky was that for my visits, he had a court order that all visits were to be at his house so, there we were—Pres, my new Dad, Bessie, Pres' wife, Cory, my stepbrother and Cory, me."

Bobby finally found a parking space about a block and a half from the restaurant. As they walked to the restaurant, it started to sprinkle. "That's a really strange story. You swear that it's real?" asked Bobby.

"The story gets weirder. Yes, it's true. My Father was a serial eater.' Cory laughed.

"A serial eater. I told you that it would get weirder. He'd read the San Francisco Chronicle, the Oakland Tribune, and the San Jose Mercury News to see when society people would take cruises. He'd break into their homes and cook a gourmet dinner with their food. When I was eight, he went to a gourmet market and bought some Beluga caviar, the ridiculously expensive kind. He left a small caviar spoon, he was a fanatic, with caviar and his fingerprint on it. He was arrested and my Mom, Bess l, bailed him out. He got probation. Bessie ll divorced him and he remarried my Mom, Bess l. Are you confused? I think that I'm getting the story right. He was arrested again for breaking and entering and petty thief. He spent only a few weeks in jail. Cory, my step brother owns four gourmet restaurants and five garment markets. Each Christmas, he invites himself to my parent's house, I come, and he brings a ham, turkey and, a goose for Christmas dinner with all the trimmings."

Once inside Alioto's, they had to wait forty minutes for a table. "I guess that I should have called ahead for a reservation." Bobby told Cory. When they did sit at a table, Bobby ordered an Old Fashion and Cory, a beer. "A Porter, if you have one." Cory told the waiter. They both had coffee. The waiter left menus.

Cory spoke up first. "I think that I'll have the lobster. What're you having?"

"I think that I'll have the same thing. Cory, you remember Jimmy, don't you. plays keyboards? Was a side man for a while?"

"Yeah, I remember."

"Well, he's recording for ABC Dunhill with a rock band. (Cory knew this — 'Three Dog Night'.) He's doing alright, too. I can't saw that I approve of the music he plays but he's doing fine."

"Well, Bobby, you've always been a jazz man."

The waiter walked over to the table and Cory ordered. "We'll both have the lobster, and steaks, New York, medium rare."

"And I'll have another Old Fashion, please."

"Thank-you, Gentlemen." Then, the waiter walked away.

"Want some gum?" Cory offered Bobby.

"No! No, thank-you."

"It's spearmint."

"No, thank-you."

"Well, okay. It's here if you decide different." Cory put a piece into his mouth.

"I heard some news about your old drummer, Cory."

"Sonny, what about?"

"He's going through cold turkey. He's been on junk for six years."

"Sonny hit the pipe? He only did grass when he and I was in the group. I hope that it wasn't skee. I sure hope that it wasn't. Was he pin shooting?"

"I don't know, Cory."

"I ran into Nicky 'bout a year back—played lead axe."

"I remember Nicky."

"He's got the ral, Bobby. The kid's dying if he ain't dead by now."

The waiter brought their salads. Cory took the gum out of his mouth and put it under the table. Bobby looked at him sternly, like a father would his son. Cory just laughed it off. For the next few minutes, both were quiet while they ate their salads. It was an awkward silence, though, because neither one could think of a thing to say. Bobby was the first to speak.

"That was a good salad. I wish that they had asked me what kind of dressing I wanted. They usually do. I guess that we just weren't paying attention. Italian was fine but I'd much rather have had Roquefort."

"Yeah, but I liked what I got, a little spicy but I liked it. Italian, you say?"

"Uh-huh!"

Cory pushed his plate away from him. "This is a pretty classy place you picked out. Come here often?"

As a matter of fact, I do. They've got terrific food. Next time that you come here, try the prime rib. It's out of this world."

Cory mumbled to himself, "At these prices, it better be!"

"Did you say something, Cory?"

"Huh? Oh, no, just thinking out loud."

"Did you read the papers yesterday or watch the news?"

"I didn't. I stopped the paper. It just piled up on me and I don't have a TV."

"You're kidding! Everybody owns at least one TV. Anyways, the Zodiac Killer struck again at Lake Berryessa. A young couple was parked at the lake. The guy survived almost ten stab wounds. I wonder if he'll be able to I.D. the guy."

The waiter came to the table and poured the two another cup of coffee. Bobby ordered another Old Fashion. The waiter took the salad plates. Bobby took a sip of his drink. "You'd better be careful. You're drinking an awful lot!" said Cory.

"If I can't handle it, I'll just call a cab. I guess that we should have brought your car."

Cory had been holding the collection of poems on his lap. The booklet slid to the floor. Cory reached down, picked it up and put it on the table. "What's that?" asked Bobby.

"It's a book of poetry that my good friend at the coffee house that we were at gave me that he wrote. I'm going back to catch their act."

"Are they any good?"

"I don't know, yet. At rehearsal, he read some and they were good. I showed him a trick or two on the piano and this book was his way of paying me back." Cory lied.

"Bobby, do you remember Geoff? About a month ago, a guy that looked just like him saw me on the street and called me by name. It really freaked me out 'cause Geoff's been dead for almost six years, or is it seven? It turned out it was his baby brother.

"I still have dreams about Nam and wake up in a cold sweat. I still can't get over Geoff being killed and me finding his body. He was my best friend in the Army and he had to die in the war. That's what Nam does to you. I'm sure as hell glad it's over."

"I never knew Geoff and I never was in the service. It must have been rough on you."

The waiter brought Bobby's drink and the steak and lobsters.

"Thank-you."

The next twenty minutes was filled with small talk while they ate. "Bobby, this afternoon I was in a drugstore this afternoon and I overheard a telephone call between a wife and her husband. She sounded nervous. 'Honey, I can't get the car started. Can you come and get me?' "She told her husband the name of the drugstore." 'Where's the car?' he asked. 'In here!' she said." It took Bobby a few seconds to catch on to the joke but then, he laughed. Cory finished his beer.

"Cory, are you sure you can afford this? It's going to be awful expensive. Listen, if you cant. I can . . ."

"No, I invited you for dinner and I'm going to pay. Say, listen, I'm not poor you know. Not Cory Davis, jazz pianist extraordinaire. If you'll remember, I was one of the most respected and well paid musicians in my own class at seventeen."

"That's just it, Cory. That was ten years ago. Nobody remembers you today. When you left to go overseas during the Vietnam War, your career just faded away. Be realistic about it."

"I was hoping that you'd be my manager again. I want to get back into the business again. That's why I wanted to meet with you tonight."

Bobby took another sip of his drink, ignoring Cory's request. "Are you sure that you don't want me to pay my part of the bill?"

Cory ignored the question. Nothing more was said until the both had finished eating. A bus boy came over and cleared the dishes. Then the waiter came back. "Would either of you like dessert?"

"Not for me, thank-you. Bobby replied. "How about you, Cory?"

"Not for me, either. I'm full. Thank-you! Bobby, could I borrow you pen?"

"Sure, and keep it. Someone was looking for handouts and when I dropped some change into his cup, he gave me this."

"Well, I've got to be going. Are you ready, Cory?"

"You go ahead. I've got to meet a friend here in about a half an hour. Don't worry about the check."

"It was really good seeing you again, Cory." Bobby left.

After Bobby left, Cory opened the poetry book to the inside cover and wrote,

> 'Cory, you're a real special cat. Thanks for jamming
> with us. Your hands are your gift.
>
> Stay cool, Coy (Ken)'

About ten minutes later, the waiter came over to the table and poured Cory another cup of coffee. "Pardon me, sir, but are you driving a white Mustang. The lights are on."

"Why, yes I am." he lied. "Thank-you very much. I'm expecting a friend named Noel. If he comes in asking for me, please show him to this table. Be back in a sec."

Cory walked out of the door and down the street. He hitched several rides and eight hours later, he was in Redding—for no other reason than to get out of the Rider.

ALMOST A LOVE STORY

Some people call me K.B., short for 'Keyboards'. A high school friend, a drummer named Scot Stein, gave me the nickname. I play keys at Heder's, a bar and grill and, this is almost a love story. One night after Heder's closed, Lenny, the bar waitress, and I went out for coffee.

"See that guy over there?" she pointed, "Oh, never mind, that's not him.

"Not who?"

"Well, about eight or nine months ago, before you came here, we had a guy come in to Heder's for about three weeks straight, every night. Called himself, Butch. He's go up to the bar and just get water and put sugar and a squeeze of lime in it to make it look like a drink. Didn't cost him a cent. Then, he'd go sit with people." She laughed. "When they left, he'd pore what was left of their drinks into his glass and then, pocket my tokes . . . um . . . tips that they had left. Well, one night he was carded. He was under age so they eighty-sixed him. He only had about four or five months before he was twenty-one. So, I expect to see him again soon.

I laughed, "Sure!"

"You don't believe me, huh?" I only smiled.

One night, I saw him! After he pocketed the toke and refilled his glass, he walked over to the piano bar. "Hi!" he said to me. "Butch Mahoney's the name."

Sometime later, I had a band. Players would come, jam, and go but three stayed. Ron played bass, Kier, guitar, and Bernie played traps (drums). Bernie's doing session work in L.A. now. I hadn't seen him in a long while until he stopped in for breakfast one morning at a nearby diner. I was having chorizo, eggs, and coffee and finishing a poem on a napkin. Now, I'm still sitting in the diner most weekday mornings. I'm writing this story on 'paper towel' napkins.

We talked about old times and he bragged a little about how well he was doing and then, he asked me if I remembered Maggie. She was the second Maggie that I knew. He said that she was doing fine. I asked him to give me her address and phone number the next time he saw her.

When we were playing Header's a couple of years ago, after we were through for the night, I'd walk over to this diner and write. I met Maggie on the third morning of the graveyard shift. Every once in a while, she'd ask to see what I was writing. She always seemed really interested when I showed her.

Since she worked nights, she would naturally sleep days. Sometimes in the early evenings, her mornings, she and I would walk down to Jack London's Square, looking at the Fisco lights and talk or just walk around and always watch the sunsets. They were beautiful.

Maggie once asked me to write her some poems. I did and my Dad made a cover for the book out of walnut with brass hinges. I was so proud of that book. I gave it to her one early morning at the diner. She reached over the counter and kissed me—four times. I titled the book '4:14 a.m.'.

I drew pictures for her, too—mountains. The trees were an inverted 'V' from a green felt tip pin. And she told me that she framed them and hung them on her wall. I don't know if she really did or not but it was something nice to hear.

I remember one time when she went on vacation for three weeks. I can count on one hand the times that I went into the diner during those three weeks but, I knew the night that she'd be back. I was there waiting for her. I think that she knew that I was excited to see her back and I think it made her happy.

I knew Maggie for about four months before she was switched to days. I meant to go in and see her but, I never did. Someone told me that she got married and moved to Florida.

I've seen her since then, twice, and her little girl. The first time was by mistake. She was waiting for a blind date and I was wearing the same brown and blue Hawaiian shirt that he was supposed to wear. We talked about 'old' times and small talk and what each one if us had been doing. She told me that she had moved back into the Rider District, that she got a job waitressing at a steak house in Jack London Square, and that her husband had died of leukemia, and she was moving to L.A in a week and a half.

Cont'd on the next page ☞

4:14 a.m.

By
Ken Martinez

I'm sitting in the doorway
of Groan's bookstore,
drinking thermos coffee,
trying to keep dry.
I have time to do a lot
of thinking . . . about
memories mostly . . .
but some of these are bad so,
I'll just turn my collar
to the damp
and walk until
I'm tired.

A girl just drove by and yelled,
"Hey, honey, you're cute."
About a half an hour ago à fella
who looked like Beaver Cleaver's
brother, Wally
drove by and threw
two beer cans at me.
He missed the second time.

The nice thing
about today is that
nobody has used it up yet.
It's all brand new.

4:14 a.m.
I'm just sitting here outside
smoking my pipe and thinking
about everything and nothing.
It's raining hard and
the batteries in my radio
are going dead
but it's a nice feeling
because I'm where I want to be,
doing what I want to do.

Her name was Dana.
She bought me coffee this morning.
While walking to her apt.,
she gave me her key
then asked for twenty dollars
so, I left

i drew a flower on a
popsicle stick
and sold it to a drunk
for a quarter.
i gave him his money back
but he kept the popsicle stick

the feeling is layback
and nice
and wet from the rain.

I want this to say 'I love you'.
I'm writing this in pencil
on a Hersey bar wrapper
that I found in the gutter
but, it's all I have . . . and
I want this to say 'I love you'.

I'd like to write you a symphony,
to play my life—
in all twelve keys,
not just in the key of 'C'
or sometimes, in Em.
Mornings will begin with an oboe
⩽ because, I like the oboe ⩾
and the days will end with an oboe
because, it will be the same time,
twenty-four hours later.

if I could cork up time in a bottle
and hold it for today . . .
it's five-thirty a.m. and i'm
very tired. I really don't know
what I'm writing.
if you're reading this
and I'm wasting your time,
        i'm sorry.

I'm home now.
I just watched the test pattern,
the morning prayer and
the farm report on T.V.
Now, I think I'll sleep for the day.

A BLUE LOVE STORY

*T*he *Velveteen Rabbit or How Toys Become Real* is a children's novel written by Margery Williams and illustrated by William Nicholson. First © 1922 by Avon Books—All Rights Reserved. Now, it's Public Domain. It chronicles the story of a stuffed rabbit and his quest to become real through the love of his owner.

This is a love story . . .

She called me Skipper, not Captain. For as long as I've known her she always called me Skipper. I really don't know why, except that Skipper is a character in a story that I wrote for her. Betsy Bogsinagn was seven.

Today was Easter morning. I read my poems and told my stories and sang my songs with my guitar to Betsy and to other children at an orphanage. It was the first time I performed, ever, as a poet/singer and it was the first time I've been accepted by so many people, ever.

Sandy, the orphanage director and a member of my church asked me to come to the orphanage that Easter and I asked her to sing—she did. My favorite song that she sang was on the piano, Ray Stevens version of 'Jesus Loves Me'.

As I read my poems and told my stories and sang my songs, I couldn't help to wonder—would the Easter Bunny find them this morning?

When we were done, the children, Sandy, and I ate lunch together. While I was finishing lunch, Betsy ran up to me, hugged me, and gave me a picture that that she had colored. After the Easter egg hunt, we talked and joked and she asked me to give her my address, I did and then, she kissed me on the cheek—good-bye.

I didn't expect her to write. In fact, I didn't expect her to even remember me past the next day, but she did. A few days later, I received a letter from her. She told me how lonely she was. I wrote back and waited for a letter but, it didn't come . . . for a month, anyways. She told me how lonely she was and then, asked me to marry her and that her birthday was June 2nd.

From then on, we wrote back and forth, exchanging colored pictures and poems and we would pretend things that we had done or would do.

I sent her a pink toy puppy for her birthday and she sent me a pretty smooth stone for mine. I tried to visit her each week but time got in my way. I was twenty-one and in college. When I thought of her, the possibilities were endless. And, my time and the things I did were dedicated to her. She became my little girl.

I speak of Betsy in the past. When I think of her, I become a lone person because I don't have a girl to love me anymore. It seems so worthless.

One Saturday, I received a letter. It told me that Betsy was found dead. By her side, was a Xerox copy of the book, *The Velveteen Rabbit*. These passages were marked with a pink felt tip highlighter.

The Skin Horse had lived longer in the nursery than any of the others. He was so old that his brown coat was bald in patches and showed the seams underneath, and most of the hairs in his tail had been pulled out to string bead necklaces. He was wise, for he had seen a long succession of mechanical toys arrive to boast and swagger, and by-and-by break their mainsprings and pass away, and he knew that they were only toys, and would never turn into anything else. For nursery magic is very strange and wonderful, and only those playthings that are old and wise and experienced like the Skin Horse understand all about it.

"What is REAL?" asked the Rabbit one day, when they were lying side-by-side near the nursery fender, before Nana came to tidy the room. "Does it mean having things that buzz inside you and a stick-out handle?"

"It doesn't happen all at once," said the Skin Horse. "You become. It takes a long time. That's why it doesn't happen often to people who break easily, or have sharp edges, or who have to be carefully kept. Generally, by the time you are real, most of your hair has been loved off, and your eyes drop out and you get loose in the joints and very shabby. But these things don't matter at all, because once you are Real you can't be ugly, except to people who don't understand."

"I suppose you are real?" said the Rabbit. And then he wished he had not said it, for he thought the Skin Horse might be sensitive. But the Skin Horse only smiled.

(A few pages later) *There was once a velveteen rabbit, and in the beginning he was really splendid. He was fat and bunchy, as a rabbit should be; his coat was spotted brown and white, he had real thread whiskers, and his ears were lined with pink sateen. On Christmas morning, when he sat wedged in the top of the Boy's stocking, with a sprig of holly between his paws, the effect was charming.*

For a long time he lived in the toy cupboard or on the nursery floor, and no one thought very much about him. He was naturally shy, and being only made of velveteen, some of the more expensive toys quite snubbed him. The mechanical toys were very superior, and looked down upon everyone else; they were full of modern ideas, and pretended they were real. The model boat, who had lived through two seasons and lost most of his paint, caught the tone from them and never missed an opportunity of referring to his rigging in technical terms. The Rabbit could not claim to be a model of anything, for he didn't know that real rabbits existed; he thought they were all stuffed with sawdust like himself, and he understood that sawdust was quite out-of-date and shouldn't ever be mentioned in modern circles. Even Timothy, the jointed wooden lion, who was made by the disabled soldiers, and should have had broader views, put on airs and pretended he was connected with Government. Between them all the poor little Rabbit was made to feel himself very insignificant and commonplace, and the only person who was kind to him at all was the Skin Horse.

In her vest pocket was a note. It read, 'I tried to be real and loved. I really tried. Skipper, if Jesus loves me, why doesn't anybody else?'

I read the letter and cried. I still do.

SACTO, CA

Bo was four. He was riding his trike in the driveway. While he was riding his trike, he saw a man, in his early twenties walk by.

"Hi!' Bo said.

"Hi!" The man smiled.

"What's your Name, Mister?"

"Regan!" the man said, still walking.

"Want to play, Regan?"

"Not today, kid."

Bo's voice was getting louder as Regan was getting farther away. "My name is Bo. Come by tomorrow and let's play, okay?"

"We'll see."

"Bye!"

"Bye!"

Regan kept walking down the street. When he reached the corner, he turned. He passed a girl hitchhiking—and as he passed her, he turned and looked at her. She was very good looking.

Her cardboard sign read SACTO.

Skipper was driving down University Ave., Berkeley. He pulled over to the curb, reached over and unlocked the passenger door. (Car door locks were by the windows in those days.) She opened it.

"Hi!"

"I'm going to Union City first but then I'm going to Reno, going through Sacramento. Want a ride?"

"I don't know. How long will you be in Union City?"

"Just 'bout a half an hour, long enough to get some clothes. It's up to you."

"What time is it? Can we be there by ten? I have to be at work by ten."

"No sweat! It's 4:15 now. I'll have you there. Like I said, it's up to you."

"Alright, if you're sure that you'll get me there on time."

"Come on, hop in. We'll have time to spare."

She put her suitcase in the back seat of the car and then got into the front seat, right next to him. He was surprised but then he smiled.

Several minutes later, "Hi . . . I'm Kari." She smiled.

He didn't. "I'm Skipper."

"Skipper! I like that. It's different. I like it."

"Real name's Frank." He smiled a quick smile. "Four years ago, I was a counselor at a summer camp and I wore a ship captain's cap. The kids started calling me Skipper. The name stuck."

"I like it. Does your radio work?"

"No, it's broken. Been meaning to have it fixed but haven't gotten around to it yet." He did a quick look at her. "Do you live in Sacramento, Kari?"

"Uh-huh! For about fourteen years. I'm eighteen, now. I hitchhiked to Redwood City to stay with my folks for my Mom's birthday. It was nice, a real nice three days but it will be good to get home. I haven't seen my parents for about three years, ever since they moved to Redwood City. It was nice seeing them again.

"Some black guy picked me up. He scared me. I think that he wanted more than just to give me a ride, if you know what I mean. I just told him to let me off in Berkeley, that this was as far as I was going. Then you picked me up. Thanks! I really love you for it, all the way to Sacramento, I mean."

Frank smiled but didn't say anything. They were both quiet for a few minutes and then Kari started to laugh.

"What's so funny?" Frank asked.

"Nothing, I just thought . . . just thought of something funny that happened yesterday." Kari laughed again.

"Oh!"

"Well, aren't you going to ask what?"

"No, 'cause it's none of my business."

Kari was a bit surprised at his answer. She couldn't think of anything to say. After a few minutes, she put her head on Franks shoulder. "You don't mind, do you? I'm tired."

"No, I guess not!"

"What's your name again . . . your real name?"

"Frank"

"Frank, what?"

Frank snickered. "You wouldn't believe me if I told you."

"Try me!"

"Sinatra"

"Sinatra? Frank Sinatra?"

"Yeah, that's me!"

"You're right!"

"About what?"

"I don't believe you."

"Okay!"

"That's all? That's all you're going to say?"

"Yeah! If you don't believe me, you don't believe me but listen—with all the millions of people here in the states, there has to be other Frank Sinatra's, don't you think?"

Kari smiled. "I never thought about it. I believe you. I never met a famous named person before. It's kinda funny." Then, Kari got serious. "Could we stop somewhere and get something to eat. I'm getting hungry and you did say that we had time to kill. I'll pay since you gave me a ride."

"Sure! As soon as we get to Hayward there're plenty of restaurants off the highway, Okay?"

Kari didn't answer. They were both quiet for a while and then he asked, "Frankie would you like to make love to me?"

"Huh?" Frank gasped.

"If you've got ten dollars, I'll let you make love to me."

"No thanks, sweetheart."

She cuddled next to Frank a little bit more. "Frank?" she spoke softly, almost a purr.

"Forget it! You're not getting any money. I'm not into that game."

"Alright, Babe, we're still friends?"

Frank smiled. "Yeah!"

Kari reached up and kissed him on the cheek. Frank looked at her and smiled.

"The second turnoff from her is Marina Boulevard. Turn off there, okay?" asked Kari.

"How come?"

"It's such a nice day, let's go down to the Marina and look at the bay." Frank was puzzled. How did she know where the bay was if she practically said that she had never been in the Bay Area before or, was he mistaken? "We won't be able to look at the lights or anything. It isn't dark enough yet."

Frank sighed. She was begging to annoy him. "Okay!"

"You're sweet, Frankie!"

After Frank parked the car along the side of the bay, Kari reached over and opened his door. "Come on, let's get out and walk around for a little while."

"I thought that you were in such a hurry to get to work!"

Kari smiled and sing-songed, "Don't worry, Baby. Everything will be alright."

"You like the Beach Boys, huh?"

"Love 'em!"

After they had walked awhile, Kari took Frank's hand and turned him so that she was facing him. She kissed him. She smiled and kissed him again . . . and a third time.

He smiled at her. "You're still not getting the money!"

I . . . I didn't even mention anything about that. That hurts." Kari was pouting. "That really hurts.

Frank turned from her and walked away. Was she faking and trying to get money again? "Hey, I'm sorry, okay?" Frank kept walking without looking at her. Kari caught up with him and took his hand, neither one said anything.

They walked until they came to a house. Kari picked up a small rock and started to throw it at the house. Frank grabbed her wrist.

"Hey, what do you think you're doing?" He asked. Frank was upset.

She pointed to the roof. "See the weather vane? I'm going to try and hit it." She threw the rock but missed. It landed on the roof and slid three-quarters of the way down. "You try it." She said, looking at Frank.

Frank changed his attitude. He picked up a pebble and threw it, hitting the vane. He smiled a proud smile at Kari. She picked up another rock, a bigger rock, threw it, and hit a window. Frank grabbed Kari's hand. "Come on! Let's get out of here!"

"No! Wait! Wait! I want to see the people when they come out of the house. I want to see their reaction."

"You mean, just wait here?"

"Yeah, they can't see us over here."

They waited for about ten minutes but nobody came out of the house. Kari picked up another rock. "Maybe they didn't hear the window break. Maybe the TV's too loud."

Yeah, maybe, but you're not going to throw another rock. I'll leave you here first. Now, throw it down! She did. "You're crazy! You know that, Kari!" This was not a question.

She grinned and nodded 'yes'.

"Come on, Missy, it's getting late. Let's go! Frank turned and started towards the car.

"No, I wa . . . okay." she backed down. "Hey, wait up, would you?"

Franked stopped and waited for Kari, and then they walked to the car. When they got in, she hugged and kissed him. "You're really sweet, Frankie." She smiled at her.

Frank didn't smile or say anything. He started the car and they drove to the freeway. After a few miles, they reached Hayward. He pulled off of the freeway at 'A' St. and drove about two blocks until they reached a Sambo's coffee shop. He pulled into the parking lot. Frank was still upset and flustered.

I'll tell you what, Kari, if you want, you go in and I'll go get some gas and some clothes. Go ahead and eat, anything you want and when I get back, I'll pick up the bill.

"But, I told you that I'll pay. When are you going to eat?"

"I'll make a peanut butter sandwich."

"How long will you be gone?"

"Only twenty minutes, a half hour, tops. I only live a couple of miles from here, okay?"

"Alright!" She got out of the car and started to close the door.

"You forgot your suitcase."

"It will be safe here."

"You're sure you want to leave it in here?"

"Yeah, why not?" She blew him a kiss.

"Bye, Kari,"

Frank drove back to the freeway and Kari walked into the coffee shop.

Kari sat at the counter and ordered a burger and fries and iced tea. Iced tea came with refills. Almost an hour later, Kari asked the waitress if she had a paper.

"It's the 'San Francisco Chronicle', if that's alright." The first article that she read was about the Zodiac Killer. Donna Lass, 25 was last seen at Stateline, NV, near Tahoe on Sept.6, 1970. This article said that the Chronicle received word about it on March 22, '71.

After a while, I came in and sat at the counter, two stools from Kari and ordered coffee. A stool was missing but the bolts were still in the floor.

"What happened to the stool?" I asked the waitress.

"We don't know. It was stolen. We're open 24 hours and there is usually always some-one in here, staff and customers. It happened last evening" I laughed and the waitress left.

I worked for an inventory company and I had to meet my co-workers at 10:30 p.m. We're doing a Safeway store. I needed the coffee.

"Hi!" said Kari to me. "Do you have the time?"

"It is a few minutes 'til nine."

"Oh, dear — he's not coming back!" She looked like she was about to cry.

"What's wrong?" I asked.

"A man picked me up in Berkeley. I live in Sacramento. I need to be at work at 10:30. He told me that he was going to Reno and he would drop me off there *BUT* he needed to come back here to get some clothes. I agreed. I was stupid. He dropped me off here so that I could get some-thing to eat and he'd be right back. That was quit a bit ago."

"Can't you call your work and explain things?"

"I don't have enough money to pay for the call and pay for the food. They won't accept collect calls. I'll lose my room and I have clients waiting."

"What kind of work do you do?"

"At a massage parlor — I'm a masseuse. Next September, I'm going to start beauty school."

"No offense but, you look only around fifteen. How old are you?"

"I'm eighteen. How old are you?"

"I'm twenty." I reached into my pocket and handed her a five." Get some change and make the call short.

"You're sweet! What's your name? I'm Kari."

"I'm Ken."

"What do you do for a living?"

"I work for an inventory company. We're doing a store tonight and I'm meeting my co-workers at 10:30 here. I'm on a break from college for a year or so. I'm an English and music major."

"Do you go to Chabot College?"

"No, Pasadena College in Pasadena."

"Do you plan to be a teacher?"

"No, I've substituted and taught Sunday school but I I don't have the patience to teach, I'm a writer, a poet and I write short stories."

"Have you written anything that I'd know?"

"Probably not. I've had some of my poems published in literary magazines, along with other writers. I've written a poetry book called 'Bey' that I'd like to see published."

"Is it about the ocean?"

"Oh, no—It's spelled B-E-Y, not B-A-Y. I have a poem called 'Bey' about a girl named Karen Bey. I like the word so I titled the book, 'Bey'."

"Well, I'll go make my call."

When Kari returned, she asked for another iced tea.

Kari turned to me. "For $60, I can give you a massage and a . . ."

"I don't think so."

"It was worth a try.

"Well, there's my group coming in." The three men and two ladies came over to me and ordered coffee to go. I asked for a 'go cup' and another cup of coffee. I introduced them to Kari. They all shook her hand. Before I left, I gave Kari an Ellery Queen magazine to read. I forgot about my change.

The next morning, when it was light, Kari paid her bill and left the restaurant . . . alone.

THE PORCUPINE

The boys were back in town in '74. The boys were back in town for the funeral—Kaz Waulker's funeral. They were staying ay Judy's house, on Porter St. in Fremont, CA. She's Kaz's ex-lady.

The funeral was beautiful. Several hundred people attended. It was a closed casket ceremony but Kaz wasn't in the casket. Nobody will claim who, if anyone was in the casket and nobody will claim how the switch was done but, Kaz wasn't dead. He had toyed with the idea of attended his funeral by sitting in the balcony like Huck Finn did but, he found that there was no balcony in the church.

Later that day:

Kaz was listening to a Neil Young album, 'Harvest' in the back bedroom. The songs were recorded soft but the record was turned up loud. He didn't hear the knocking at the door. The door was unlocked so, I just let myself in. I walked through the empty house to the back bedroom. Kaz was sitting with his back to the door. Besides the record player was another record and a 45, a few other small things on the floor, and Kaz, the only things in the room.

"Hi!" With the record as loud as it was, I was definitely not whispering. It was a good record. Kaz didn't hear me. When I reached out and tapped him on the shoulder, it startled him and he jumped.

"Hi! Didn't hear you come in. Have a seat."

I sat on the floor facing him. One of his eyes was red, not from crying. It was just bloodshot. He said that it didn't hurt any. "You look sexy." I said.

"What!"

"Well, when I dress like that, T-shirt and levies, I tell myself that I'm sexy. I need to buy that record." I did in '79.

The record played through and then Kaz turned it over. When that side was finished, he turned it over again. Kaz and I sat through two and a half sides of the record without talking. When that side was through again, Kaz took it off of the turntable and put it back into the Jacket. Then, he looked over at me. "Young's good. Good record, huh? **B**etter than The Springfield — well, maybe not. I did have a friend who was hooked on heroin 'Needle and the damage was done' (referring to the song). Want some lunch?"

"No, I've already eaten."

"What was the funeral like? Was it nice?" asked Kaz.

"It was real nice — real nice. There were a lot of people there and a lot of . . ." I sneezed.

"Bless you!"

"Thank-you! Um, there were a lot of nice things said about you."

Kaz smiled. "That's nice. Want some coffee? I'm going to have a cup."

I sneezed again, probably from the dust and dirt.

"Man, bless you, Ken."

"Thanks, I'd like a cup, black."

"I thought that you used milk and sugar?"

"I do, a lot. Black just sounds good. I had a lot of sweets at the funeral luncheon."

"Lunch?"

"A lu-u-uncheon! It was fancy with fancy cheeses and nuts and cold cuts, sparkling cider and a huge cake."

"Wow!"

Kaz stood up and left the room. He was gone for quite a while. He finally walked back into the room with two sandwiches.

"Here, Ken, I hate to eat alone. It's Kielbasa."

"Okay! I'll eat it. I love Kielbasa. The only sausage that I don't care for is Brats — a little too bland for me. There's another German one that I don't care for but I don't remember what it's called. It's almost white and it's boiled. I'm not hungry though, you know." I took the sandwich and took a bite of it."

"I don't know what it's called either but, I'll be back with the coffee."

When Kaz came back with the coffee, I asked him if he had any mustard.

"Oh yeah, sorry."

He left and returned with a tiny jar and two knives. I sat my coffee on the floor. "This is Chinese mustard, Ken. It's hot! It will clear your whole head so only use a little."

"Ahhhh!! It sure did!" I started coughing. "I need some water."

"No! You need some alcohol or milk. That's the only thing that will ease the hurt. I'll get you some." He returned with a fifth of vodka, almost a quart of milk and two glasses. I downed the milk and another glass.

We ate the sandwiches and more milk for me—vodka with milk for Kaz.

Kaz started mumbling but he soon became progressively clearer. "As a kid, we either had tuna or peanut butter sandwiches at every lunchtime. We were poor and couldn't afford much more for lunches but we always had milk and Basco. Or, my Mom would buy a package of straws that had flavor in them. I'd suck on a glass of milk and magically it would be chocolate or strawberry milk."

"I remember the flavor straws and Basco. I like Olvatine. Go ahead, finish your story."

"Being poor, at Christmas, we'd go to Christmas Eve service, yes—I went to church. We're Methodist and then go home and open presents. One Christmas, it snowed. I was probably four or five and I never seen it snow before. My Mom and Dad would buy us kids a toy or two that they could take apart and they would wrap them in five or six boxes and we'd have six gifts instead of one or two."

"Do you ever still go to church?"

"Not for many years, I haven't. I still pray nearly every day and I remind and thank God and Jesus for all the good things that they've done for me."

I asked Kaz where the bathroom was.

"Down the hall, and to your left."

"Okay!"

"Yeah, go for me, too."

After a few minutes, I walked back into the room. "Did you go for me?" he asked.

"Yeah, I was going to but you didn't have to go."

"Well, thanks anyways, Ken." Then he laughed—I smiled. "Did I ever tell you about my DUI? I got it in Hayward."

"No, I don't think so."

"Well, I was in a bar called Red River. Remember that name, it's important. I was drunk and so the bartender named Emily, I'm surprised I remember her name. Well, Emily called a friend of mine to come pick me up. He only lived a couple of miles away. Well, I started drinking just coffee. I was talking to a girl at the bar when her husband or boyfriend came in drunk and mean. He didn't like the fact that I was talking to her and he started threating me. I told Emily that I was going to wait in my Mustang until my friend got there. Well now, the girl's boyfriend followed me out. I unlocked the car door. I got in the car and locked the door. The others were already locked. He picked up a rock or a brick and started pounding on the window and the windshield. I was scared so I drove off. I knew that there was a 24 hour restaurant a couple of blocks away and I knew that Kenney, same name as you, huh, would probably go there looking for me if he didn't see me in the parking lot. We went to that restaurant quite a bit for pie with cheese. I drove slow near the curb but about a half-a-block away a cop pulled me over. I explained to the cop what happened and where I was headed but I had to spend the night in jail, anyways.

"I demanded a trial so, 'bout a week before the trial, I went back to the bar and the bartender was there. She remembered me and I told her my story. A while later, the girl that I was talking to came in. She was friends with Emily and we both talked to her. She agreed that her husband, he wasn't her boyfriend, was very jealous and he was mean when he drank and that she would testify on my behalf in court. Emily would, too.

The morning that I got home from jail, I called Kenney. He had gone to a bar called River Run in San Lorenzo to pick me up. He said that he'd testify, too.

"Well, the judge said that under the circumstances, that I could have been seriously hurt by that guy, the case was dismissed. He believed me. I *was* telling the judge the truth, Ken!

"You came up here from L.A. didn't you, Ken?"

"Yeah, from a college reunion, not mine. How come?"

"Where did the other guys come here from?"

"Gee, I don't know where they all live. I just assume that they were still in the Fremont area. How come?"

"Just wondered if we'd ever all get together again someday. Concord is a little too far to hitchhike and I don't think that Judy would welcome me after what I just did."

"Sure, we will. Look, I'm going over to Judy's later. I'll hint around and try to fill her out without giving you away. Shoot, why don't you just come over with me and explain things? They'll be glad to see you resurrected from the dead like Lazarus." I laughed. "It will be a real surprise. A *real* surprise! They were all at the funeral."

Kaz smiled. "Yeah, it sure would be a surprise. I can't go over there. I'm going to miss her and I'm sorry about that. When you see them, don't tell them that you saw me, okay?"

"Alright, if you want. Hey, Kaz?"

"Yeah!"

"How come you went through all this and, who's in the casket."

Kaz gave me an attacking look. "I just did, okay?" There was a little pause. "Okay?" he was smiling, I'm sorry that I got mad with you. No one is in the casket, just heavy bags of stuff. Man, it's hot in here. I'm going to open a window and put on some cutoffs." He did and another T-shirt (There was a mustard stain on the one that he was wearing.) and put his long, dark hair into a ponytail.

Kaz put on a 45 record from '63, The Squires (Neil Young's first group, released only in Canada). The song was called 'The Sultan' and then he put on a Paul Horn record and turned the record player down. "Kenny, I'm gay, bi-sexual but mostly gay. If Judy and the guys knew, it would kill me. I had to get out." I didn't know what to say so I picked up a magazine from the floor and thumbed through it. It was a fish and game magazine. Kaz grew a surprised look on his face. "You never knew, did you?" I knew that Kaz understood my silence. I knew that he knew that we were still good friends. I could feel it.

"Hey, Waulker, anything good in here?" I held up the magazine.

"Don't know." I only read one article. It was about porcupines. Man, they're dirty animals. They'll live in their own filth and eat it if they have to. You can corner them up a tree and they'll stay up there for months without moving. When they do eat, they'll eat anything. They're worse than a billy goat."

I read the article. When I put the magazine down, I looked over at Kaz. He had just lit a cigarette and was burning hairs on his leg with it. I finished my cooled coffee.

"How about one last cup of coffee with a spoon of sugar and some milk, if you have it?"

"Yeah, okay! Ouch! Son of a . . ."

"What happened?"

"I burned myself. I'll get the coffee. Two spoons of sugar, right?"

"Two this time, It was a little strong, and some milk."

"It's been sitting in the percolator all morning just bubbling away. I add some water to it every once in a while. I like that bubbling sound it makes in the morning when it's being made. Seems like they'd come up with a way to keep coffee fresh with-out getting stronger or more bitter. Want another sandwich? Kenny, didn't you live overseas for a while?"

"In '62, a few years after my twelfth birthday, we moved to West Pakistan. My Dad got a construction job. They were building a dam near the India border. My Dad went over three month before my Mom, sister and I did. The three of us stayed in Honolulu, Tokyo, and Hong Kong for a few days each. We lived there for two-and-a-half years. I've been to India three times. I saw the Taj Mahal three times — once by air, once by train and the first time, by being on the grounds and inside. It's beautiful. And, we went to East Pakistan. On the way home to the States, we went to Istanbul, Bagdad, the Holy Lands, Egypt, and Greece. In Rome, my Dad picked a Mercedes that he had ordered from Stuttgart, Germany and then we drove through Europe for three months."

"Did you like living there?"

"Oh my, yes!"

"What was your favorite country?"

"Oh, gosh! That's a hard one. I like Hong Kong. I loved India. I guess on the way home I liked Greece and Istanbul the best, and Bagdad. Austria was beautiful. I like London. That's a hard question. I liked everywhere that we went to."

"You're lucky, I've only been to Tijuana but, I was there three times. Smoked Cuban cigars which are illegal here." Kaz smiled and chuckled.

"The nice thing is that my sister and I were old enough to enjoy and to remember it all."

"How'd you get here from L.A.? I mean, you didn't drive, did you?"

"No, my water pump went out. I wanted to get her for the funeral so, I hitched a ride, well, several rides. I left yesterday morning."

"How'd you know that I lived here in Concord?"

"Oh, word gets around — just like I knew you didn't die. Say, you don't have any other records besides Neil Young and that one, do you."

Kaz shook his head 'no'. "I had a ZZ Top but I cracked it, sat on it."

"How'd you do that? Were you drinking?"

"I just forgot that it was there and I sat on it."

"How about a radio?"

Kaz shook his head 'no' again. "Why? Don't you like Paul Horn?"

"Yeah, but I'm kinda getting tired of it."

Kaz picked up his sandwich from the floor, brushed the bottom of it off and started eating it.

"Do you still play guitar, Kaz?"

He shook his head 'no' and finished his sandwich. He took a sip of coffee. "No!" he said.

"No, what?"

"No to your question. I don't play my axe anymore. When I left the Header's bar, I had to pawn it off and the amp for a hundred. I needed money."

"That's all you got? You shoulda come to me! I would have given you more than that with the option to buy them back with payments."

"Sure! On what you were making there. You had a girlfriend to look after. You couldn't spare a hundred."

"Lenny and I didn't live together and she had a good job. We were only good friends. I've got a girl named Carolyn but she wants to get married. I don't know. I don't think so."

"Get out of here! You may have someone back home but you can't tell me that you and Lenny didn't love each other. What about that lady in Kansas City or wherever?"

"She's just a friend, someone to write too. I've only met her once. Man, why are you on my case about women? Get back a little!"

Kaz smiled. "Just like ol' times, huh?"

"Yeah, Kaz and I hated it then, too." Kaz laughed and then, I did.

"Man, I don't know how we made it back then"

"Back then? It was only a few months ago, not more than a year. You make it sound like it was years ago. I thought that it was good times. Where else could you work for five hours a day? A musician's life was the life of Riley."

"Yeah, all for just $22.73 each a night. Did anyone ever figure out why the seventy-three cents. If the band was still together, we could get several hundred a week each, at least."

"Yeah! That's why I quit, Kenny. Not enough bread. If my Grandma didn't leave me this house, I don't know what I'd do. But, we did have some good time though, didn't we?"

"Yeah, I miss it. That life was a habit. Say, what do you do with yourself all day, Waulker?"

"Just sit here all day in my filth of mind, the memories. I don't want the past things to catch up with me. It was to filthy but the memories will always be there."

"After you and the others, one by one left the group, I left Heder's . . ." I heard a loud scream outside. "What was that? Some ones hurt!"

"That's Mariam next door. She's taking some kind of scream therapy. She's alright,. Well, she not hurt. She'll be singing opera, bad opera just as loud in a little while. She screams better than she sings. So, what about the bar?"

"After you all left the group, I up shopped and left Heder's, too." Another few minutes of silence and then I asked, "Are you seeing a girl now, Kaz?"

"Yeah, for a few days now but I don't want to talk about her. You wouldn't understand about Dana."

"May I ask why?"

Kaz ignored the question. "Man, those were the best days of my life at Heder's.

"I want some more coffee and another sandwich. I don't know why I'm so tired or hungry. Want anything?"

"No, thanks!"

"Okay! I'll be right back."

I picked up the magazine and started thumbing through it again. After just a few minutes, Kaz walked back into the room eating another sandwich but no coffee.

"Kaz, I gotta leave in a little bit."

"Okay! I used to work in a winery up north, not in the Napa Valley. It was on the highway past Sacramento, on the way to Redding." Kaz stopped talking. Outside, we heard singing, opera. "See! She can't sing, huh, Ken?"

With a sneer on my face. "Man, she sounds like a she's singing through a phase shifter with a distortion pedal or something!" We both laughed.

"Well, anyways, we'd also grow and sell olives with different types of fillings, garlic, anchovy's, just different kinds of fillings, even with just the pit—mostly green olives. All of the wines came from the same vineyard. I'd go to other wineries and compare the different personalities of their wines with ours.

"When are you getting married, Ken?" Kaz smiled.

"That's something that I'm staying away from if I can, for a while. Hey, we need to stay in touch. Boy, that lady is annoying!"

"I don't know where I'll be. I can't collect unemployment or welfare because I'm 'dead'. Maybe if I change my name, I don't know. Let me get the coffee. It should be done by now."

"I'm coffeed out! Kaz, let me ask you this. What would you like to do with your life. You're a heck of a mandolin player and guitar player. You could play anywhere."

"I need to change my name and get a new ID and I want to learn cello. I want to play rock or jazz on it, but classical is a must. I have an instruction book by Christopher Parkening. He's really into Back. I need to learn classical guitar. I need to start that guitar book. I like Bill Evans and Béla Bartók on the piano."

"Cello?" Kaz left the room. I looked around the empty room. In one corner were a red blanket and a pair of Levis on the floor, forming a pillow and bed. I hadn't noticed them before. I guess Kaz slept there. Near the Levis' was a copy of 'Jonathan Livingston Seagull', written by Richard Bach, about a seagull learning about life and flight, and an account about self-perfection. The room was exceptionally dirty.

"Kaz!" I yelled into the other room.

"Yeah!" He walked into the room with two cups of coffee. He handed me one of them and set down, setting his cup on the floor. I did the same. "I remember a few years ago, I went home to Straton, Oregon and surprised my parents. I got there almost midnight. My Mom made hot chocolate and we all talked until two in the morning. They live on a dairy farm and also grow Bing cherries and boysenberries. He, my Dad don't have any farm hands and he had to get up around four a.m. That morning, he let me sleep in but around 9:30 he came into my room. 'Let's get some coffee.' He said. I knew he wasn't talking about in the kitchen. I got dressed as quick as I could and put my hat on. We had biscuits and gravy and talked, just talked. Soon, the waitress came with the lunch menus. I was surprised that it was a quarter to twelve. We had lunch. Even though my Dad is very busy with the farm, he gave up his time for me. I know that they love me very much but I feel like I'm a big disappointment to them. I know that I'm not."

I looked down and then back at Kaz. I was touched my his story. After a few minute, when I felt that it was appropriate, I said "I'm going back to L.A. in a couple of days to pick up my car and I have a four day gig. I could use a guitar player. How about it?"

"We'll see. I doubt it. I'd need to find a guitar."

"I wish that I could help you out more. Why can't your brother help you out?"

"He's not my brother. He's my mother and my father's other son."

"I got to go. I wish you well. I love you, brother. We'll see you, Buddy

Sometime after I left, Kaz left his house and hitched a ride over to Oakland, MacArthur Blvd. As he walked down the street, a lady yelled out, "Hi, Kaz!"

"Hi, Pat! How ya doing?"

"Okay, I guess. I just got back from a funeral."

"This must be the season" he thought to himself. "Man, that's a bummer. Was it a relative?"

"No, it was a girl that worked out here on the streets." Pat nodded towards the street. "She was robbed and murdered."

"I'm so sorry to hear that. I'm sorry to do this but I really have to get going, Pat. We'll see you later, huh? I really don't know what to say. Try to cheer up."

"Sure, bye, Baby."

Kaz walked down the Boulevard about another block.

"Hi, Love."

Kaz turned around and smiled. "Hi, Dana. How's business tonight? Are you doing okay?"

"Slow, real slow, but I guess that's how it goes when you're only seeing men that you know. It's getting scary out here now. How are you?"

"Fine! A friend that I haven't seen in a while stopped by unexpected. We started talking about church."

"Oh, yeah, church? Nobody's been walking by and hell, the cops are all over the place tonight. It's making it real tight. My man's going to be mad when I tell him I didn't make any money tonight."

"What kind of trouble will you be in, Dana?"

Oh, probably just won't do anything except slap me around some and yell a lot. And probably, I won't get to sleep with him tonight. Tonight's my turn. I don't want to lose my turn.

"Someday, I want to take you someplace real nice for dinner. Are you dating tonight, Kaz?"

"I don't think so."

"Why? How come?"

"I don't have very much money. I was just planning on seeing you, talking to you here for a little bit."

"That's sweet! How much money do you have?"

"All I have is fifteen."

Dana frowned. "Okay, Come on, Love."

"Dana, let's go for some coffee."

"My pimp, he might be in the restaurant. O.k. and some pie. Say is this church thing bothering you."

"It just brought back lots of memories and I started to think, maybe I should start going again. I really enjoyed . . ." They kept walking.

PORTER ST.

This was an un-family reunion after a previous day's funeral. I was expected yesterday. I don't know exactly what time I arrived at Judy's house. I wasn't wearing my watch at the time. The door was open so I just walked in.

"Hey, is anybody here?" I heard music being played inside.

"Yeah! We're back here in the kitchen." someone hollered.

I took my cap off and walked back to the kitchen. Judy, Bob, Larry, Karl, and Jerry were there. Jerry had a beard half way down his chest, wearing bib overalls. Larry looked like he belonged on Beale St., Memphis with his black shiny suit and tie, white shirt, shades, and fedora. Judy, pigtails, a muu-muu and barefoot was singing and playing autoharp with Bob, hair down his back and ponytailed, on guitar. The others and I wore Levis, T-shirts and baseball caps. I was raised not to wear a hat indoors. The others, probably not. Everyone had some kind of instrument.

"Hey, Dude!" from Karl.

Judy smiled. "Hey, Sweetie, I've missed you. Pull up a chair 'round the table. Want some coffee?"

Yeah! That sounds good. Cream and a spoon of sugar, please." I told Judy.

"Yeah, I remember. I have real cream, not that powdered stuff unless you want skimmed milk." I shook my head, 'no'.

The phone rang. "Hello!" answered Judy. (Pause) He'll meet you at 7:00 a.m. (Pause) Go to 30th and P." Everybody in the room began laughing. It tool Judy a minute to catch on. "Good luck, good-bye." She said, still laughing.

I sat at the table and rested my elbow on the table with the beer cans and the flies. Judy sat a mug of coffee and a small pitcher of cream by my arm. The coffee was a little strong so it wasn't sweet enough for me.

"Thanks, Jude."

"Yeah! You're welcome. Hey, I wrote a song the other day. Let me play it for you, ok?"

"Ok!" some said.

"Play it with me, Bobby. Put in some of that fancy stuff you do."

"What are we playing?"

"'Dancing In the Street!', not the R&B version."

"I don't know that."

"Yes, you do! We've played it together before. You know!"

"Judy, I don't . . . I don't!"

"Bob . . ." She played it by herself and then, everybody clapped.

On the table was a dingy white tablecloth with green embroidery. I took a sip of Judy's coffee.

"Want a beer?" Karl asked.

"No thanks!" I said. "I don't drink."

"Yeah, I know what you mean. Sometimes I'm not in a mood for a beer, either." Karl added.

"No, it's not that. I don't drink."

"No matter, it's not important. Let's sing and play another song, all of us." Judy smiled.

"What'll we do?" from Jerry.

Larry mentioned 'Will The Circle Be Unbroken' but nobody knew it. I was surprised.

"Then, how about doing 'Freight Train'?" I said.

"Nope, don't know it." said Larry and Karl, almost together.

"I thought that all folk musicians knew that one." I said.

Judy smiled. "It's a good song to know. We'll have to learn it sometime."

"Yeah, we do!" from several.

Judy looked across the table at me. "Do you play guitar or anything besides piano? I forget."

"Yeah, a little."

"O.k. There's a guitar, and a mandolin hanging on the wall behind you. Take your pick."

"My main instrument is piano, if you have one . . ." I told the others. "and banjo. I play four string a little and ukulele."

"Really! Larry, get Ken the 5-string out of the closet in the hall, would you? Don't worry, Ken, the top string is broke off."

I tuned the banjo to the same as a slack key guitar and then we did a Hank Williams tune, 'I Saw The Light.' With me on banjo, Judy on autoharp, Bob on guitar, Larry on harpoon (harmonica), Karl doing rhythm on the table, and eefing and ham-bone by Jerry. Judy and Bob sang the verses and we all joined in on the chorus. We sounded pretty good. After that, Jerry picked up a fiddle off of the floor and we did 'Orange Blossom Special'.

"You can play that one but you don't know 'The Circle Be Unbroken'? I asked.

Jerry put down the fiddle and then he looked over at me. "I know you from someplace. Did you have a beard?"

"Yeah, but I've been over here playing before."

"Yeah! And you set shop in a place called Cachino's down in L.A. playing piano, too, huh?"

"Uh-huh, It was Pasadena, in college. I'd play for tips and for the greasiest, best chili I ever ate. Pools of grease floated on top. They'd put in hamburger, ground pork and ground bear meat. Bear meat is sweet but greasy."

"Yeah, I remember. You wouldn't remember me 'cause you probably met all kinds of people but I used to come in sometimes. The chili was greazy and good."

I only smiled. Very few people came into that bar and grill. I'm surprised that they stayed in business the two years that I'd go in. I took another sip of coffee. It was cold. Someone burped from the beer. "Excuse me!" but nobody noticed, or nobody said anything

Larry loudly cleared his throat. "Down the road a piece, north, is a bar, O'Reighly's Irish Pub. I know one of the bartenders named Joey. He asked me if some of my musician friends would want to come down on a regular basis and play for tips and beer. How about it, guys—and lady? Irish Gaelic music is just like bluegrass."

"I do that at a pizza parlor in San Leandro on Mondays and Tuesdays, except for the beer." I told them.

. Judy asked if we knew 'Me And Bobby McGee'. We all said yes. Bob said no but he'd try to fake it. Larry asked what key it was in and Judy said 'G'.

"Could you do it in 'F'? My harpoon is in 'C' and blues cross harp would make it in 'F'." I had no Idea what he was talking about.

"I can't!" came Judy.

"Sure you can." I said. "Use your index finger like a capo."

"Yeah, it's only F, B♭ and C." Larry added.

"O.k. I'll try it."

The song went o.k., not great, just o.k.

"Hey, Honey," Judy said, smiling at me. 'how ya doing? Haven't seen you for a while. What have you been doing with yourself?"

"Nothing, really. College awhile back. I'm going up to Redding. I have a friend up there that's real sick. Another friend wrote and said that myfriend wanted to see me. After that, I don't know what I'll do. Maybe go down to L.A. again."

Jerry started talking. "That's pretty country up by Redding. A buddy of mine lives in a place called McCloud, on a ranch, I think, and he loves it. Man, it's pretty up there. I wouldn't mind living up there."

Jerry continued. "Last night I saw a movie called 'Murphy's War'"

"Yeah, I saw that." said Karl.

"Judy looked over at Jerry. "What's it about?"

Jerry and Karl both started to answer. "It's about . . ." Karl kept talking. Jerry gave up. ". . . this dude whose ship, I think it was a ship, is blown up and he's the only one who lives. He gets hold of this plane and bombs a sub but it doesn't sink it. At the end, he's on this barge and drops a torpedo on the sub but it sinks the barge which he didn't intend for it to do and he dies. It was a good movie. It had Peter O'Toole in it."

"Thank you mister movie critic." said a sarcastic Jerry.

"Want some more coffee or beers?" Judy asked.

"No thanks, maybe later." I said. The others took the beers.

"You're staying for dinner with us, aren't you?" asked Judy.

"Anyone know where's Ross?" Bob looked around waiting for an answer.

"Yeah, he's at the beach, Santa Cruz." answered Jerry.

"Who's Ross?" I whispered to Judy.

"He's this cat that plays a mean guitar. He makes Bob look like a beginner."

"Thanks, Babe. Say, listen, I'm not that good anyways. Bob looked over at me. "I'm really not. I can be sloppy, making a lot of mistakes like Jimmy Page in Zeppelin. He's sloppy if you really listen to him."

"He really is—good, I mean. Bob, not Page I'm talking about." Judy said. She lit up a cigarette and started playing her guitar. "First one I've had today." She said, holding up the cigarette. I'm trying to quit but it's hard. You don't smoke, do you Kenny?"

"Never have, drugs either."

"You're lucky. I'm proud of you, Ken." praised Jerry.

"I have good parents that raised me right,"

"That's good, really good!" Judy started singing a song that she wrote. I didn't care for it much. When she finished, we all started in on 'Foggy Mountain Breakdown' with Bob doing the guitar part and Judy and Larry both doing the banjo part on the autoharp and harmonica. They were excellent.

When we finished the song, we all clapped for the trio, giving them a standing ovation. Judy, Larry and Bob smiled at each other. "You know, guys, we should do it again. That was fun." Everyone said o.k. so, we did—and the song just went on and on, everyone doing a solo. After what seemed only a few minutes—it was more like twenty—the song ended. It just sort of fell apart at the end. Nobody knew how to end the thing. For the few minutes that followed, we all just sat there, not saying anything to anybody. I think that the song just wore everybody out. Some lit cigarettes and sipped beers. Judy reached for her cigarette but it was just ash. We both just sat there. The feeling was layback. Then, Karl yelled a 'Yeah!' and then it was quiet again for awhile.

Larry was the first to break the silence. "Karl?"

"Yeah, Larry."

"When did you, I mean, where did you see that movie?"

"Murphy's War?"

"Yeah!"

"On T.V. last night at nine. It was on VHS but I forget what channel it was on—probably on 20. I was at my ol' ladies house and we watched it on her set. She didn't like it. It kinda started out bad, you know, boring but it picked up as it went along. It was a good flick. See it if you can."

"Yeah but, you ruined the ending. Dude."

"Sorry, Dude!"

Larry took a sip of his beer and a drag on his cigarette before putting it out. He looked to his left at Bob and then, across the table at me.

"What?" I I questioned. I probably sounded annoyed.

"Say, Ken, how would you like to judge a dance contest? I was going to but I have to go into Oakland to court in the afternoon. It's day after tomorrow and I don't think I'll be back in time. How 'bout it?"

"Tuesday?"

"Yeah, It's . . ."

Jerry was sitting to the left of Judy. She didn't look at him when he spoke, "Where's it going to be, Larry?"

"Huh? Why do you ask that?"

"It's not an amateur contest at the Hip Hugger, is it? That's the only place around that I know that they have dance contests."

"Ken, you don't want to do it. The Hip Hugger is topless and it's sleazy."

"I'm not going to be in town anyways Even if I was, sorry, but I'm not interested."

"Alright, I'll get someone else. Just thought I'd ask."

Judy looked over to me. "I used to dance go-go at a bar in Newark and that was bad enough but in a topless dive. That's what they are, dives. Want some more coffee, Love?"

"No thanks, Jude. Hey, Judy, how old are you?

"Never ask a lady her age. Kenny. I'm thirty-two."

"Really? I took you for twenty-one or two."

"Excuse me, Karl." Judy accidentally kicked him in the foot. She looked back to me. "Yeah, I know, Ken. I don't mean to brag but a lot of people think that. When I'm fifty, maybe I'll look thirty-five or something. You look young yourself. How old are you, eighteen? No, you have to be at least twenty-one. How old are you?"

"I'm twenty-four, just turned." I sat the banjo onto the floor.

Karl tilted his chair back so that he could see me past Jerry. "Don't do that, Ken. We'll be playing again in a sec." He looked at Judy. "Have you got any crackers and some cheese to go with it? I'm kinda hungry."

"Sure, we got Monterey Jack and Brie, if that's o.k."

"Sure, fine, anything, I'm starved."

"What's Brie?" asked Jerry to Judy.

"It's for the Avant-guard society folk and it tastes like mushrooms. It's my favorite cheese but I don't get it very often because it's expensive."

"Anybody else want some? Need to know how many knives and plates to bring over."

Bob doesn't like cheese but the rest of us said yes. Karl asked Judy if she had any wine to go with the cheese and crackers.

"Only Thunderbird and Cream Sherry."

"Yeah! Bring those over, if it's alright."

. . . she did

then she sat down.

The phone rang and with a mouth full of cheese and crackers, she answered the phone. "Hello . . ."

Jerry started staring at the ceiling. I looked up to see what he was looking at. I didn't see anything. I looked at Jerry, sitting next to me, and then, back up to the ceiling.

"What are you looking at?"

"Nothing, just the ceiling. Say, Larry, what's this about judging that contest?' still staring at the ceiling.

"If you're interested, just show up by a quarter to ten and tell them . . ."

"Go to hell!" We all turned to see Judy slam the receiver down. "That guy has been calling me for three weeks and I'm getting sick and tired of it! He just hangs on without saying anything. What can I do about it?"

Bob giggled. "Just keep a whistle by the phone and the next time he calls, just blow the whistle into the receiver. He'll quit calling."

"Ow! That hurts just thinking about it." she said.

"Yeah, Jude, but it'll make him quit calling you. Trust me, Babe!"

"O.k. Where can I buy a whistle?"

Jerry, still looking at the ceiling looked down and over to Judy. "I'll get you a plastic one for 39 cents."

"Where?"

"At any dime store like Woolworths."

"Really? You can just go into a dime store and buy a whistle?"

"Yeah, I'll have it for you tomorrow . . . no charge."

"Jerry, your generosity overwhelms me!"

"Think nothing of it, Judy Honey."

"Oh, I won't, Jerry Honey! Don't worry about that because, I won't." They both snickered. Judy accidently spit, which made her laugh harder, and then, everyone else laughed.

Jerry sipped some cream sherry. "You know what we need? We need Bob the Younger here with his bongos. I wonder why he didn't come."

Judy went over to the counter and opened a drawer. I have his number. Let's call him." Everyone shook their heads, 'Yes'."

Karl asked Judy, "Does he still love Rueben sandwiches with extra Russian dressing?"

"I have no idea. How would I know?" asked Judy.

"I don't remember him." said Larry. "Why do you call him Bob the Younger?"

"You should. You probably remember him as Rob." replied Judy.

"Oh, sure, before he went to calling himself Bob."

Judy dialed the number. After a few seconds pause, Judy started talking. "Bobby, this is Judy, Did you get my letter? The guys are all here jamming."

Karl interrupted, "Ask him if he still loves Rueben sandwiches with extra Russian dressing."

"Just a minute, Bob. There's a distraction in here."

"Ask him if he still loves Rueben sandwiches with extra Russian dressing."

"No!"

"Ask him if he still loves Rueben sandwiches with extra Russian dressing. Ask him . . ."

"I'm back. (Pause) "That's too bad. Say, do you loves Rueben sandwiches with extra Russian dressing? (Pause) Oh, I was just reminiscing. I'll let you go. I love you. (Pause) Thank-you, Baby, bye." Judy hung up the phone. "He's sick. He's got something called Valley Fever. I never heard of it." Everybody agreed.

I asked "Why do they call him 'Bob the Younger'?

Because he's younger then this Bob.' someone said.

Larry finished a glass of Thunderbird wine and then looked over at me. "Hey. Dude, you said that you were going to Redding and then back to L.A.?"

"Yeah, I'll probably go back down south. I have family in Pasadena that I haven't seen in a while and my car is down there with a busted water pump . . ."

"Are you going to set shop at Cachino's again?"

"No but I'll stop in to visit if they're still in business. There was no money there. How come you asked?"

"Just wondered. Might come down there again. I'd like to see if I could get some session work playing. It would be nice to work at a recording studio. I could use a ride."

"Alright, but I don't know when I'll be down there. I'm on my way up tp Redding, then, I don't know what. I have a friend in Concord that might go down with me. I have a friend, Bernie that does session work in Hollywood. He plays drums, traps. Speaking of work, what do you all do? I do telemarketing."

Judy took a sip of sherry. I'm on welfare." Except for Karl, they all said the same thing.

Judy looked at Karl. "What do you do?"

"Let's just say that I'm an entrepreneur."

"A what?" asked Larry.

"I supply things to people for a lot of bread."

Karl changed the subject. He sounded nervous. "My best buddy just got married Friday. We had the rehearsal and dinner the day before and the wedding, Friday at eight. I was the best man."

"Lives just beginning and Kaz's just ending." Judy said with a troubled look. Judy asked what the colors were.

I think that they were green and yellow."

"You think! You were there and you don't know?"

"Yeah, I do. They were. It was a real nice wedding. There leaving today at five-thirty" Karl looked at the clock on the wall. "In fact, they're leaving about now. They went to Hawaii, Kauai for their Honeymoon."

"Hawaii!" Judy was excited." Marry me, Kenny and let's go to Hawaii."

"O.k. You know what I'm going to do in a few months? For the past two years, I've been writing and calling a girl in Kansas City that works with my sister and she's going to fly her out to see me. I'm sending her the ticket. She doesn't know it yet. It's going to be a neat surprise, don't you think?"

Judy smiled. "I sure do. That's so romantic."

Bob look straight across the table at me. "Say, um . . . I hate to mention this, man, and spoil your surprise but, what if she can't or doesn't want to come, spending all that bread for nothing."

"Oh, she'll let me know if she's coming out here or not before I buy the ticket. I'll check with her, first."

"Yeah, Ken, you better. The way you told it, it just sounded like you were just going to send her the ticket out of the blue." Bob took a sip of his wine and a slug of beer. "Yeah!" Bob continued. "I think that that's a good idea. It might save you a lot of cash. Where is she coming to, Oakland or San Jose?"

"Gee, I didn't think about that. I'll have to pay for her motel and I should help out on her meals, shouldn't I?"

"No, I wouldn't pay everything. What is she, poor? The trip is a big expense. She'll appreciate that, I hope. Just let her shack up with you."

"I wouldn't have no room for her. Well, we'll have to just wait and see. I don't even know if she's coming or not."

"Bob, when you said 'out of the blue', it reminded me of a song that we all use to do, 'Beyond The Blue Horizon'. Let's do it." We did.

I watched Judy starting a cigarette and putting it down. "That's a pretty ring, Judy."

"Thanks, Babe. My ex gave it to me."

"Kaz?" someone asked

"No, my husband."

"I didn't know you were married."

"Yeah, twice. My first ol' man told me that he didn't care . . ."

Jerry took a small, round cardboard box from his vest pocket. He opened it and took a little of something that was brown and moist. He placed it 'tween his cheek and gums. This happened while Judy was still talking.

". . . if I went out with other men and he could go out with other women. The first thing that I did was to divorce him and marry my lover, well, the man I really loved. I never was unfaithful to any of my men."

Jerry passed the little round box to Karl, on his left and Karl passed it to Larry, then Larry to Bob and Bob to Me and then Me back to Jerry. Larry was the only one who took any. He did just what Jerry did, placed it 'tween his cheek and gums.

Judy was still talking. "That's all he was good for, making love. Not that I have anything against that, goodness no. It's just that, he wouldn't work or anything else. He's the one who gave me the ring. Made it himself. It was my wedding ring. We wanted something different, that nobody else had, you know? He would have been a fine jeweler if he had applied himself but, he was lazy."

While the box was being passed around, I must of looked confused or *something*. Jerry looked over at me. "What's the matter, kid? Never seen stuff before? Here, try some. It's flavored with wintergreen."

"Maybe in a T.V. commercial. No, that's o.k. I'll pass. Hey, it's getting late. I've got to get going."

Judy looked over at Jerry and Larry. "You better go outside and spit with that stuff. I swear, my first ol' man would spit in dishes, cups, anything that was around so that he wouldn't have to get up and go outside. That stuff is gross and messy."

"Don't worry, Jude," Larry smiled and then walked to the back door. He went outside. When he returned, he had a sour look on his face. "That stuff is terrible! I had to spit the whole wad out. Where did you get that stuff?"

"First time?" Jerry laughed.

"Hell, no but, that's the worst that I've tried."

Judy looked over at me. "If you need to, you can crash here tonight. Either shack up with me in my room, I trust you, or over there, on there, on the couch." She pointed into the living room.

"No, I can't. I need to stay, I mean, get going. I'm heading north tonight. Thanks, anyways."

"Yeah! At least, stay for dinner."

"What are we having?" asked Jerry.

"Liver and onions and eggplant with parmesan cheese and pesto, if someone will go to the store for me."

"That sounds good." said Karl. I just said "No thank-you! I can't".

Bob smiled. "I'll go to the market for you. What's the matter, Ken, don't you like liver or eggplant?"

"No really! I've never had eggplant and I don't intend to for a while, either. Besides, I really have to get going."

"It's great stuff how Judy makes it. Pesto is a great sauce."

I stood up. Judy stood up, hugged me, and then she took my hand. "Let me walk you to the door, Kenny."

Everybody said 'Bye!." Just when we were getting to the door, Jerry hollered. "See you in L.A. unless I can't get a ride, Judy has my number."

"Yeah, and I have her's." I hollered back.

Judy looked at my eyes. "You better be careful, you hear? You best call me when you get there. Call me collect if you want to." With another, tighter hug, she kissed me on the forehead. "My second husband split with some chick, got too busy with her. I never saw him again. Just 'tween me and you, I really miss the guy. Don't get to busy with anything that you don't come back, you hear, Baby."

I smiled big.

Well, Kenny . . ." She put her arms around my neck and hugged me again and kissed me on the lips.

"Bye!" I said. I turned and walked outside. The screen door slammed behind me. Half way down the walk, I turned, saying 'Good-bye!' but Judy was gone so I turned and walked away, teary eyed. As I did, I heard fiddle and harpoon music from inside, and Judy started singing a 60's Sonny and Cher song, 'Baby, Don't Go'.

A STORY CALLED 'ROOM'

The room smelled of urine and sweat. It wasn't a hospital room, or a motel room. It was just a room; the room Cory stayed in before he died. I walked in at about two in the morning and found Cory on the floor, on a mattress and a sleeping bag. He had a high fever and a six day beard. Brubeck was on the radio. This is before he died.

"What's your name?" he asked. Cory spoke slow and deliberate and his voice was soft and weak, almost a whisper. It was an effort to hear him.

"Ken!" I said. He said nothing.

After a few minutes, even though I was kneeling next to him on the floor, he motioned to me with his hand. "Come here. I want you to read to me." Cory held up a thin soft cover book. It was my book. I wrote and sold the poetry book at a two night gig at a San Francisco coffee house in North Beach, that I did with my best friend. We were billed as 'Coy & Sloan' — I was Coy. Cory was there one night. After that, he and I corresponded because we were both jazz pianists.

> In the early morning,
> among the green and mist . . .

"Are you reading it out loud? I can't hear you." I just put the book down.
"Tell me, have you ever written a story or a poem?"
I nodded, 'Yes'.
"That's good. You'll have to read me some sometime, if you want to."
I nodded yes and smiled.

Cory smiled and then he closed his eyes and slept for several hours. I just sat on the floor beside him, trying to sleep, and waited until he woke up.

"Hey, boy, what time is it?"

"Six-thirty!" I replied.

There was a long pause of silence. Again, Cory asked, "What time is it?"

I held up my arm out so that he could see my watch.

"Six-thirty — tell me, is it morning or evening? When you're sick, one loses track of time. Sometimes, time goes by fast and other times, so slow.

"What is your name?"

"Ken" I told him a second time. I spelled it out in ASL, finger sign language but he just looked at me in confusion. I took two semesters of ASL (American Sign Language) at a junior college.

Again, another pause, and then he spoke. "Well, if you don't want to tell me, I guess it doesn't matter. My name is Cory, Cory Davis but you don't have to remember the whole thing — just, Cory." He extended his hand. I took it and shook his hand. He smiled and then, I smiled. Obviously, he couldn't hear. I was hoping that it was an ear infection, something that could be easily cured with meds.

Cory lifted himself on one elbow, groaning, and pointed, with the other hand to a chair across the room. On it, there were several objects, carelessly placed. "In my jacket are my cigarettes. Bring them here . . . please."

I did but when I placed them beside him, He was asleep. I sat against the wall and waited once again for him to awake. I didn't want to move his stuff from the chair without his permission. I didn't know his state of mind — what may set him off or what wouldn't.

Cory slept for, perhaps, twenty minutes. I really doubt if he had slept, just rested. Then he looked up. He thanked me for the cigarettes. It was a guess but Cory asked, "You don't smoke, do you, son?"

I shook my head, no.

"You're a smart boy. It won't do anything for you but kill you. Maybe that's why I'm dying. I'm dying, you know. The doctor didn't tell me that but I know that I am. He wanted to put me into the hospital or into a nursing home but I wouldn't go and I fired him. Maybe I smoke too much. Used to smoke a pipe. Better for you, you know. I gave it up though. Darn thing kept going out on me—too much trouble keeping the fool thing lit. Smoked good, expensive cigars, too but, it got too expensive. I miss a good, a great cigar. Then I rolled my own cigarettes. Smoked less then and, it was cheaper. Hell, it took so long to roll them; you didn't have time to smoke as many. Maybe I should have stuck to rolling the darn things, might not be dying now. But then, maybe that's not what's wrong with me. I hope not.

"My drummer, I played keys in a jazz band in the '60s, taught me to roll my cigarettes. He'd smoke marijuana. Kept getting himself arrested.

"Did you know, I smoked a pipe at one time? Did so for fifteen years. Started when I was eighteen, in college." Cory laughed a hoarse laugh. "Man, I thought that I was so sophisticated back then with my pipe, my beard, tweed sports jacket, and brown and white saddle shoes. Black and white saddle shoes weren't cool. Anyways, I had over six hundred bucks invested in pipes. That's over a thousand in todays cash. Threw them all away. I should have kept them or sold them. I had one little toy that cost me eighty-five dollars. I had it made special. Was carved in the shape of a head. I had it carved that way out of meerschaum. I loved that thing; it was my toy—smoked real cool. It was the only one I kept. Had the tobacco special blended for me, walnut flavored. It was the only worthwhile thing I ever did, smoking that thing—that, and playing piano. I wish I had hung onto it. I know what you're going to say, 'I thought that you held on to it'. Well, I'll tell you, I lost the thing. I looked for it a few years ago but I didn't find it. Still haven't. Kinda of wish I still had it so I could give it to you . . . but, you don't smoke, though, do you. You're a smart boy. Won't do anything for you but kill ya.

"Say, I'm hungry boy. In my jacket is some money. Get it and go get something to eat and then, bring me back some chili—no beans, just chili and hot sauce and some coffee with a little cream. Nothing else, just some cream."

I went to the chair and picked up his jacket. In his pockets was thirty-seven cents. I checked my pockets and found eight dollars so, I put his change back into his jacket and walked out the door. "I'll be back shortly." I hollered back, forgetting that he couldn't hear me.

I was in luck! At the corner of the block was a café. It looked like a small log cabin. I ordered buckwheat pancakes and coffee.

I was gone just a little over an hour. Cory was reading out of the book that I had given to him. When he saw me, he put the book down.

"Good, you got my chili." Cory sat up against the wall and I gave him his chili and coffee.

"You know, the guy that wrote this book, his name was Ken Martinez, has some nice thoughts here. He isn't a philosopher and his thought have all been said before many times but he says things nice. I'm quiet now. It's a good feeling."

Cory had fits of awareness. This was one of them "All my life, I've been conning people, especially after I fell from grace in the jazz circuits. People just didn't want to hear me no more. I wouldn't con them out of money, just mainly their time. I told people that I was famous people. Once, I told people that I was Dylan—not Bob . . . um . . . Thomas and they believed me. I didn't look a thing like him and without an Irish brogue, too. This was in the 60's and he died in the 50's and people should know that. I was playing piano then. I did interviews under different names. I did it just to see people's reactions. I made a lot of people happy 'cause they thought that they had met someone famous. I used to make up stories about my so called adventures and people would sit and listen to me for hours. No one ever caught on that it was a bunch of bull, as far as I know. I guess I have a good imagination. As far as I know, I never did anybody any harm. Just made folks feel good. You can con anybody if you want to. Now, I'm quiet and I'm not conning no one. It's a good feeling and now, I'm dying. Wish I could live with that quiet feeling a little longer. I guess that everyone has their time and this is the time God set for ol' Cory Davis. Moral: be yourself. People have been saying that for years but nobody listens. Everyone's out to be someone else, not being satisfied with what they are. Why don't they aim to be what they want to be and not just make it up out of their heads? It's a hell of a lot simpler. I know, I was there. Do me a favor, Pal?" I raised my head a little. "Change the world for me, would you?"

I laughed a little and shook my head 'no'.

"I know" Cory went on. "you can't but, I wish you could.

I only smiled. I pointed to the food.

"Yeah! I'd better eat it before it gets cold, if it isn't already. Want some chili?"

I shook my head 'no'.

"Say, this is good chili! Thanks for getting it for me."

I smiled and nodded.

"I haven't eaten for a few days. Maybe that's why I'm sick." I had a hard time hearing what Cory had just said. A motorcycle was revving up outside.

Without a break, Cory continued. "About two weeks ago a friend of mine called and said that he was in trouble, that he wanted me to come over and help him out. I hitched a ride in the rain. Took me two hours to get a ride and when I got there, he wasn't there. Don't know what happened to him. He told me to meet him at Blue Gum Road. Now, there's a name. Its south of town a ways. Had to hitch a ride back. It's cold in the rain, know that? Then the heat was off here when I got back. I couldn't pay the gas bill. They'll turn off the electricity soon. Just stick around, you'll see. Had an attack, too and seizures. That's what laid me out here. All I know is, I'm dying.

Cory finished his coffee and then fell asleep. While he slept, I picked up the poetry book (The book was titled '4:14 a.m.') and began reading through it. Even though I had written it, it had been sometime since I had seen it and I had forgotten what I had written. Inside the front cover, not in my handwriting, was written:

Cory, you're a real special cat. Thanks for jamming with us. Your hands are your gift.

Stay cool, Cory (Ken)

Things were starting to come back to me now. I didn't give him the book. He came into the coffee house when Ron and I were rehearsing. He made a pest of himself. I must have given him my card. He must have just taken the book without paying for it from the back table because he wasn't there that evening for our show. The thing is, through his letters and me seeing him this day, laying there sick, I liked the guy.

4:14a.m. is continued on the next page→

The lilacs are what I'm allergic to. My throat
   clogs up and I sneeze a lot. I like sweet peas.
   They're pretty. When I was in second grade,
   My Mom had sweet peas and daisies growing
   in the front yard. I used to pick my Mom's
   flowers and sell them for a penny a piece. She
   didn't like it much.
When Jan and I went hiking in the hills, I'd sneeze
   a little from the lilacs. She would laugh at me,
   making fun of my misery, but I didn't mind
   because I like to see her laugh. Then, she would
   tickle me and I would end up chasing her until
   we both would trip and fall. Then, she would
   kiss me on the cheek.
That was summer. Now that winter and rain are
   here. It's hot chocolate by the fire and television.
   She still tickles me but I tickle her
   back and she still kisses me on the cheek.

Last night before I went to bed
I lit a candle Bayberry, I think.
It didn't lit up the whole room,
just the small corner
where it burned.
I wish that you could have seen it.
It was pretty
. . . and quiet
. . . and soft.
You would have liked it.

I love you.
Gee, it's nice
doing that.

11:57 p.m.
I just said goodnight to you.
on the phone.
I wish that I could do it again
but
I'll wait five minutes
I'll call to say good morning.
I love you that much.

Alone
it's nice
with you.

loving you is nice.
having you to love
is nicer.
          -make sense?

                                        Jesus loves you
                                        with or without memory
                                        and without association
                                        of time gone by . . .
                                        Today is new
                                        and more important
                                        than yesterday.

It's quiet and
I'm alone.
It's four a.m.
The radio is on,
and sitting in a pool
of hot tea
is my cup of tea.
I'm reading Albee's 'THE SANDBOX'
and a fly is crawling
up the drapes.

Ken Martinez

In my quiet times
I dream of ideas
most people would
laugh at.

I think of being
heroes
and presidents.
I think you do, too.
I think everybody does.

Even the mountains
are free
just to sit and do nothing.

Cory broke the silence. "Some years ago, boy, when I was about eight, I wassitting on the street corner. I was throwing rocks into the gutter and building a dam with my foot. You know, blocking the gutter water with my foot. I wasn't paying much attention to my surroundings. It was Saturday and there wasn't much to do. Sky King and all of the other shows that I liked on T.V. were over. After a while, I noticed a man sitting down the block a ways eating a can of chili—a can of cold chili at that.

"'Hey, Mister' I called out. 'Can I come over and talk with you?'"

"Why, of course, my good man."

I wondered over and sat on the curb next to the man.

"Hey, Mister, are you a hobo?"

"On the contrary, sir, man of the world, I am. I travel the world, dine with kings and duchesses. The world is my home and the sky, my roof. I travel it as I please.

"What's your name, boy?"

"Cory" I told him.

"Cory, I'm mighty proud to meet you. Mike Chase is my name. Er . . . um . . . Cory, would you have a dime for a cup for coffee on you? I seem to have forgotten my my change purse."

"No. I don't," I told him. "but just a second and I'll go ask my Mom. Now, stay here."

"When I returned, empty handed, he was gone. You know, I think every young boy is influenced by stories about hobos and tramps and their casual way of life. I know I have. Perhaps, I'll eat a casual can of chili, if I live long enough." Cory smiled at me. He took a bite of chili then he looked at me. He smiled and then, he fell asleep again and I picked up my, I mean Cory's book, again and began reading. 'Bey' and another poem, 'Little Rag Lucky Jeff Zebra' were missing.

When I had finished reading book, I set it back on the floor, next to the sleeping bag. Cory was looking right at me.

"Writes some good thoughts, doesn't he. I met Ken a while back.

Me and a buddy of mine were going to open a laundromat to supplement my income. This was a few years back. The Nam war was going strong so, decided to get the service out of the way first so, we both joined the army.

"Say, hand me my cigarettes, would you?

I reached near his shoulder and grabbed the cigarettes then, I handed them to Cory.

"Thanks! Well, because of this Buddy Plan that they have, me and Jeff were able to get into the same outfit together.

"You know, boy, it wasn't the killing that got to me. Shoot, I got used to that. I never killed nobody face to face or even seeing the little kids starving with their stomachs bloated. No, you know what really got to me? After the battles, I was the one that went out to drag in the bodies to ship back to the States. We'd take their dog tags, put them sideways in their mouths and hit their jaw, jamming them into their teeth. Even this was o.k. as far as things go until I found Jeff's bod . . .

"I remember seeing a bullet from a AK47, that's a Gook's M16, coming towards me. I can see it, slow motion, just grazing my head and it didn't hurt. Then, I blanked out.

"I have a dream, a nightmare most every night. I see a sphere, a . . . a . . . circle, blurry at first but it gets sharper and sharper, brighter and brighter. Then, a face appears. It might have an ear missing or the whole side of his face missing, blown off. And then, another scared face appears and another until there are thirty-eight. Then, I'm walking down a street at night. I come across an alley and find my girl, Janet there.

"'Hey, Darlin', you're going to get killed by the Cong if you stay here!' I yell at her. 'Get the hell out of here.' Suddenly, her face turns white. I look behind me and number thirty-nine is holding his machete, ready to swing it at me. I grab Janet's arm and we take off running. At some time in my dream, I turn around and see all thirty-nine people, broken faces and all, chasing us. They just about catch us 'cause I can feel their breath on my neck. That's when I wake up, screaming and in a cold sweat. It's a bad trip, man. That's what war does to you. Stay away if you can 'cause it just ain't worth it!

"They sent me home for psychic rehabilitation. It took four years. Four years of my life wasted.

When I did get out, my friends had pity on me. They meant to be kind but they were cruel because they wouldn't let me forget Nam or the hospital. Finally, I couldn't take it anymore so I came up to the Bay Area. That's when I met Ken. If I ever saw him again, I doubt if I'd recognize him. He was a nice boy, though. About twenty-one or two, I think. He was traveling, he and a friend of his. Name was . . . Sloan. I'm surprised I remember that. Anyways, he was reading poetry and playing the piano, jazz at a coffee house. His friend was a drummer. That's when I got this book. I used to play jazz in clubs, nice clubs. People knew me, too.

"If I could have another name, I'd want it to be Cotton, Jim Cotton but folks would call me Cotton."

I must have looked at him funny because he answered back, "I just wanted to change the subject, that's all." I smiled.

"Hey, boy, what time is it?"

I held my watch where Cory could see it.

"Does that say, five after eleven?" Cory asked.

I shook my head yes,

"And it's still morning?"

Again, yes.

"I couldn't read if it was a little after eleven or one o'clock.

"When Ken gave me those poems, I recopied them in my own handwriting and gave them to a girl and she thought that I had written her some love poems. She sure loved them. If I could do it over, though, I'd tell her I didn't write them. I didn't tell her that I wrote them but, she thought I did. I didn't lie to her but it's still isn't right. Mar-tinez didn't get the credit. He should of, you know."

I only smiled.

"You smile a lot, don't you? You must be happy. I like that, people that are happy. You know, a lot of guys think that it's sissy or queer to smile. They think their Joe Stud or something. They think they're cool. I like people that smile a lot—makes me happy.

"I just came up from Venice, California, not Italy. It must have been a couple of three years now, I don't know. Stopped and lived in Oakland for a while. Didn't like it much. Then I . . . well, you'll see it going south. When you get to the Stoneyford turnoff, look to your left." Cory started coughing hard and spitting up. Then, he continued. "Turn to your left. That there is the smallest mountain range in the world. It's just a little, bitty thing. Hell, I don't know what they call the darn thing but you can see it before you get to Willows until clean past Dunnigan. Look back and if it's clear, you'll see Mount Lassen. Only active volcano in the states, the continental U.S., that is, except maybe Mt. St, Helens. I don't know. There's a truck stop along there, too called Olive City. We spent the night there on the way here. Just got tired so we pulled into their parking lot and went to sleep. Was about four in the morning and we slept until about six. Trucks woke us up so we just moved on. I was hitch hiking.

"Hey, boy, a guy named Earl Hughes lived in a town called Fish Hook, Illinois and when he was ten, he weighed three hundred and seventy-eight pounds. I don't know who he was. I read that somewhere. That's a lot of weight to be carrying around."

Then, Cory was quiet. It was the type of quiet when someone is trying to think of something to say. Then, he went on. Talking about Willows, every year, May I think they have stock auctions. I went the last time. I wouldn't bid on nothing, the rams and cattle but . . . aaaaaaah! Help me! It hurts so bad! My chest . . . Lord Jesus, help me. Forgive me my sins, Jesus, please."

He then closed his eyes and slept . . . and I did . . .

I was awakened by a loud scream. I sat up quickly, shaking.

"Kipper! Kipper! It was bad . . . the dream . . . this dream. They had me undress to the waist. It was in the fifteen or sixteen hundreds. It was in the cold. A pound of gunpowder was tied to my legs and a pound to each of my arms. I was tied to a stake . . . the one I was to be burned at. The fire was brought on a torch, but the wood was green. The dry straw only burned for a few minutes until it was blown away by the wind. A huge flame would paralyze the nerves right away but a little one or a slow fire was torture. That's freaky 'cause I don't know how I knew that. Then they took off the gunpowder from me and then threw on more wood . . . green! Again, they tried to light the fire. This time, my face was singed and scorching but again, the flames went out and the hot, damp sticks smoldered around my feet. I cried out, 'Let me have dry wood! Have mercy! Let me burn quickly!' Again, for a third time, wood was laid around me and the gun-powder was replaced between my legs and under my arms. This time, the powder exploded but was either wrongly put or wasn't enough. 'Have mercy!' I shouted. A few minutes later, the post to which I was tied burned through at the base and fell backwards, pulling me down into the glowing woo . . .

. . . it was terrible. I don't want to die! Do you think Jesus heard me asking forgiveness? I didn't do it in fear, not entirely. I was sincere. Do you think he heard me, Kipper?"

I smiled and nodded yes. I've never been a Kipper. Cory doesn't even know my name. I became very concerned. It seemed that he was becoming delirious. I didn't want this worry.

"I hope so!" Then, he smiled. His voice was beginning to become even softer and weaker. It became more of an effort to hear him. "You know, we're going to meet again when things are better. You'll be there, won't you?"

I nodded yes.

"In this poetry book, he wrote that Jesus will love me wi . . . aaaaaaah! Help me! It hurts so-o-o-o aaaaaaah, bad. My chest, it hurts so bad!"

He reached out and grabbed my hand — so tight that it hurt. He was obviously in pain. He was crying, almost screaming.

"Hold me, boy, hold me. It hurts so bad!"

I lifted Cory to my chest. He still held onto my hand very tight. He coughed and that's when he died.

I laid him back down onto the sleeping bag and then, walked out of the room. That's when I cried.

SMOKEY JOE'S CAFÉ

I never was fast on my feet. Spina-bifida had its toll on me. My other reflexes were actually pretty good. I guess that this was the reason that I was hired to work in a kitchen—a four stool, two table diner on Broadway in Buhl, ID, across the street from Jackson's Kountry Kitchen. (I won't make you groan by saying 'My first time on Broadway,') This isn't the original name of the cafe but I don't remember the cafe's original name. Maybe it was The Buhl Café. Back again across the street, down on the corner was a bar and grill. Every time I ate there, an annoying but catchy Leiber and Stoller song by the Robins, 'Smokey Joes Café' would sing through my mind. The Robins became the Coasters and, I like the Coasters. Now, back to the Mom and Pop diner. I was their dishwasher and seldom, a cook. A Mom and Pop and their high school daughter owned and ran the place.

After washing and sterilizing the dishware and cookware, they developed a strong smell and taste of bleach. I used a shower hose and two sinks. The wares would be cleaned with the shower hose with the combination of the garbage disposal. Then, they were washed again in the first sink in very hot, very bleachy water and then put soaking in cooler plain water. This piquant flavor didn't sit well with the customers. I was frustrated, to say the least but that was the way that it had to be according to the owners.

One day, on my day off, I decided to hitch hike to Twin Falls, maybe fifteen miles east. My car's electrical system was out of whack. I caught a ride from the fifth car that went by. She told me that she was turning south at the junction going to Jackpot, NV. I said that it was fine so, I ended up at the casino town with $8 in my pocket. On the way down, I decided that I needed that money so when we arrived there, I bought a dollar hot dog, crossed the street and headed back to Idaho.

A couple of hours later, I decided that my luck may better traveling the other way. The first car stopped for me. "Hi! We're heading for Sacramento. Where you headed?"

"I don't rightly know." I said. "I'm just playing the vagabond lover." This caught the ear of the lady sitting in the backseat. She smiled at me. I got in to the backseat next to her.

The trip was quiet—to quiet. The backseat lady, after she grew tired of flirting with me, and the boy up front, just read. The driver just sang with the radio the whole trip. There were no stops for meals, just the 'rest stop' breaks.

After midnight, I was left off on the side of the freeway in Sacramento near a small grove of trees. I walked into the grove and sat down behind a tree facing away from the traffic and fell asleep. The morning sunrise woke me up. I hitched a ride into Oakland. The driver had a cooler of food and drink that he shared. I was left off by the Hyatt Regency Hotel around five o'clock p.m. I thought, 'Happy Hour Time. Maybe they'll have free food, a buffet. The lounge had a baby grand piano so I asked if I could play the piano. There was a large brandy glass on top. A fellow named Nick put a ten dollar bill in and requested a song from the forties that I did not know but Nick just walked away, leaving the ten. I played 'Summertime'. He did this four or five time.

This little adventure happened during a heat spell. Nick invited me to his table where he told me that his AC was out so he just checked into the hotel for the duration. He was twenty-three years old. A couple of years ago his Mom died, he told me. His Mother left him three million dollars and he bought the apartment house that he lived in. He asked me where I was from so, I told him my hitch hiking story. He said that he had two beds in his hotel room and I was welcome to spend the night.

The next morning, Nick asked me to breakfast. Oh course, I said 'Yes!' He drove me to his apartment house. We both went in and then Mike took a foot locker from under his bed.

"You are not going to rob me are you? I guess if you did, I couldn't stop you." Mike replied. He opened the trunk and it was full of twenty dollar bills. He took out a bundle. I thought that you and me and two girlfriends of mine could go out to lunch. Edna will be with you. Here's some money so you can pay for both of you. I'm not a pimp!" Mick handed me a stack of twenties and told me to keep the change. This amounted to $240.

That afternoon, the four of us went to a restaurant on the Frisco Bay. We had crab legs and claws AND lobster.

After lunch and good-byes, I took BART (Bay Area Rapid Transit) to Hayward and I spent the next night at Ron's, my best friend, on the living room couch. The next morning, before he went to work, we had coffee.

"How long do you want to stay, Kenny?"

"I'm leaving this morning" I didn't have any place to go but I went. I felt funny about staying with Ron's wife alone because in high school, I had a serious crush on her.

Heading further south on BART, Fremont was my next stop. When I lived there, I was in the habit of going into Lyon's restaurant every day for coffee. It was here that I met Lilly, a waitress. This was a couple of years back. When she saw me, she screamed, dropped a plate of onion rings, and grabbed and hugged me. She brought me a hot fudge sundae and coffee and then she told me to stay until she quit work at ten. "You're staying at my house tonight, Kenny." she demanded with a smile.

I used to sit in on Keyboards with her boyfriend's 60's, 70's cover band.

One night at Lyon's, she told me that Steve asked her 'to be her bride'. When she asked me if I should accept, I said, 'That's an out-and-out NO! I like the guy but he's a jerk. He'll hurt you, not physically but, he'll hurt you.'

The next time we discussed the subject, she told me that she said 'yes' and that she wanted me in the wedding. "Steve's band mates are going to be his ushers and best man and Jaime (his keyboardist) is going to do the music."

"That's ok! Just being there is important."

"No!" Lilly interrupted. "You need to do something."

"I could have people sign the guest book and collect the gifts."

"No, Kenny, you need to do something important! I know . . . no, you won't do that."

"What?"

"You could be my . . . no, that's alright."

"You want me to be your maid-of-honor, don't you?"

"Yeah, I do! You" Lilly smiled and hugged me. "You are my best friend, aren't you?"

"I think so."

"I know so!" Lilly said.

I was her maid-of-honor wearing a shirt, bow-tie, and cummerbund the same color as the dresses and a tux the same as guys.

Now, I was spending the night at Lilly's, sleeping on the top bunk of a bunk bed. The next morning I met Lyman Penning, a high school classmate of mine for breakfast. I sort of invited myself as his guest. I used to be good at doing that.

"I went to the bus company and bought you a ticket back to Buhl." I feel that you're down on your luck." Lyman told me.

"No, I'm fine." Lyman gave me a 'Yeah, sure!' look. "I am, really."

"Well, I can't return the ticket so, it's yours. (Maybe he lied. Yep! I'm sure that he lied.)

The breakfast went fine — long but fine. Lyman was quit a talker.

After breakfast, I caught a county bus and other transportation to Los Gatos to visit my Uncle Leo and my Aunt Margret. The next morning, I acquired another bus ticket. At the bus station, I cashed in one of the tickets for cash.

Eight hours later, I was home in Buhl. From this fanastical fun trip, I developed this story and 'The Char Ms.'

One of the two barber shops in Buhl was owned by Keith, a member of my church. After I came back from my trip and, after losing my job, I spent hours in his shop just visiting. One day he began telling me that I should attend the Barbers College. After much conversation with Keith, and after much thought, I began looking into the opportunity of a barber career. After all, I was a baritone. Keith sang 2nd tenor in the church choir.

Vocational Rehab decided to put me through the nine month course. The school was in Boise. The same day that I drove to Vocational Rehab, when I returned to Buhl, I headed for 'Smokey Joes Café' for an iced tea. The counter was full so I went into the next room and sat at the bar. How'd I know there was a party goin' on? A couple of my friends came over to me and told me that it was a wedding reception for Grace Holland and that she wouldn't mind if I stayed since I knew her. I didn't. I didn't remember seeing or meeting her at all. "Hey, Kenny, get some food — roast beef, ham, chicken. The mustard is real good on the ham or beef. I did. I spread the mustard on thick.

I rejoined my friends that were laughing. Just about the time I was to ask them to repeat the joke, I took a bite of the ham and tears rolled down my cheeks and my sinus' were suddenly cleared—the mustard was Chinese mustard. The laugher became much louder. "I'm sorry, Ken, but we couldn't resist." I won't tell you what thoughts ran through this good Christian mind of mine. Now, in 2012, I love the stuff on sandwiches.

Seven weeks later, I was living in a flat in a converted Victorian house on State St. in Boise—across the street from Sears. The only bathroom was up the stairs. Years later, while writing 'Just Jokin'', I had this place fixed into my mind as Joey's home.

I had a two month wait until school started. I began spending my evenings at Sambo's restaurant, reading. Soon, the evenings melted into the wee hours of the morning. I became friends with the graveyard cook. Soon, I was spending my afternoons at Dan and his wife's apartment. Dan and I spent hours playing Othello and chess. When school began, we played during the evenings.

During this time, I met Butch, Paul Revere's (of the band fame) drummer brother-in law. He and I hit all of the bar's open mike nights. Sometimes, we'd win—usually, if not cash, a case of beer. I gave the beer to Butch since I didn't touch the drink.

Butch introduced me to Revere and twice, the three of us jammed. Once, Paul Revere & The New Raiders invited me to join them on stage at the Holiday Inn to play 'Louie Louie'.

A few months later, I decided that I couldn't stay on my feet all day, especially Saturdays. I had to drop out. I began going out to Sambo's again. One night, the dishwasher didn't show up for work. Bob, the assistant manager asked me if I'd wash dishes for a steak dinner. I did.

The next night, Déjà Vu but with a shrimp dinner. The next night, I was hired. By company policy, steaks and shrimp ended for employees—too expensive.

Work was *hard* work, very hard work. The first two nights, my helping hand nights, the work was skimmed down quite a bit. Now, I had to do pots and pans which required a lot of scrubbing and scouring. I was slow enough that after a couple of three weeks, I got wind of the fact that I was about to get fired.

The next night (Yes, there was a next night.) I overheard that they needed to hire a counter waitress. I talked Bob, the assistant manager into giving me a try. I did alright and soon, I was waiting on tables and soon, I was a cook trainee. Thus began a career.

Six months or so later, I got a call from my sister saying that our Mom and Dad was sending her and her family, Russ and their toddler, Jennifer, and their baby, Todd, and myself to join them in Rome and then a trip to Majorca, an island off of Spain—the former home of composer Frédéric Chopin and writer/activist Amandine Lucile Aurore Dupin, a.k.a. George Sand, his mistress. The next day, I looked into applying for my passport and I also told Sambo's management of my plans.

Rome was as I remembered it almost fifteen years earlier. One thing that we, the adults remember is that even the children drank wine. My Dad and probably Russ reasoned that the drink was grape juice. Every table had a complementary bottle of red so for dessert we had berries in 'wine' and a glass of the potent potable. It WAS wine. Todd loved the two and cried for more as a two year old would.

Majorca, I loved more than Rome—maybe because I had been to Italy and knew what to expect. Majorca was new and exciting and full of a new type of history than I had heard or learned before. I discovered barrel-aged Colheita Tawny Port wine there.

My favorite composers are the biggie BCDD's—Bach, Chopin, and Debussy & Dvořák. I truly enjoyed visiting the monastery where Chopin and George Sand lived.

Back in the USA at the customs line at the NY airport was Richard Burton in front of us. He was very pleasant and polite.

Back in Boise, I called in to work that I was back. I asked for Bob, the assistant manager. I was told that he was now the manager of the Sambo's on the 'Bench', near the Boise airport. I called him there and the next afternoon at two o'clock, I was working for Sambo's again but as a waiter.

A requested to cook on the graveyard shift and although I was still fairly new as a cook, I soon had it although sometimes I would cook or wait tables on the swing shift.

One afternoon, my waitress and my dishwasher walked out. As soon as I could, I called Bob on his day off. He said that he'd call to have some people come in and that Neil would be there by dinner. Neil was a trip. He knew or maybe pretended to know everything. If he was pretended, he was very good at it. One day we were talking about the Donner Party and if they were cannibals. I made the statement,

'I wonder what human flesh tastes. Neil knew this, maybe. He said "Pork! It tastes like pork!" Maybe he was right.

Neil liked to confuse people. One day he was a Buddhist, than, a Satanist; a Druid; a Christian; a Bahá'í. One day I asked him if he knew where he'd go when he died. He said that he didn't know. He asked me the same question. I told him, "When I became a born again Christian, God exchanged my soul for a new one. I'm a new person." I reached into my pocket and took out my copy of the Four Spiritual Laws and shared it with him. We talked about God and Jesus from time to time but I didn't notice any changes in him. I just trusted that God would make Neil a new person, too.

Sambo's kitchen was behind a chrome-topped brick wall about shoulder high. Behind it was a grill with two large griddles on each side. The finished meals were put on top of the chrome. Sambo's had no heat lamps so the meals had to be picked up quickly. Except on Friday and Saturday nights, the graveyard cook worked alone with one waitress or waiter. I seldom worked weekends.

One night, when I went to work, three unforgettable (to this day) events happened. The kitchen floor hadn't been mopped and the swing shift cook made a speedy exit. As I was walking to my cook station, passing the other station, I slipped on the greasy floor and I could see my hand heading towards the griddle. I panicked as the palm of my hand hit the griddle. It wasn't turned on.

The second was when a waitress kept dropping and breaking plates when she picked them up to be delivered to our customers. I finally told her to take a fifteen minute break. When she returned to the floor, I had an empty dinner plate on the chrome. As she walked by, I tipped the plate and it fell to the floor, shattering. She smiled a huge smile. "Thanks, Kenny! I needed that! You're a real sweetie."

Also that night, two regulars came in after work. They were married. They were security guards. I wish that I could remember their names. They were both extremely nice and they were both extremely good looking. Every night they would order scrambled eggs, bacon, pancakes, and coffee—a Sambo's Special. I went to their table to greet them. She told me that she wanted something to nibble on but that she was not hungry for the Sambo's Special. "I'll make you something special that I think you'll enjoy. I tool a piece of bacon and cut four pieces widthwise. The pancakes were actually silver dollar size as was the scrambled eggs. I served it on a saucer with one stem of parsley. She loved it!! Sometimes my sense of humor scares me but other times, like then, it's so much fun.

I took some time off, about a week for some minor surgery. During my recovery time at home, my Mom came to visit. Towards the end of that time, I received a call from work.

"Ken, it's Bob. How are you feeling?"

"A little weak and tired. A bit sore"

"I could really use you for three or four hours. Neil didn't show up. You'll be gone before the bar rush, I swear and when you're not cooking, you can sit down, It's Sunday night so it will be quiet."

A semi-regular customer, a lady, a very annoying nameless lady came in with a very pretty lady. They sat at the counter where the nameless lady always sat.

After they ordered and when the food was out, I went over to them. "Ken, this is my friend, Beth. She's from Ketchum and she'd been staying with me during a women's church retreat." Beth smiled and said 'Hi!'

The three of us, actually, Beth and I talked for a long time until said that she had a long drive home so that they had to leave. A few days later, I got Beth's phone number from her friend, my regular. Beth would come to Boise on weekends and I'd go to Ketchum on my days off. Her two children were visiting their Dad for the summer so I slept in Joanna's room. A month later, I took my vacation at her house, staying in her son's room for the next two months.

Beth worked at the valley cable company. Story has it that the actor, who lived north of town couldn't get any TV channels—no one could—so, he personally financed the cable company. Sometimes I'd see him riding his Triumph motorcycle around town.

After a couple of months, I was cooking breakfast and lunch at a restaurant in Hailey, twelve miles south of Ketchum. They were famous for their Monte Cristos, a fried ham and Gruyere cheese between egg battered bread. We served it with clotted cream and preserves. Many people used plain maple syrup. I never ate one until a few weeks after I started working there and then, I was in love again.

It was while working there that I proposed. A few weeks later, August 18th, we were married. The restaurant made the wedding cake and supplied finger sandwiches and other goodies as a wedding present to us. A waitress supplied the punch, complete with floating rose petals.

The summer tourist season ended and I was laid off. Every day, I read the want ads for any kind of a job. I soon found a job as a bookkeeper trainee at the Sun Valley Hospital which since has moved and now is called St. Luke's Wood River

Medical Center in Ketchum. My first day, the electricity went out. Computers and calculators that should have had batteries didn't. I called out. 'Does anybody remember math or how to think?' No one raised their hands. How odd and sad *but* I'm sure that no one took me seriously.

The first time that I did the payroll solo, everybody was paid exactly half to the penny. I had no idea what I did wrong but soon on this late Friday afternoon, a long line of angry employees conjugated around my office door. I felt liking crying but I didn't

Monday, I read the 'Hospital Opportunities' bulletin board and something almost missed my eye but it didn't. The kitchen was looking for a cook. At my desk, I called the kitchen and made an appointment for that day. I got the job and I was told that I didn't need to give my two weeks noticed in payroll.

Cooking there was a trip. We cooked in bulk for thirty something patients. Very little is any seasonings were used. Cooking in bland food in bulk was new to me. I was trained to read one 'ticket' at a time. I had to be at work at four a.m.

One day I heard that Robert Redford had broken his ankle or leg while skiing Baldy Mt. I told Beth that evening that we should do the Christian thing by representing our church by dropping his hospital room for a visit. She just laughed at the idea. The next day, I dropped by his room, telling him that I was from the kitchen and I wanted to see if everything was alright. He and I had a nice chat.

One day I was called into the kitchen manager's office. She told me that they had to 'downsize' and that that day would be my last. She apologized by saying that she was sorry that it had to be done between tourist seasons but 'What had to be done, had to be done.'

Next day I applied for unemployment. Work was scarce. I was out of work for about six weeks by then, I was a taxi van dispatcher. The office was only about two blocks away from our country home. I worked the swing shift. Basically, it was a shuttle for tourists to get around and to and from the Twin Falls airport, ninety miles south. When a driver called in, signing out and coming in to clock out, I was asked if I wanted anything from the store. I almost always told them, Snickers. Soon, I'd get a call on the radio. "This is Tom. I'm signing out and coming in and I'll get you your Snickers." I had friends.

All too soon, the season was over and being the new kid, I was laid off. I spent my days playing darts and I was back in the unemployment line for just two weeks when one day I answered the phone. I was told that a four star restaurant was looking for a chef—a chef. I worked there for a few months until Beth began divorce proceeding. The strain was too much for me and my work suffered, I was laid off with a very good recommendation.

During and after my divorce, I took a cut in pay in my next job by becoming a prep cook at Louie's Pizza. Now, I'm not downgrading prep cooks. Their work is important. Prep cooks seldom cooks. They cut and dice, among other important duties. I also made bread and pizza dough. I made two cheese cakes a day and also Biscotti.

The uneasiness of seeing Beth in town almost every day (We moved into a condo about two blocks from town a while back.), especially for her, as I was told, was too much so, I quit my job and moved in with my sister and her family in Palo Alto, CA.

This was not the end of my cooking career but these were my most cherished memories. From my first time cooking in a restaurant until to the end, I had a reign of maybe twenty-two years, off and on. I enjoyed most of those times and miss all of those times.

LONE

(A book of poems and love about my ex and stepson)

While I was walking down the street
    this morning,
    my thoughts were on you . . .
    nothing else mattered.

~and the rain came down heavy~

**Poems
and memories
of six days shy of two years.**

I wish that it wasn't over.
It was time well spent.

When I think of you,
the possibilities are endless.
And my time and things
I do
are dedicated to you.
When I think of you,
I become a lone person
because I don't have anyone
to love me.
          It seems so worthless.

As I passed a certain yard,
a dog barked
and startled me . . .
interrupting my thoughts.
Nothing else changed.
The rain still came down . . .
. . . the world went onjust
the same.
But soon my thoughts returned . . .
Soon the rain stopped . . .
and I was still thinking of you.

We were parked about ten miles outside Wasco, CA. when I asked her to marry me. We were on our way to Frisco. We ran out of gas. After she said, 'Yes' we hitched a ride into Wasco. We had to put a $5 deposit on the two gallon gas can. She wanted to keep it, so we did. About three weeks later, we threw it away.

Every once in a while, I'll think about dumb things like,
like even, 'who wore the pants that
I'm wearing
before I bought them?'

We were married on Feb. 14.
               (St. Valentine's Day)

I started putting my first collection of poems together
during this time.
It was,
      'MICHAEL . . . a love book.'
Michael isn't my son except by marriage
      but, I love him as if he were mine.
As the philosopher, Sonny Bono has said —
      many times in song & verse —
         'The Beat Goes On'.

We couldn't afford a honeymoon
but we did spend the day in Berny Falls.
The following week, we pressed flowers
and painted pictures on pebbles
and spray painted the pine cones that
that she found.

The first time I ever played
Jazz professionally, my check
was in five figures . . .
                    $159.95

One night she was watching an
old movie on T.V. while in bed.
I was reading a Vonnegut Jr. book.
She hit my shoulder and asked,
          "You know I love you,
              don't you?"
I smiled, meaning 'yes'.
A few minutes later, she hit me again.
          ". . . and I really like you, too."

Today
I watched a boy
kicking a can
down the street,
ate a chili dog,
and time to
read over some of my
poems . . .
        . . . and
I enjoyed
my day very much
but, I still miss you.

The year before we were married,
I made 34,000 dollars . . . after taxes.
We spent our wedding night in an empty apt, 'cause
we couldn't afford any furniture.
We spent the evening cutting out valentines for
each other and paper dolls, too.
We slept in a sleeping bag on the floor.
We both weighed 129 lbs.
She's lost 23 lbs. since.
I've gained.

"Have you ever been to Catalina?"
She said 'no'.
"It's a beautiful, beautiful island off the coast.
It's nice, really nice.
I'm going to take you there on our first anniversary.
That will be our honeymoon, too, ok?"
She smiled.
"You'll love it . . . wait and see."
She poured me another cup of coffee and we finished breakfast.

I'm thirty.
Timmy's six.
He came over for
a spare rib dinner.
That's when I found out
he doesn't like spare ribs.
I went to the store
and bought a
mushroom and sausage pizza.
I brought it home,
cooked it.
and he wouldn't eat it, either.

Ken Martinez

We had our month anniversary in the car.
We ran out of gas on the way to the restaurant.
She forgot to put gas into the tank when she borrowed the car.
We had smoked salmon sandwiches and milk for dinner.

We watched a lot of T.V.
We never really got out to do anything else.
The thing is, though, we never got bored.

I gave her a dog for her birthday.
Two days later, he ran away.

I bought a yo-yo to play with.
The next day, she cut the string
so that the little boy, Timmy down the street
could play with it.
She never did understand why I was mad

I played my trumpet this morning
for the first time in about a year.
I did alright, too.
My lips swelled up but, I did alright on it.
This morning, the mailman asked me
who hit me in the mouth?

Ken Martinez

I wish that I could explain the lone feeling I feel, but I can't.
All I know is that I wish she were here with me.

. . . because I love her, I have the right
    to miss her,
    and go through what I'm going through.
. . . and cry, and . . .

About twice a week, every other week, she'd put on a record,
turn out the lights in the living room, and just stare out the window.
She always put on the same Elton John record and just stared out the window and cry.
She told me that it brought back memories.
She never told me what. I never asked her.

Ken Martinez

I don't have anyone looking over my shoulder, annoying me when I write, anymore…
. . . and that's annoying!

She always puts strawberries
in red bowls,
chocolate pudding in brown bowls,
peaches in yellow bowls
and chili beans in lavender bowls.

About six weeks before she left me, we bought
a house. It wasn't much—just two rooms and a bath.
It was like a studio apartment but it was a cottage. It
was beautiful because it was our first home. The baby
slept in a crib in the kitchen and she and I slept on a
hide-a-bed in the living room.

　　　Every once in a while, I'll walk by the house.
in the front yard is an old junk washing machine and
a '57 Chevy, stripped, and a little red trike. I guess
that they have a little boy or girl. I wonder if their
kid sleeps in the kitchen, too?

In the evenings, we would sit on the
same side of the couch and hold hands
while watching T.V.
. . . even after we were married.

I bought Michael a small pocket radio. The first
time I put the earplug into his ear, he thought that it
was funny. He likes to listen to the news and to
people talking.
If the earplug isn't in his ear, he's putting it
into someone else's ear so that they can listen.

She and Michael and I had
Kings hockey jerseys alike.
I was #19.
She was #78
and Michael was #2½.

In the morning,
with the baby crying,
I'm grouchy and I don't
love anybody . . .
but by evening,
                    watch out!

She gave the little boy
down the street
a horse that she made
out of pipe cleaners.
            He thought it was a dog.

Ken Martinez

I like Jazz . . .
      She doesn't.
I like fish . . .
      She doesn't.
I like to read . . .
      She doesn't.
I like the color green . . .
      So does she.

Sometimes she's dingy.
Sometimes, she's smarter
then me . . . and then
I'm her little boy.

I think that we were together
    a little more than we should
    have been. She kept saying
    that she needed some time
    away from me.
    . . . now she has . . .

The reason she left me
was stupid . . .
    really stupid
but a lot of stupid things
are important to me, too.

When she left me, I went to Wasco to spend a little time. I spent my first three years of my life in Wasco. I go back and visit from time to time. I haven't been back for about seven years.

They say that when you go home where you grew up, it's not the same . . . but it was. The same people were there, working in the same places, living in the same places. It was a comfortable feeling.

The night that she forgot her keys, I didn't hear her
knocking 'cause I had the stereo headphones on.
It was raining heavy. She was at the door for
Over an hour before I heard her.

That's the night that she hurried home to tell me
That Michael ran in front of a car.

How do you tell a two year old
that he's going to spend a long
time with a cast on his arm?

She laughed at my beard
    when I grew it.
    When I shaved it off
    she asked me 'why?'
    And raised a big stink
    about it.
    One of these days,
    I'll figure her out.

I interviewed a pole vaulter a few months ago.
I also knew personally the winner of the of the
'76 Burney Falls spitting contest.
Things like this impressed her.

I like RC Cola and Pepsi—not together but just
to drink out of the bottle. We used to save the
bottles for the dime deposit. I like tonic water
and lime but the T.W. bottles are non-deposit.

We had saved over $10 in pop bottles to return.
She gave them to a little boy down the block.
We stayed home most of that week. We didn't
Have gas money.

That's the week Timmy came over for dinner.

I found a book titled 'Lone'.
I picked it up and opened it
                to the first page
                        It read, 'Dedicated to Beth'.
                (I smiled)
The second page had an image of me.
                . . . I was crying—
                something I hadn't done
since I was a boy.
It was nice because
                it
                showed that
        I cared.
The third page pictured Beth.
I don't know if she was crying
                or not.
                Her back was turned towards me.
I tried to turn to the next page
but the pages were either glued together
or uncut
                and I couldn't turn the pages.
I guess that I'll never know
                what will happen.

MICHAEL—A LOVE STORY

There's love inside here —

most definitely.

. . . two years old . . .

I met Michael when he was eighteen months old. I married his mother when he was two, Her name is Lydia. Every night, Michael and I and Lydia will sit and watch T.V. together until it's time for Michael to go to bed. When I tell him to go to bed, he does without a fuss . . . after our little ritual. He has to kiss everyone in the room goodnight, starting and ending with me.

I'm a musician and a poet that sometimes writes short stories. I upshop the coffeehouses and saloons where I performed when I got married but, I do occasionally still play the coffeehouses. It's nice to see my friends who are still working in shop. Sometimes I'll be gone for a week-end. I always call home and when I do, Lydia will put Michael on the phone. He hardly talks but he always laughs when he hears my voice.

When I do get home, usually three or four in the morning—tired, very tired—I'll wake him up just to let him know that I'm home. Lydia doesn't like it but I always let him stay up for a while. We'll play trucks or watch the end of a movie on T.V. and always have a bowl of oatmeal going to bed. Michael's real good about going back to sleep. We have a terrific time, I think that I get more excited than he does.

To know that you love me
is important
and knowing that you know
that I love you
is much more important.

When I was a little boy,
two,
I sat with my Dad,
pretending to read
the newspaper.
My little boy likes to
sit with me and
pretend to read the newspaper.
For some reason,
that makes me happy.

Our little boy
found a Scrabble tile.
I drilled a hole through the top
and put it on a string.
Now, Michael wares a 'J'
around his neck.

Babies are nice
to have around—
especially my baby
because he needs me.

Michael drew (he actually scribbled) a blue and black picture for me. I framed it with a cardboard frame and hung it in the kitchen. It's Michael's toy zebra, Lucky Jeff.

He wanted to share his French fries with me.
He picked one up and handed it to me, but it
slipped out of his hand and slipped into
the dirt. He picked it up and handed it to me
and waited for me to eat it,
I did . . . after saying, 'thank-you'.

'I love you, Daddy!'—
    said with a burned match.
He knows that I collect matchbooks.

Ken Martinez

'Kaw-kuh' means dirty,
or no good . . .
    . . . like, food that's been
dropped on the floor.

In my spare time,
I like to kick back with
        a cup of coffee,
        Procal Harem on the stereo
        and, a book
        (usually by Kurt Vonnigut Jr.)
Most of the time
my little boy kicks back with me.
He'll hold my hand or
put his finger in my ear or
pretend to read magazine.
        I love him.

I'm not Michael's father.
I wish he were mine because
I love him as if he were.

. . . he's mine.

Michael's two.
When Lydia and I moved,
We let him carry a plate
so that he could help.
He dropped
and broke it.

. . . at four & five & maybe six . . .

I see my little boy on weekends.
He's almost five.
He and Timmy, the little boy down the street,
and I go fishing.
I made Michael a fishing pole out of a
stick and a piece of string.
The only time that he caught a fish,
the fish pulled the pole right out of Michael's hands
and into the water.
It scared him at first but when he saw that pole
gliding across the water,
he really started to laugh.

I'm teaching my little boy
to count.
He always skips seven.
One, two,
        three,
        four, five six.
        nineteen, eight, nine,
        ten.
                He's four.

"Daddy"

"Yes, Michael?"

"How old are you?"

"Thirty-two, why?"

"Just wondering. I'm five so how long before I have a little boy?"

"Oh, it'll be a few years at least."

"When I have a little boy, I'm going to be the best father in the world . . . next to you."

"I'm sure you will."

"Yes sir, I'll just remember all of the nice things you did for me and I'll do the same."

"Michael, I love you."

"I know. Daddy, how much money do I have" He put his hand into his pocket and pulled out some change,

"Let's see . . . thirty-eight cents."

"Come on, I'll buy you a Coke."

"Ok, come on."

"Dad!"

"Yes, Son?"

"I love you, too."

"I know!"

> Curb-walking is walking
> the entire length of the
> block on the side of the
> curb without losing your
> balance.

"What's this called again, Dad?"

"This is called curb-walking. If you step into the gutter, you lose the game. Those are the rules, Michael."

"I'm a tightrope walker."

"Well. I'm a tightrope walker, too."

"We're walking over Niagara Falls."

"I know."

"Now, I'm a ladybug, Dad."

"And I'm a ladybug, too."

"And we're walking around a teacup, huh?"

"That's right!"

"We're going to have to stay up here forever, Dad."

"How come?"

"Cause it goes 'round and 'round and 'round and never stops."

"I guess so, then."

"Dad!"

"Yes, Michael?"

"Let's go home."

"We can't . . ."
"But, I'm tired."

"You should have thought of tha before we got up here on top of the tea cup."

"I was just kidding about being a ladybug."

"You were?"

Yeah, we're still crossing Niagara Falls."

"As soon as we get to the other side, Michael, we'll go home, alright?"

"Alright!

       "Dad!"

       "Yeah, Son?"

       "Uh . . . never mind."

       "I love you, too, Michael."

       (a big smile) "Honest?"

       "Honest!"

Dear Jesus,
Please make Mommy and Daddy friends again so I can see Daddy more than once
a week.

Amen

"Daddy, do you love me just when you see me
or do you love me all the time?"

When we're together,
it's our time . . .
a special time . . .
an ordinary time,
doing ordinary things . . .
but together.

Sun. afternoon after church
"Want to go to the zoo?"
"No!"
"Then, how 'bout the park?"
"No, let's do stuff we used to do."
I sat up Michael's train set and he
played with it while I watched the
golf game on T.V.

. . . when Michael stopped crying . . .

"Michael, I've told you not to leave your bike in the front yard. If you'd kept in the garage, it wouldn't have been stolen."

He stared at the floor and pretended to be mad.

"If you promise to keep it in the garage, I'll buy you a new one. We'd better get you a lock for it, too." Michael still stared at the floor then, he smiled.

"Yeah, and we better get a big chain to put around the garage so no one will get in. But if they do get you boy, they better watch out 'cause I'll clobber 'em. I'll sock then in the stomach and then hit them in the head with my fist and knock them out. We better move my bed out there, too, so that I can watch for them."

"Hey! Slow down. Come on, let's go get your bike."

The new bike was yellow with red training wheels.

Michael and I were sitting on the bathroom floor, floating sailboats in the bathtub. Without looking at me, he said, I kinda love you more than I like you."

Without looking at him, I smiled.

Michael looked up at me and patted my knee. "Don't worry, Daddy, I like you a lot."

"Come on, Sport, let's dry you off and get you to bed. It's way past your bedtime."

"No!"

"I let you stay up until eleven. Come on. Now."

Sigh, Alright,"

. . . after midnight
        on a rainy night . . .

"Dad . . . Dad . . . wake up!"
"Wha . . . ? Michael, what's wrong?"
"Just thought I'd come in here and sleep
with you just in case that ol' thunder
was scaring you."
"No, it's not . . . um, ok, Sport, crawl in."
"Good-night, Dad."
"Night . . . and thanks!"
"Shucks, it's alright."

If I were to say how much you mean to me,
I couldn't say, "I love you'.
It's more than that.
You mean more to me than I could possibly show . . .
        . . . more than I could even comprehend . . .
        . . . and more.

JUST JOKIN'

Prologue

*N*arrated *by the lady at the next table at O'Reighly's Irish Pub and told to Tres (pronounced Tray) Payr who told it to me. He (Tres) got his name from being the third of four sons. I'm surprised that they remembered so many details to the story.*

I spent the better part of two hours talking to the lady sitting at the next table of Jack-In-The-Box. She said that she had to go and then threw me a kiss. I had come in to get an iced tea, a couple of tacos, and to read but, I didn't read. I put my two books into my backpack, threw away the remains of my lunch, walked out the door of Jack-In-The-Box, unlocked my bike and started to ride. The sky was overcast. After fifteen feet riding down the parking lot, it started to sprinkle. By the time I reached the other side of the parking lot, I was drenched from the rain.

My name is Harry. I went into a bar to get out of the rain and ordered a tonic and lime. Fleetwood Mac's 'Tusk' was playing on the jukebox. I asked if I could park my 18 speed inside. They said, 'Yes!' The lady at the next table was telling her story to a couple of guys.

"Single malt whisky faded into blended whisky, fading into a double. Soon, Joe died drunk, while running a red light on his moped after work here. We will always mourn him".

This is the rest of her story, as best as I can recollect.

CHAPTER 1
⁓ **❋** ⁓

O'Reighly's Irish Pub
Established in 1882

Joe and Ty sat drinking at O'Reighly's, where Joe bartends. Today wasn't Joe's day off but the pub was empty. In his spare time, Joseph Kehn didn't drink. He rarely had any spare time to speak of.

"Here's one I read this morning. 'Never touch your eye but with your elbow.' I think it's an English saying or proverb." Joe said. Ty laughed.

"How about this one, Joey? 'Never put a razor inside your nose, even as a joke'."

"By Johansen, huh?"

"Man, your good!" Ty again.

"Not that good. I hear things at the bar. Here's a couple more, 'Catch a man a fish, and you can sell it to him. Teach a man to fish and you ruin a wonderful business.' Karl Marx" Then, there was a long silence as each one just sat.

"Hey, Joey, about the second one?"

"The what?

"The second one!"

"Of what? Oh, yeah! Well, I forgot." They both giggled. "Hey, Ty, how's about me buying us another round of Scotches?"

"No, I better . . . well, alright, and I'll play the box. Anything you want to hear?"

"Yeah! 'Tusk' and (laughing) some ABBA."

"Yeah, right! Oh, and how 'bout some Bay City Rollers, Joey?"

"Hey, we just got in some new old Skynard and ZZ Top and, oh yeah, CCR's 'There's A Bathroom On The Right'."

"Who's CCR, Joey?"

"Serious? You'll see."

"Yeah! Let's go for it. Wanna another whisky?"

"Sure, why not." They both sat there listening to someone else's dollars on the juke box without Joe getting the drinks.

CHAPTER 2

Today is a month later. This night, back at the O'Reighly's Pub, Joe's only day off, he kept busy by bumming $10.25 worth of quarters from customers and deciding what he would play on the juke box. He chose four songs before he forgot what he was doing; too much drink.

This night, sitting on a bar stool, Joe got up, swiped a $58 bottle of single malt Scotch from the liquor store room then, called a cab for home. Twenty-five minutes later, the cabbie was calling out, "Cab for Joe Kehn". Joe hated his name. Finally at home and the cabbie walking Joe to the door, Joe staggered and tripped into the small cottage and poured himself a scotch then, passed out, not paying the driver for the ride.

When Joe woke up the next morning, he cursed the bright muggy morning and then, he finished his 18 year old plus a day older glass of Scotch from the morning before. Joe, head throbbing, looked around the room rather confused—he didn't remember when or how he got there or to bed. Joe poured himself another glass, a full tumbler of the Scotch to sooth his head, taking about an hour drinking it while getting dressed, putting on his favorite Pink Floyd sweatshirt (He has six) and watching part of an 'Adam's Family' marathon, falling and waking from sleep a couple of times. Finally, he headed for the door. The door wouldn't open. He shook it hard, hearing metal on the other side. The harder he shook the door, the louder the clanking metal. Joe went to one of the two living room windows to open it but it was stuck—so was the second one, and the kitchen window, too. The bedroom window slid open. Joe crawled out, walked down the sides of the cottage and noticed that each of the other windows were screwed shut by bright yellow screws at the window frames. He crawled back into the bedroom, found a screwdriver and putting it into his back pocket then headed for work. His moped wouldn't start. Right now, he was two hours and twenty-five minutes late for work.

Ty was sitting on a bar stool. A girl from last night was sitting next to him. Joe opened the front door of O'Reighly's but he didn't go in—couldn't see in, in the dim light. Joe finally went in and sat by Ty. The lady said, "Hi! Do you remember me? I am Elaina".

Joe didn't remember if he remembered her or not so he just said, "Hey!" and half smiled.

She smiled back. "How do you feel today? You were doing pretty good last night."

"I feel Okay"

She laughed a sigh. "Man, I would be so sick today if I did how you did last night". Joe was annoyed and let it be known by his look. "Hey, Ty, get me another gin & tonic and I will pay you back when I get back from the little girls room, all righty?" Then she left, stepping and tripping on her foot.

"Hey, Joey", said Ty, "she won't, you know. How're ya doin'?"

A lady came into the bar riding an electric wheelchair, a power chair. One leg was amputated at the knee. "Excuse me! My battery is about dead. Should I plug it in for an hour or so? I don't have money to drink." Joe showed her where to sit and plugged the chair in with the power cord she had in a pocket on the back of the chair than he bought her a drink—tonic and lime. That's all she wanted. When Joe returned with her drink, she was staring at some type of an electrical device.

"What's that?" asked Joe, looking at the device.

"It's called a Nook, an electronic reader."

"What are you reading, if I may ask?"

"It's a book on anthropology, nutritional anthropology. I'm going for my Master's degree."

Joe looked at her square in the eye. "How old are you?"

"I'll be twenty-three next month."

"Wow!" he exclaimed.

"Hey, Joey, how you feel?" continued Ty.

"Good but I needed some help from Jameson, ya know." No smile except from Ty. Joe ordered a coffee & whisky instead of his usual scotch.

"You know, Joe Kehn, (Joe scowled) It's pretty bad when we have to drink at nine in the morning to make it through the day, ay."

"Yeah! And I'm never going to do that again, but I will." No smile. "I had to walk to work. My bike wouldn't start. I was almost three hours late. I doubt if they'll let me slide. I'll probably have to work until five. I'll hate it but I guess I'll deserve it."

"No quotes today, huh? What a minute, Turn up the TV, please. Never mind. It's over. There was a picture of George Harrison. He died today."

"Who?" asked Joe?

"You know, George Harrison from the Beatles."

"I thought that you said Woody Harrison from 'Cheers'."

"That's not Woody's last name. It's . . . uh, I can't think of it right now. Harrison was a heck of a guitar player. Hey, I'm going to play darts tonight. Want to come and watch?"

Joe shook his head, "No! I didn't get much, if any sleep last night. I've never played. I should try. How expensive for darts?"

"I paid $75 for my good set but you can get by for fifteen. A good board is expensive, too. You can make money at it, too if you're good—not just trophies. It wasn't hard for me to get good enough for tournament play. I'll give you a set if you want. Do you ever play anything?"

"You'll laugh." smiled Joe. "I used to play bridge and I'm good at cribbage and backgammon when I can find anyone to play. They used to have them here at the bar but they got taken. I enjoyed the people that I played bridge with but I never got the hang of the bidding. Oh! And I'm good at the dice cups and liar's poker. Make good money at that but you have to be careful not to get caught here. It's illegal and the bar can get fined or even closed down, I hear. Say, I just started watching a show called 'Mythbusters'. Ever hear of it?"

"Yeah! I like that show. Comes on 'bout six times a day. See the MacGyver show?"

"MacGyver's still on reruns. I watch it if I'm up early enough."

"No, not the show, the Mythbusters MacGyver show?" Joe shook his head 'No'. "They show clips of the show and then see if the stuff can be done in real life. Most, they can't."

"I saw him on a talk show a long time ago and he (the front door opened) said everything could be done. I believed . . ."

"Joey, I think you have a customer. I'm getting kinda warm. Could you put my jacket behind the bar or someplace?"

"Yeah! I am, too." Joe took off his jacket, took Ty's and still talking, he went behind the bar. "I believed whatever his name is — MacGyver . . . uh, Dick Anderson said. I think that they researched on the things."

"Rich uh . . . um . . . Richard Dean Anderson. Do you sell food?"

"Yeah! You know that we do, dummy. I have chips and hot link sausages cooked in porter beer and, chili . . . on the house as usual. You just wanted me to say that didn't you?"

"Yep, I did. Chili, please" Ty said.

"Chili with an 'i' or a 'e'?"

"What's the difference?"

"'E' is a pepper and 'i' is beans, I think. We have both with corn chips or rice."

"I'll have a couple of those sausages with mustard.

"Okey doke! Let me get this guy first." Joe gave the customer a beer and then talked to him quit a while before giving him a couple of sausages. When he got back to Ty, "He kept arguing when I told him two-fifty. He said I said they were on the house so I finally gave in and gave them to him. With my luck, I'll have to pay for them and then he'll stiff me on my tip. Here! Do you want regular or hot mustard?"

"Ho boy, too many choices, too early in the morning, too much hangover. I've been up since ten last morning. If you mean hot dog mustard, uh, regular. Elaina isn't coming back. You want her drink?"

"No thanks! I better not but, thanks anyways." Ty downed it in one gulp. The ice was melted.

Joe got busy working for the next hour and a half. Because of the way he felt after last night, it probably did him a world of good to keep busy. He didn't notice Ty leaving until after noon-time. The guy with the sausages 'on the house' with a $3.25 tab left him a $16.75 tip. Joe got a phone call asking him to work until 10 pm but they settled on 5 pm.

Elaina came in shortly before noon, asking for her gin & tonic. Joe made her a fresh one. "Thank-you!" She winked and smiled. "When did . . ."

"I don't have time to talk now, to busy. Wait around I'll talk to you later when I'm not."

"Would you like some lunch? I'll buy."

"I'm busy! He said, scolding her.

Ten or twenty minutes later Joe came back and leaned on the bar, in front of Elaina. Stirring her unfinished drink with her finger and not looking at Joe, she began talking. "I was talking to a fellow here after Ty left (*the 'sausage on the house' guy*). I met him before. He is named Mike or Mick or something." She giggled. "He tells a very interesting story that might be a lie but some of it is true because I was there for a while and a friend of mine told me some of it. Mike or Mac is twenty-three years old. A couple of years ago his Mom died. I was applying for an apartment where he lived. His Mother left him three million dollars and he bought the apartment house that he lived in. Another fellow I knew went into the Hyatt Regency during happy hours hoping to get some free food. They had a piano there and my friend, I do not remember his name, asked if he could play the piano. There was a large brandy glass on it. Mike or Mick put a ten dollar bill in and requested a song from the forties that my friend did not know but Mike just walked away, leaving the ten. He did that four or five time. This was during a heat spell and Mick told my friend he could stay in his room. Mick's AC was out so he just checked in the hotel for the duration. Must be nice, huh?"

"Sorry but I have a group of people I have to check on. Finish when I get back, Okay?" Joe found the story boring and was hoping that she would forget about it but she didn't.

When he came back, without looking up she started in. "The next morning he had my friend drive him to his apartment house. They both went in and then Mike took a foot locker from the closet.

"You are not going to rob me are you? I guess if you did, I could not stop you." Mike asked. He opened the trunk and it was full of twenty dollar bills and took out a bundle. I thought that you and me and two girlfriends of mine could go out to lunch. Here's some money so you can pay both your ways." Mick handed my friend a stack of twenties. I do not know what my friend said and he did not rob Mick or Mike.

Mac or Mike and my friend picked us up and took us to a restaurant by the bay, the ocean. We had crab legs and claws AND lobster. I would like another of the same, please." meaning a drink.

Joe gave her another drink and then went to the other end of the bar, pretending to be busy but soon he got curious about the Mike, Mick, Mac story.

"Crab and lobster? How was it prepared, boiled or grilled?" asked Joe.

"The lobster was in a salad and also in a burrito with pepperoncini and banana chilies and sweet, probably Walla Walla onions. The crab legs and claws were served with lemon and melted butter. They were so delicious. Best food I had since probably when I used to cater private parties."

"Sounds like it. I love crab better than lobster and I love banana chilies. So, you used to cater?"

"Yes, in Hollywood. I lived in Laurel Canyon in a cabin four doors from where Frank Zappa used to live. I had to move out because of a fire so, I came here. Talking about food, you know, a well-fed cat doesn't hunt is a myth. The play of a kitty is really hunting behavior. Pouncing and leaping at anything that moves like, your finger, a ball, or a leaf is a sign of this. I know a thing or two about felines. I used to work with them."

An old man sat down in front of Joe. "Hey, barkeep, what's up? And she said that she'd never leave me for the studs. She left me for the studs. She said that it was drinking that made her leave me but I was dr-dr-drinking when she met me. This is such a wonderful birthday."

"Today's your birthday? Happy Birthday!" Joe said.

"You know, my de-de-dead end street . . . the hills, I never saw what was on the other side but now I can imagine anything that I want to imagine on the other side of those hills.

"Stu-stu-stupid cat! Get away! Get away! You know, before I du-du-die, I went fishing and was shot—wounded. A d-d-doctor was fishing and wanted to help but I turned him du-du-down. I d-d-didn't think that it was necessary. He called a paramedic but I d-d-didn't think that it was necessary so I turned them d-down. When I d-d-died, I asked G-God, 'Why!'

"I have to go now. (He smiled) Sorry but I'm drunk! Thank you so much for your courtesy, su-su-sir." Joe was relieved that he didn't have to ask the drunk to leave but I don't think Joe would have had the nerve or maybe been that polite, depending.

Joe walks back to Elaina. "Strange man, very strange. If I didn't know he was drinking, I'd say he was crackers. I was going to give him a birthday drink but, Na-a-h!

"What's that book there? It looks old or used."

"It is! Mama sent it to me, an autographed edition of Allen Ginsberg's 'Howl and other poems'. She sends me autographed books quit often. She told me that she hung around with Allen Ginsberg and Ferlinghetti and Jack Kerouac and other 'Beat Poets' in Times Square in the 50's. She spent the three days at the Woodstock Festival, too. She has been around in her many years. She was forty-three when I was born and I am twenty-six."

"Elaina, that's interesting. That really is. Maybe we can get together sometime for coffee and you can tell me about her adventures." Joe gave Elaina a five to put in the juke box and poured her another gin and tonic. He poured himself another scotch but didn't have time to drink it. The front door opened and a crowd came in.

"Our tour bus broke down. You'll have a bunch of customers for a while." said one of them. Do you serve any food?"

"Where you from and where are you going?" Joe asked.

"Redding! Vegas!" the customer said. They stayed for a few hours which kept Joe busy.

Ty came back into O'Reighly's just around five. "Hey, Joe!"

"Hey, Ty! Want a drink? Elaina's here."

"Wow! It sure gotten crowded in here. No! I want to be sober for tonight. Change your mind about the darts tourney? Where is she?"

"Yeah! Maybe but I'm so tired from last night." Joe looked around but she was gone

"How about some chili with an 'i'?"

"Coming up. Red or green hot sauce?"

"Neither, but with crackers."

Ty sat on a bar stool. "A man just came up to me, talking about Jesus. He gave me this pamphlet. I used to go to church twice on Sunday and on Wednesday night. My uncle would pick me up and take me. I really liked Sunday school. I had a little girl friend there. I loved the night time church music, too. Little ol' ladies would cry and wave their handkerchiefs. They weren't funny. They were inspirational."

"Yeah! I don't have time for that stuff." Joe uttered.

"Why not!" asked one of the bus passengers. "My work keeps me busy and, my friends. I used to go to church on Easter and Christmas and the other Easter holidays. My Grandparents go and they always pray for me so, I guess I'm covered."

"God doesn't have Grandchildren. Just because your family are righteous and go to church, that doesn't make you a Christian." The man had a paper name tag that said 'Jim' stuck to his sport jacket pocket.

"But I'd have to quit the things that I love to do.", argued Joe.

"I don't drink or gamble but I enjoy going to Vegas with my friends." said Jim.

Ty put his hand on Jim's shoulder. "You mean that Jesus . . ." Joe walked away. Ty and Jim talked until the bus driver announced that the bus was leaving in ten minutes.

Ty walked over to where Joe was mixing a drink for a customer. "Real interesting guy," said Ty to Joe. "and funny. He's very passionate about what he believes, too. Very convincing. He was . . ."

Joe interrupted. "How long will the dart tournament last tonight? I have to be back here a little bit before six because I open."

"Let's see, it starts around seven. I guess three hours or there abouts, never noticed. I have an extra set of darts if you want to give it a try. It'll cost five bucks to enter. There'll be at least two beginners from last week — if they show up."

"That's awful late. I don't think . . . yeah, I'll go. Give me a ride home?

"Sure!"

Ty ate his chili and Joe did his backup work, a little bit of shelf stocking, and ate a bowl of chili with Frito's. When they were leaving, the 'sausages on the house' guy was walking back in to the pub.

"Sit back down and I'll buy each of you a drink, whatever you had for your last drink."

"I drink Glenlivets but it's expensive, $9.75 a snifter."

"That's expensive brandy.", said Mac.

"No, it's single malt scotch, better than blended. Tradition has it served in a snifter with no ice, with a splash of water for flavor. The splash really works."

"I drink Glenlivets, too", Ty lies.

"Good, then we'll all have one. What's your name? I remember you working here earlier, right", he asks Joe.

"Yeah! I'm Joe and this is my best friend, Ty. Do you know what single malt scotch is?" The word 'whisky' caught the attention of some people that were sitting or standing around the bar.

"No, I don't."

"I learned this on the Discovery channel on a show about distilling." Joe seemed proud about this fact. "Scotch is whiskey spelled without an 'e'. All others are spelled with it. Blended scotch is produced by a blend of single malt whisky with one or more whiskies produced with cereals and it is the most common Scotch whisky. A premium blend never contains less than 25 different types and the average is made with 30, even though there are some blends containing more than 40. (People were losing interest in this conversation fast) Now, single malt is produced by a single distillery and uses a blend of only single malts only. Many people think that single is very harsh tasting. Trust me; it has very unique taste that I love. A fifth of sixteen year old costs $78 here.

"Thanks much for the drinks but we have to get to a dart tournament Thank-you again!" Joe says while shaking his hand. Ty shakes his head 'yes' and smiles then, they leave without finding out the guy's real name.

Ty drove a '56 T-bird with the portholes on the back of both doors. He didn't work but he always had money. He always had enough to do anything he wanted to do but he was cheap, mooching off of anyone, getting free drinks from Joe.

They arrive at the bar, maybe it was a pub, where they were going to play. To Ty, "A very strange thing happened to me during the night or this morning. I was passed out from last night so I didn't hear nothing. When I left this morning for work, the door wouldn't open. I kept shaking it, hearing metal on the other side.

A waitress interrupted them. "What would you two like?"' she asked.

Ty order a glass of beer. "I'll have a Glenlivets, please."

"A what?" she asked.

"Glenlivets . . . scotch."

"We only serve wine, beer, and soft drinks."

"Okay," said Joe. "then I'll have a Froch Heather Ale."

"We don't carry that. How about a Bud?"

"Do you have Guinness?"

"Good choice, sweetie. I'll be right back."

"Anyhow, I kept shaking the door, hearing metal on the other side. The harder I shook, the louder the clanking. I went to a living room window but it was stuck — so was the second one, and so was the kitchen window. The bedroom window slid open and I crawled out. All of the other windows were screwed shut, with bright yellow screws. I crawled back into the bedroom, got a screwdriver, and then went to work. My moped wouldn't start so I was over two hours late for work. I have no idea who or why they did this."

"You know, Joey, darts' a simple game—after a lot of practice." Ty chuckles. "No, it really is after you get used to throwing them, but not hard. You'll ruin the board. They play singles 301 and partners 501 tonight. The score each turn is added up and subtracted from our score before play. A bull's eye is . . ." The waitress brought the beers' Ty still talking, "A bulls eye counts 50, the outer ring from the bulls eye is 25 and a dart in the double or treble ring counts double or treble the number in the pie. The object is to be the first player to end up with zero, the only thing being is that the last dart must go into a double or the bulls eye. If not, you bust and you go back to the points of your last turn. You have to win two out of three games. We're playing partners, 501 and you'll shoot first.

Okay! You know what, Joey, I went to a record/CD shop and asked for CCR's 'There's A Bathroom On The Right'. They laughed at me and played Credence Clearwater's 'Bad Moon Rising. I could hear 'the bathroom on the right'. I laughed. It was funny. It does sound like they're singing that. I don't think I knew them as CCR. I don't know."

Joe shot first. He hit the top edge of the board the first two throws but then hit a triple 'one', not the 'twenty'. Because of Ty, Joe and Ty won the first game. The second game, Ty had to get a fourteen to win—he busted. He hit a double fourteen. "Your next turn, Joey, aim for only a fourteen. Don't do what I just did", he said to Joe. When it was his turn, Joe aimed and missed the fourteen but hit a double seven. They won! They came in second but Ty was still excited, 'O-o-o! O-o-o! O-o-o-ing!' and dancing a football touchdown dance, with high fives in the air. Mac, (not the 'sausage on the house' guy), one of the guys they were playing against was so upset that he broke off all of the aluminum shafts, crushing the flights, and walked out the back, forgetting about the pitcher of beer he had just bought.

Joe and Ty sat down at Mac's partner's table. Joe looked at him, "That guy that broke the shafts of his darts, he's a pretty poor loser. By the way, what's your name, stranger?" said to Mac's partner.

"Oh, yeah! Jonesy's a real poor loser. He thinks that he's better than anybody else and, the thing is, he usually is. He's a great fiddle and mandolin player."

"I thought that he told me his name was Mac. You know, either I've seen him before or he reminds me of someone. When you said 'mandolin player' . . . how well do you know this guy?"

"His name's actually Jack Jones, like the singer. He doesn't like the singer so he either goes by Mac or Jonesy Jack. He's from here but he stays with his girlfriend sometimes in Fremont."

"Yeah!" said Joe. "I used to go to a lady's house in Fremont. Her name is Judy Porter and she lived on Porter St. I play blues harp and a group of us, sometimes twenty, sometimes six of us would sit in her kitchen and jam. We'd call it Porter's kitchen on Porter Street. The thing is that his name wasn't Jack Jones. Can't remember what it was but it wasn't Jack or Mac."

"A few years ago, he thought that he witnessed a murder but he was mistaken. He was so scared that people would be after him that he faked his own death to hide. The funeral was very nice."

Ty split Mac's beer between him and Joe, the other player said 'no', that he didn't drink.

After only one beer, both Joe and Ty said good-bye to him. He smiled, shook their hands, then said, "Jesus love you." Ty took notice of what he said but Joe felt uncomfortable about it.

Joe and Ty drank one glass then left. Ty put in Pink Floyd's 'Dark Side Of The Moon' in the CD player and they just listened while Ty drove.

When Ty dropped Joe home, "Need some help getting in?"

"No! I have my screwdriver." He holds it up. "Thanks, though, Bro."

"When do you have to get up for work in the morning, Joey?"

"Five-fifteen—my moped wouldn't start this morning. I have to open the bar at six. I'm probably going to have to walk to work. You know, there'll be about six or seven old guys waiting at the door to get in when I get there for their coffee and whisky shots. They'll leave about ten a.m. or maybe before dark tomorrow evening. They seldom eat or go out to get something."

"Well then, so long. Sleep tight. Maybe I'll come in in the morning and check on you."

"Yeah! And get free drinks." Joe thought. But he didn't mind. "One of these days I'm going to get caught giving free drinks, probably, and taking single malt."

Ty drove off.

CHAPTER 3

⚜ ***** ⚜

With screwdriver in hand, Joe went for the door and unscrewed the latch and padlock. The door wouldn't open. He shook it hard, hearing metal on the other side. The harder he shook the door, the louder the clanking metal. "Not again!" he cursed very loud."

Joe went to one of the two living room windows to open it but it was stuck — so was the second window. He went to the kitchen window. The window slid open so he climbed inside — getting his foot wet in the dirty, soapy water in the sink below. Joe poured a tumbler of single malt with a lemon peel that he brought from work.

Twenty minutes later, after his scotch was gone, Joe walked into each room and noticed that each window was screwed shut with orange screws. The door was padlocked from the inside.

Endnotes

⚜ ***** ⚜

Most of the people in this story attended Joe Kehn's Memorial and then quietly went their separate ways, some many miles and a state or two away. I don't know how or who kept track of them. I don't know how a committee tracks down graduates for school reunions either but please, read on.

Ty quit drinking indefinitely on the day of Joe's funeral. Eleven days later, he was arrested for pimping and possession of Turkish black opium — the finest, some say (Ty actually took it away from a friend but was arrested before he turned it in to the authorities.). After a while, Ty found Jesus and soon became instrumental in the prison ministry and studied for the ministry. A few months later, he was let out on a technicality that his lawyer had discovered. A while later, the owner of O'Reighly's found Ty. "I know that you need a building for your church. If I didn't open on Sundays until 2 p.m., would you like your people to meet here? There's only one condition. I won't charge you any rent but I insist on hosting Sunday dinner once a month for your people." Said Ty, "And I have one condition for you. I have several recovering alcoholics in my congregation. I need for the booze to be locked up." They shook on it and a deal was made. Some of the people play darts and cribbage after church every Sunday.

Mike, Mick, Mac the 'Sausage on the house' guy's real name is Nick. Nick lost all of his money six weeks shy of two years after he inherited it just by spending too much of it. He lost his apartment house but still lives there rent free as part of the sale. Today he's a successful telemarketer selling tickets to real estate seminar dinners. He's a want-a-be bass/keyboard player. Many times he tells fantasies about his talents and uses musician's names as his own. He's smart, not crazy.

Elaina conned Nick out of a lot of money. After a while, she felt guilty about it. She donated most of it to the church of Scientology but then, got it all back somehow. She then donated a third to D.A.R.E., Drug Awareness Something Something, a third to a small church in the San Joaquin Valley, and the other third — $40,000, she kept. Elaina is patterned after an ex-girlfriend of mine. She's never conned anybody. She's either very honest or scared or both. People at my church and work really liked her. I honestly don't remember her name. I guess in that way we're alike. She asked me to marry her and then told me to think about it before I could give her an answer. A short time later, she moved to Florida and got married. They came back to California and she went back to work at the same restaurant chain but a different restaurant in town. I moved to Arizona but every year and a half or so, I'm in town and I stop to see her. And yes, her name is Elaina.

Nick is featured in my story, 'An Untitled Memphis Tale'. After squandering his fortune on useless possessions, all with-in three years, he settled into the Chicago blues bar life — but not as a performer. He did do two grand deeds before Chicago. (See my stories 'Pabadoe' and An Untitled Memphis Tale')

The drunken old man's name is Hylo Greer. He has no family. He had a stroke on his barstool one evening. Now, he lives in a hospice.

The early morning old men outside the bar, I passed them on my way to work. One afternoon I stopped in to meet them. Some were very out of it, not necessarily drunk while others were sober, alert, interesting, and funny.

The tour bus co. put O'Reighly's Irish Pub on their Redding-Las Vegas-Redding route as a meal stop for chili and beer hot link sausages. The bus stops there once a month both ways.

I only wrote the story of Joe Kehn but I miss him. I liked him but I didn't like his ways. I liked my two friends that I blended into Joe's character. Alan was my local best friend in Fremont, Ca. He was a heavy drinker but one day he just quit without notice or with anyone's help. He started going to church with me. He isn't Ty at all. Paul (real name), looked enough like the singer/songwriter to be Paul Williams (not of The Temptations), the singer / song-writer. I knew in Boise. He was a working musician—a classical/jazz guitarist. He was an alcoholic. He died the same way that Joe died. After playing and drinking one night in a steak house lounge, he ran a red light on his moped in a hit-and-run.

A MADDENING SILENCE

(A Study Of Deaf Classical Composers and Musicians)

When I went on disability, I started going back to school full time. I was in my late forties. Before I knew it and at a great surprise to me, I earned two masters in nutrition with emphasis on life science and also, anthropology. This is my term paper for my American Sign Language 1 class. I got an A+.

I. King Jordan, president of Gallaudet University made this statement, "A deaf person can do anything a hearing person can, except hear." I decided to challenge this statement by choosing the topic of 'deaf and music.' Boy—was I wrong. Beethoven is infamous at composing after becoming deaf, but, I wanted more. I told myself that if I couldn't find information about other deaf composers or musicians, I would change my topic mid-stream. I did find two others, Glennie & Smetana. Here is a brief bio of each one.

Thou shalt not curse the deaf, nor put a stumbling block before the blind; but thou shalt fear thy God: I am Jehovah. Lev 19:14 (ASV)

LUDWIG VAN BEETHOVEN was born in Bonn, Germany on December 16, 1770 and died 1827. He was the second-oldest child of the court musician and tenor singer Johann Van Beethoven. His mother was a singer in the service of the elector of Koln (now Cologne).

As a youth of 17, Beethoven became a court musician in the Bonn court orchestra in order to support his family. He held a position as harpsichordist in the court theater and assistant organist in the electoral chapel, where he obtained his first lessons in composition from the court organist. His early compositions under the teaching of German composer Christian Gottlob Neefe, particularly the funeral cantata on the death of Holy Roman Emperor Joseph II in 1790, signaled an important talent, and it was planned that Beethoven study in Vienna, Austria, with Wolfgang Amadeus Mozart. Beethoven was granted a paid leave of absence in the early part of 1787. Mozart predicted that Beethoven's music would leave a lasting impact on the world. Beethoven did become the first important composer not obligated or supported by the court or by the church. He received a regular salary, making it possible for him to call the shots and compose whatever he liked.

As his career was reaching its peak, he began growing deaf. The first reference to this was in a letter (dated 29-June-1801) he wrote to a friend. "For two years now I avoid all society for I cannot say to people, 'I am deaf'" He continued, "At the theater I must sit quite near the orchestra in order to hear fellow actors." His deafness became progressively worse and by 1817 his deafness was total and a way of life. Beethoven relied on small "conversation books" in which visitors wrote their remarks to him. He withdrew from all but a steadily shrinking circle of friends.

Beethoven, before his deafness, was by nature, impatient, impulsive, unreasonable and intolerant. Deafness added cynicism and paranoia to his temperamental, troubled life. At one point, he considered suicide. His troubled mind began to produce music that aroused and terrified his contemporaries. People wondered how he could write such beautiful music even though he was deaf. Beethoven wrote the 'Choral' Symphony (the monumental Ninth Symphony) in 1823, with its choral finale based on Schiller's Ode to Joy. He did conduct the 1st performance of this work, not being able to hear the music. The soprano soloist had to take him by the arm and turn him towards the audience to see the applause that he couldn't hear.

Today, the diagnosis for Beethoven's deafness is otosclerosis, a progressive growth of spongy bone around the stirrup bone in the middle ear. This ailment restricts or prevents the vibrations leading to the inner ear. Otosclerosis is curable today.

Musicology legend has it that, while on his deathbed one fierce stormy day, Beethoven did react to a loud crash of thunder by opening his eyes and sitting up. He shook his fist to the sky. He then fell back, dead. Beethoven died in Vienna on March 26, 1827. His last words were reportedly, 'I shall hear in Heaven.'

In that day the deaf will hear the words of a book, and out of their gloom and darkness the blind will see my plans. 19 The meek will be filled with fresh joy from the Lord, and the poor shall exult in the Holy One of Israel. Isaiah 29:18-19 (Living Bible)

Tens of thousands witnessed Ludwig Von Beethoven's funeral procession. Among his pallbearers and torchbearers were fellow composer France Stubbier and famous pianist, Johann Humble. During his lifetime, Beethoven lived an exciting and controversial life which was intense, sometimes agonizing, and sometimes joyful.

Fredrich (Bedrich) Smetana was born March 2, 1824, in Litomyšl, Bohemia (now in the Czech Republic) and died in Prague (Czech) May 12, 1884.

In his teens he attended and trained as a pianist at the Academic Gymnasium in Prague, but neglected schoolwork to attend concerts (including some by Liszt, with whom he became friendly) and to write string quartets for friends, until his father sent him to the Premonstratensian Gymnasium at Plzen. When he failed in an attempt to launch a career as a concert pianist in 1847, Smetana decided to found a school of music. With the help of the Hungarian composer and pianist France Liszt, he established a fashionable music school in Prague in 1848.

Smetana wrote national music based on Bohemian folk tunes. Smetana was truly the Poet Laureate of his country, expressing the joys and sorrows of his people, but instead of writing prose in a language familiar only to his countrymen, he wrote in the international language of Music.

In 1866 he was appointed conductor of the newly established Czech opera house in Prague, but he resigned in 1874 because of sudden deafness, the result of syphilis. Pressure on the auditory nerve (tinnitus) made him hear a constant drone on a high E. He used tinnitus to write E minor string quartet — subtitled 'From my Life' — in 1876 and his symphonic poem 'Vysehrad' on this tone.

When a conductor, in Liszt's presence, condescendingly told Smetana that his "race" produced good violinists but no composers of any talent, Liszt sat down at the piano and played from memory the music Smetana had sent him, telling the conductor, "Here!"

Despite this handicap he continued to compose. He produced some of his greatest works in the last years of his life. Smetana eventually fell into bouts of hallucinations, suicidal thoughts, and fits of violence. April 23, 1884 he was taken to a mental hospital. He died a few weeks later, May 12, in Prague. He was regarded by some to be the founder of Czech music

On a happier note (no pun intended—yeah, right! ☺), not all 'handicapped' people live a troubled life—far from it.

Encourage those who are afraid. Tell them, "Be strong, fear not, for your God is coming to destroy your enemies. He is coming to save you." 5 And when he comes, he will open the eyes of the blind and unstop the ears of the deaf. 6 The lame man will leap up like a deer, and those who could not speak will shout and sing! Isaiah 35:4-6 (Living Bible)

Evelyn Glennie was born in 1965 in Aberdeen, Scotland. She began studying music and the clarinet at an early age. She bagan going deaf at the age of 8. At the age of 12, her deafness was complete and she gave up the clarinet and began studying timpani and percussion, focusing on visual cues and familiarizing herself with the written music. She became a member of the National Youth Orchestra of Scotland, touring the UK, Faroe Islands, and Scandinavia. She earned an Honors Degree and her LRAM at the Royal Academy of Music in London, in 1982, where she studied timpani/percussion and piano.

She has been awarded many prizes, to numerous to mention in this report but they include the Young Professional Allmusic Musician of the Year Award in the 1988 Wavendon Allmusic Awards; Junior Chamber International voted her one of the 10 Outstanding Young People in the World in November 1989; and the Scotsman news-paper readers voted her Scotswoman of the Decade for the 1980s. In February 1991, she was given the prestigious Royal Philharmonic Society Charles Heidsieck Soloist of the Year Award, and in 1991 Aberdeen University conferred on her an Honorary Degree of Doctor. She's also a Grammy Award-winning percussionist, playing drums, gongs and marimbas.

One of the world's few classical percussion soloists, Glennie has taken the classical world by storm. Although extremely deaf, she is making a deafening musical statement to audiences around the world, filling performance halls for her solo performance.

Make a joyful noise to God, all the earth; Psalms 66:1 (RSV)
And Jesus answered them, "Go and tell John what you hear and see: 5 the blind receive their sight and the lame walk, lepers are cleansed and the deaf hear, and the dead are raised up, and the poor have good news preached to them. Matt 11:4-5 (RSV)

In Nora Ellen Groce's book, 'Everyone Here Spoke Sign Language' I found these wonderful quotes:

- "As one older man on the island remarked, 'I don't think about the deaf any more than you'd think about anybody with a different voice.'"
- The author asked about those who were handicapped by deafness. The response of the hearing girl being interviewed was, "Oh, those people weren't handicapped. They were just deaf."
- "Many authors, assuming that handicaps are seen in the same way in all cultures, fail to offer a satisfactory definition of what they consider to be a handicap or disability. According to the World Heath Organization (WHO), between 3 and 10 percent of the world's population suffer some sort of disability that is congenial or caused by disease or accident.
- An impairment is any loss or abnormality of psychological, physiological, or ana-tomical structure or function. A disability reflects the consequences of an impairment, being any restriction or lack of ability to form an activity in the manner or within the range considered normal for non-impaired persons. A handicap, a disadvantage resulting from an impairment or disability, limits or prevents the person from fulfilling his or her normal role. Handicaps therefore are not determined by one's physical capabilities but rather reflect the social consequences of that disability. In short, the individual's perception of a handicap is tempered by the society in which the person lives."

Ken Martinez

References:
The Living, RSV, & ASV Bibles
The Concise Columbia Encyclopedia
Encarta '95
Deaf Persons In The Arts & Sciences by Harry G. Lang & Bonnie Meath-Lang
Everyone Here Spoke Sign Language by Nora Ellen Groce
The Internet
Panati's Extraordinary Endings of Practically Everything and Everybody
Peoples Almanac by David Wallechinsky & Irving Wallace
Peoples Almanac Vol. 3 by David Wallechinsky & Irving Wallace

In my research, some of my references differed in some dates, quotes, etc. Beethoven's last words were reportedly, 'I shall hear in Heaven.' in one source but differs in others. I'd like to think that he said this one. I used the information I found that agrees with or enhances this, my report.

Works during or after the onset of deafness:

> **1**_Let us make a joyful noise to the rock of our salvation._ **2**_Let us come before his presence with thanksgiving; Let us make a joyful noise unto him with psalms._ Psalms 95:1^b-2 (ASV)

Beethoven: 1801-1824
- 'Choral' Symphony (the Ninth Symphony)
- Sonata in C-sharp Minor (later to be called 'Moonlight Sonata)
- The _Appassionata_ Sonata
- The Fourth & Fifth (Emperor) concerti
- The second through eight symphonies
- Fidelio (his only opera)

Smetana: 1874-1886
- Consolation
- Dreams
- The Moldau
- Past Luck
- My Country (his most well-known piece)

- E minor string quartet — subtitled 'From my Life'
- his symphonic poem 'Vysehrad' (My Fatherland)
- his second string quartets, also titled 'From My Life'

Glennie:
- 01/98 Glennie, Evelyn Her Greatest
- 08/96 Glennie, Evelyn Drumming
- 09/95 Glennie, Evelyn Wind In Bamboo Grove
- 11/92 Glennie, Evelyn Rebounds/Cti Percuss

AN UNTITLED MEMPHIS TALE

Jaco sat with a group of others, both men and women in a one-time, for Jaco, counseling session. "I don't know where to start—well, yes I do. I picked Memphis, Tenn. to live because I didn't know anyone living here. I came from the south San Fran Bay Area, Fremont and Alameda, to be exact. My friend Cory Davis just died in northern California. He just died! I never found out why? He was a jazz pianist. I never heard about a funeral or a memorial or nothing. Just one person was there when he died and he wasn't family—just a guy. I don't know for sure that that guy was really there when Cory died. It's just hearsay.

"The last act that I did before moving here was spray painting on a store wall. It was to be a small review of Ivan Miller Sefter's political play 'Pine Cone Juice'. It was to read, 'I. M. Sexford's political play 'Pine Cone Juice' is a much see.' I heard the police coming so I ran before I was finished. I looked back and it looked like I wrote, 'I. M. Sex'. The paper took a picture of the graffiti and made a big joke of it. I guess that it was funny, if you think about it. Talking about running, I really need to run. I have a lunch date."

"OK, but, before you leave, let's all sing, 'Amazing Grace'." Jaco snuck out during the second verse.

Everything was true except for the lunch date. Even though Jaco had quite a bit of money in the bank, he took a bus. A few minutes later he got off the bus near Beale Street and walked into a blues club across the street from B. B. King's club. B. B.'s didn't have the oysters on the half shell that he craved every day except never. Inside, he stopped and looked at a bandstand. A few minutes later, he went to a table. It took forty minutes before the waiter walked to the table. Jaco ordered oysters on the half shell, deep-fried pickles, deep-fried cat fish, and a mint julep. On the stage was a blues singer/piano player. Jaco requested 'Buddy, Can You Spare A Dime?' and tipped the singer a twenty. Jaco asked that if he went home and got his bass guitar, could he sit in. He was turned down. "I'm Mac Davis' bass player and then played bass in a fusion jazz band called Weather Report. You might have heard of us." he lied.

"Is he still around?" the singer asked sarcastically, meaning Mac Davis. Jaco nodded, 'Right!' and then tap danced, with no taps, back to his bar stool. He sat facing the stage.

A lady sat down on the next stool. "They're good aren't they? Hi! I'm Carolyn."

"I'm Jaco! Hi!"

"Do you come here often?"

Jaco laughed. "I'm supposed to come up with that line, aren't I?"

Carolyn laughed. "I just wanted to talk with you. You're not married, are you?"

Jaco lied; she had way too much make-up to be pretty. "Yes, I am but, we can still talk if we can hear each other over the band. I'm from the San Francisco Bay Area. I'm just here for an open-ended visit."

"I've never heard it said that way before." Carolyn giggled. "Have you seen the city yet?"

"No, just this street. Tomorrow I want to see Stax and Sun Records and *maybe* Graceland. I love Sam & Dave and R&B, and I'm a big fan of Charlie Rich and Carl Perkins. I've manly stayed here listening to blues."

"Well, Jaco, I'm from here, thirteen years and then back six years ago. I came back from Weiser, ID. I use to play at the fiddle contest."

Jaco smiled. "I was there for that two times. I play mandolin (truth) but I didn't play—not on stage anyways. I'm not that good."

"Wanna dance?"

"Ok!"

The dance and the rest were slow. The drinks of choice became gin rocks with a slice of lime. Oysters on the half shell came many. They were only 50¢ a piece, just like shrimp cocktails on Frontier St in Vegas.

"Excuse me for a second." Carolyn walked up to the band and after talking to the same guy that Jaco talked to, she got up on the stage, took the mike and sang four songs. When she came back to her bar stool, all Jaco could do was to look at her head to toe and snicker. "Who are you?" he asked.

"Forget already? It's Carolyn, again!"

"How'd you get to sing?"

"I just asked. Why?"

"Oh! I just wondered. You're good!"

"Well, thank-you, kind sir. You should take a gambling boat trip up the river. They don't gamble." She smiled.

"Maybe I will. That sounds like fun."

"Jock, I mean, Jaco," Carolyn smiled, touching his knee, I have to go. I have to work in the morning. Let's meet here tomorrow, same time." She left without getting an answer.

A couple of hours later, Jaco went to B. B.'s club to hear some 'real' blues. On stage, there was a six piece band. Without a request, the band played 'Buddy, Can You Spare A Dime?' Jaco tipped them a twenty, anyways. His drink of choice was tonic and lime.

He stayed the wee hours of the morning that the band played. Afterwards, he took a long walk. The street was still crowded. Then, Jaco went back to the motel for the rest of the morning to sleep. This was Tuesday morning.

Around 11 am on this Tuesday morning, Jaco again got off the bus near Beale Street and walked into the blues club across the street from B. B. King's blues club alone. Again, he ordered the same oysters on the half shell, deep-fried pickles, no deep fried cat fish (Jaco didn't much care for the deep fried. I agree that it's much better grilled), and a mint julep. His plan was to listen to the blues band, and then go to the Stax R&B Museum, the Sun Records Museum, and then take the bus to Graceland. Jaco didn't want to pay the price for the tour bus so he took a city bus to each place. At Sun Records, Carolyn 'just happened' to be there. She stayed close to Jaco which he found annoying. After the tour, the tour guide, she said that her name was Lisa Marie, brought out an old microphone. Jaco sat down on the piano bench in the room.

Lisa Marie ended the tour by telling the people that, "When people such as Elvis, Charlie Rich, and Cash recorded here, all of the back-up singers, recorded at the same time, not using multi-tracks and they stood around this single mic. Feel free to stay and sing a song into it."

As the crowed thinned out, Jaco turned around and played and sang Jerry Lee Lewis', 'Great Ball Of Fire'. When he turned back around, Carolyn was still there. He walked up to the mic and sang Charlie Rich's, 'Mohair Sam'. He wanted to do 'Hound Dog' but other people were still waiting for the mic. Then he went out to the gift shop. Carolyn was right behind him. He dilly-dallied around until she left.

When Elvis died, many TV shows showed the inside of Graceland. The inside, to Jaco was too kitschy, too gaudy. The bus made a quick stop at the gate. The driver told a story about Elvis being so popular that he couldn't go outside the gate. She said that often she would see Elvis riding his motorcycle up and down the driveway. Across the street, one could see the tops of Elvis' two planes. The day was to end at Beale St for some ribs and some blues, with Carolyn. Jaco avoided that club — but then, maybe she didn't show.

Wednesday morning was raining, not hard, just a light shower. Today was to be a river boat (the *Mississippi Queen'*) cruise on the Mississippi River after lunch. Jaco again got off the bus near Beale Street. The rain had stopped. He walked into the blues club across the street from B. B. King's blues club alone. Again, he ordered the same oysters on the half shell, deep-fried pickles, and a mint julep On the stage was a different blues singer/piano player who was introduced as Biff Diamond. Jaco requested 'Buddy, Can You Spare A Dime?' and tipped the singer a twenty. Biff knew it and played it well.

After lunch and some listening enjoyment, Jaco took a taxi to the river. The shore from the road to the dock was all pebbles, down-hill. Jaco slipped and almost fell twice. The river boat route was down ten miles through Alabama and Arkansas. Jaco's goal was to see all 50 states and the territories. AL, AR, and TN made the count to be thirty-eight. The Captain's name was Capt. Stubbing, not from 'Love Boat' fame. He told many facts of interest (but not for Jaco) and history about the River to the passengers about floods and slaves and such.

Soon, it rained again, not hard, just a light shower. Jaco hung his head over the rail and looked up and down the river. Hardly anyone came down to the lower deck during the rain.

After the rain, Jaco went to the snack bar, bought a sandwich and a soda and then, went up stairs to the upper deck to the railing. He looked up at the sky, seeing a single cloud, not too big. He hung his head over and looked up and down the river.

"Getting sea sick?" someone asked.

"Oh!" he laughed. "I'm just looking . . ." There she was, Carolyn. Once could have been a coincidence but twice was suspect. "I'm just looking at the Mississippi. I'll be back. I have to find the bathroom. I'm not sick, though."

Jaco spent the rest of the cruise hiding and avoiding her. Even so, Jaco enjoyed the river boat ride.

That evening, Jaco went to a club for a while for oysters on the half shell, deep-fried pickles, deep-fried cat fish, and a few mint juleps then, he went to B. B. King's club down the block. He didn't like the singer so, he went to another club. The entertainment was a young black blues piano/blues singer dressed in a shiny black suit and tie, white long-sleeved shirt, fedora, and sunglasses, reminiscent of pictures of Robert Johnson. Jaco ordered a tonic and lime. After a few songs, the singer asked if anyone was from out of town and to yell out where they were from. "Bakersfield, CA" Jaco lied. "Boy, are you in the wrong side of town." said the singer. People laughed, but not too loud. Jaco stood up. "I love the blues. I play a mean blues piano, gospel blues sometimes. I used to have a music ministry." This was the truth.

The piano player smiled. "Isn't gospel blues a contradiction of terms?" Even though it was an old joke to Jaco and probably everyone else, people laughed, but not too loud. "See me during the break."

When the music stopped, Jaco went up to the riser that they called a stage. The singer shook his hand. "I'm not supposed to do this because of union rules but would you like to take the keys for fifteen minutes."

"Sure! Wow! At Sun Records, I played and sang 'Mohair Sam' on their original piano and mike—now, this!" Jaco played some improvised blues and a gospel blues song called 'No More Blues', written by blues harp player/singer Darrell Mansfield.

After Jaco returned to his seat, he decided to change his shirt (he spilled horseradish on it) so, he caught the bus from Beal St to his motel, back to Beale St, but he fell asleep for a short while on the bus back to Beale St. but, not from the alcohol. He was actually kind of tired. When he woke up, he jerked and looked out the window. He didn't know where he was at. He quickly pushed the stop tape and exited the bus when it stopped. He started walking.

A few minutes later, he heard someone groaning and yelling in a very weak voice, "Help me! Someone please help me." A Man was lying in a store doorway, bloody, with a knife in his stomach. "I was mugged. I had no money so the lady stuck me. It hurts so-o-o-o bad." he groaned. "I was on my way home from Bible study." he struggled to say.

Jaco held up his cell phone. "I'll call 911. I'm Jaco. Stay still and don't talk."

"I'm Eli."

"Stay still and quiet, Eli." Jaco dialed 911 but couldn't get a connection. Eli told Jaco that he didn't have his cell phone with him (an embarrassed lie—he didn't own one). Almost immediately, as people just walked by, not paying any notice to them, a tall, long haired, bearded man walked up holding a cell phone. Except for the fact that he was dressed in extremely clean whites and sandals, the man could have passed for a vagrant or a homeless person. He handed Jaco the phone. "My Name is Jaco . . . uh, Nick. A man has been stabbed at, oh man! Where is this place?"

"795 Poplar Ave." said the man in white.

"795 Poplar Ave." said Jaco, very excited. After the 911 conversation Jaco said, "Thank-you, sir." handing back the man's cell. "Who are you?"

"I am Jesus (*Yeh-soos*)."

"Jesus?"

"Yes! You'd better tend to this man, my brother."

"I didn't ask them when they'd be here! Let me say a prayer for you, alright?" said Jaco.

"Ok! You're a Christian?"

Jaco paused a long-short while and then smiling, answered, "Yes, I am." They prayed.

Just then, they heard a siren and the paramedics arrived. They put Eli onto a gurney and then walked over to Jaco. Jaco turned to Jesus but just like the Lone Ranger, he was gone. The paramedics talked to Jaco and then Jaco walked over to Eli. "They told me where they're taking you. I'll come see you tomorrow or the next." Then, they hugged and said "Good-bye!"

Jaco needed a quick change of emotions after tonight's adventure. He walked the several blocks to the Beale St. clubs and walked into one that was new to him. The band was on break but a guitar player was sitting on stage tuning his guitar. "Hi I'm Jaco. Do you ever let anyone sit in? I'm a bass player and I play keyboards."

"Sure, if you're any good. Yeah! We'll give you a try."

Jaco played very well. There last song was 'Amazing Grace" the third time that he heard it this week. When the group sang 'I was lost, but now, I'm found—was blind but now, I see.' this hit Jaco hard. He smiled and got misty eyed.

After the set was done, the guitar player (we don't know his name) told Jaco, "You're a heck of a bass player, Jaco. If he wasn't dead, I'd think that you were Jaco Pastorius, the bass player from the jazz group Weather Report. He died in a bar fight in the late '80's. I read his biography"

"I used to be, and to a lot of people and, I didn't read about him." Jaco said, putting his hand out to shake the player's hand. The player shook Jaco's hand, giving Jaco a confused look. "It's long story, and I don't want to get into right now. Jaco's just a nickname. My real name is Nick from Alameda . . . California. I'm going home tomorrow. I just decided that a little while ago. I have an acquaintance, Elaina, who owes me a lot of money. I pressed charges against her but I'm going to make payment arrangements with her and drop them. I think that is what Jesus would want me to do."

"You're a Christian! I am, too—Seventh Day Adventist. The band gives me part of the night off Friday so that I can get to church on Saturday and not be real sleepy. We're all Christian, Children of the King. That's why we play, 'People Get Ready', 'Are You Ready?', 'Oh Happy Day' and other gospel songs, bluesy. Who do you like?

I like early Clapton when he was with the Blues Breakers; I think that was his group and Paul Butterfield, The Blues Project, the Stones and The Animals when they were blues. Those are before your time."

"No, not really." said the nameless guitar player. "They were the best but you forgot Jeff Beck and Robert Johnson. In the Yard Birds, I liked Beck more than Page or Clapton but, I'm a big Clapton fan."

"I sure did forget Beck and Johnson! Ever hear of Darrell Mansfield?"

"Yeah! Sure! 'No More Blues' and stuff with Glenn Kaiser. Best Gospel Blues ever heard. We do some of their stuff."

"I do know that song and just recently did 'No More Blues' at a club down the street."

"Few people will let players sit in. The union isn't keen on that. Some singers and groups charge people to sit in. We usually let people jam."

"That happened to me but I didn't pay so I didn't play."

"Joco, sorry — Nick, give me your number, man and I'll give you a call. I'd like to find out how this deal went off, if it's alright and, I'd just like to stay in touch."

"Sure 'nuff." Nick smiled. "I'd like that. God bless."

"Thanks! He does! And remember, Jesus will always be there for you because he loves you."

They tapped fists and then Nick headed for the door. "Hey, Nick, need a ride?"

"Yeah! Sure 'nuff. I'd like that. Thanks, Bro!"

Nick didn't go right back to California. He felt a commitment to Eli. A couple of days later, Nick took a taxi to the Peabody Hotel for breakfast and to see the ducks. After a terrific breakfast of eggs benedicts, rye toast and marmalade, fresh squeezed orange with the pulp, and a Bloody Mary, talking to some senior tourists, Nick moved to a lobby chair to see the ducks.

A pastel blue haired lady announced what she had information from the Internet about the ducks:

'This is from Wikipedia off of the Internet. Peabody is probably best known around the world for a custom dating back to the 1930s. The General Manager of the time, Frank Schutt, had just returned from a weekend hunting trip in Arkansas. He and his friends found it amusing to leave three of their live English Call Duck decoys in the hotel fountain. The guests loved the idea, and since then, five Mallard ducks (one drake and four hens) have played in the fountain every day.

Every day at 11:00 a.m., the Peabody Ducks are escorted from their penthouse home, on the Plantation Roof, to the lobby via elevator. The ducks, accompanied by the King Cotton March by John Phillip Sousa, then proceed across a red carpet to the hotel fountain, made of a solid block of Italian travertine marble. The ducks are then ceremoniously led back to their penthouse at 5:00 p.m.'

Without excusing himself, Nick put his backpack on his chair and then went to get a coffee refill and then, to the gift shop. He found and bought a Christian devotional.

When he returned, the lady was still talking. 'Over the years, The Peabody Ducks have gained celebrity status with television appearances (along with their Duckmaster) on The Tonight Show with Johnny Carson, Sesame Street, and the Oprah Winfrey Show. They have also appeared in *People* magazine.

The position of "Duckmaster" at the Peabody Memphis is one of only three such positions in the world, the other two being the Duckmasters in the Orlando and Little Rock Peabody Hotels.'

A bell rang at the elevator and when the door opened, there were the ducks, strutting their stuff across the lobby and into the pool. Almost everybody oohed or laughed and clapped.

After the ducks, Nick took a taxi to the hospital where Eli was staying. "How goes it, Eli?"

"I'm hurting from a cracked rib and I'm on Vicodine shots, very tired. I'm on a soft diet for two more days. In a few days they're going to get me up on a walker."

Nick gave Eli two pairs of cartoon pajama pants and then they talked for about thirty-five minutes until Eli fell asleep. Nick took a piece of newspaper and wrote a note to Eli telling him that he'd be back.

For the next week or so, Nick visited Eli for a half an hour or longer, as El grew stronger. One visit, Eli told about a lady patient he had met in the patient lounge. He told Nick that they seemed to hit it off. "She's from Maryland. She went down to Louisiana to visit her Sister and her VW got hit by a trailer-tractor cab. It messed up her spine but after three weeks, she's on a walker—believe it! I'm doing very well on my walker but my shoulders and knees get sore. She and I have been keeping company every day for over two weeks. Her name's Becky.

"Nick, I'm tired. Ladies ware you out." Eli laughed and then Nick did. "No, I took a pain pill and it's kicking in, I'm tired. Sorry!"

"Hey, don't apologize, my friend. I'll see you tomorrow about 11 am." They two clinched either's fists.

The next day, Nick met Eli's Becky. The day after that, after breakfast, Eli walked to Becky's room, 312 but she wasn't there. Eli looked for some paper to write a note to Becky. While he was looking, a nurse's aide came in. "You're Eli, right?" Eli smiled and nodded 'yes'. "I was told I'd know you by your Bullwinkle pajamas. I have a note for you."

Eli took the note and the nurse's aide left the room. Eli sat down and read the note:

'Coming from Maryland, I was very lonely.
I kept you the only way that I could think of.

This morning, my husband came to take me home. I am so sorry. I do love you so-o-o-o-o much. ~Becky'

Eli was very hurt and sad but he didn't cry, not yet. He went back to his room and asked for a Vicodine shot. Before the shot had taken effect, Eli was out on the street, barefoot and in his pajamas and a t-shirt *and*, without his walker—headed for the mission. (Because of the mugging, Nick had made arrangements for the shelter to keep Eli's bed and his few possessions.}

About 10:50 am Nick went into Eli's room but, the room was empty. The bathroom door was opened so thinking Eli was in therapy, he sat down to wait.

An orderly walked in. "Hey, Nick, we can't find Eli Warner. His clothes are still here. We checked the cafeteria and lounge but he's not there. We're looking."

"How about Becky's room?"

"Her husband came before I came in to work to take her home."

"Her husband? Wow!

Nick went down into the hospital's business office to pay Eli's hospital bill and to make arrangements to any charges accrued afterwards. After business was done, he headed to his motel to pack.

PAHBADOE

Chapter 1

I want to tell you a story that ended well—about a lady that was a customer at O'Reighly's Irish Pub. You might remember or want to re-read my short story 'Just Jokin' (That one didn't end well.) to understand why I wrote what I just did write.

'Miss' Duck always wore a Fedora and always wore a duck feather or two in her hat band. Her real name was and still is Hannah Mallard who changed her name back to Torey after her husband left her. She told people that he died of a heart attack while trimming one of their walnut trees. Hannah Torey came from the 'Beat' culture, turned hippie culture. This story isn't about 'Miss' Duck nor about Hannah Torey. This is just an introduction to the story.

'Miss' Duck and Alicia Smythe, just finishing her Swisher Sweets cigar and lighting a clove cigarette, sat at a side walk cafe by the water in Tiburon, CA, espresso w/lemon peel in hand, reminiscing about their 60's adventures. Said 'Miss' Duck "At night, we would usually go to the Village Gate and then, we'd make the rounds to hear some jazz, be-bop. It was always fascinating to me how four of five cats would lock in to a groove, not knowing where they were going, improvising, until they got to the end. Sometimes we'd end up in Harlem to hear more jazz or R&B at some club.

"I liked the folk music at the coffee houses and the clubs on Bleeker Street and on MacDougal street in the Village, too, like the Gaslight, Cafe Wha?, Gerde's Folk City, the Bitter End and I can remember checking out the singers like Phil Ochs, Fred Neil, and Rambling Jack Elliot, the Mugwugs with John Sebastian and Cass Elliot, and, of course, Bobby Dylan and the beat poets like Ferlinghetti. The Gratful Dead were big fans of his or, Wavy Gravy's and Timothy Leary's Magic Bus trip or whatever they called it. That was in Frisco."

Alicia took another sip of coffee. "I saw Lenny Bruce at the Hungry I in Frisco. He was too vulgar. George Carlin was funny then, too but he's too vulgar, now. He used to be funny. I saw the Kingston Trio there, too. They were great. They recorded a record there sometime. Maybe I was in the audience but not likely. I was in the audience at Woodstock. I hitched hiked. The traffic to get there was terrible for miles, worse than L.A."

'Miss' Duck agreed about Bruce and Carlin. "I remember Washington Park then being like Frisco is now, filled with pickers and mimes, bongo and conga players and artists of all kinds and dealers, too—lots of dope dealers."

Alicia smiled, "I heard Allen Ginsberg and Ferlinghetti read their poetry in a San Franciscan book store. I don't remember which one of them, but he read his famous poem, 'Howl' once when I was there. I think that they were there at different times. San Francisco banned that poem for a short time thinking it obscene.

"I crashed Woodstock in '69." said 'Miss' Duck. "Hippies, maybe it was Abby Hoffman's people tore down a fence and I got in free and stayed the whole three days. They said that three people died there but I didn't hear about it but it sure did rain though.

My daughter's name is Elaina but she goes by Pahbadoe for some reason. She thinks it's Dutch but it's not. I think that it's American Indian from Arizona or Nevada—maybe New Mexico, maybe."

"Isn't that the name of that dictator in the Caribbean? Is he a terrorist?"

"Of course not! His name is Baby Doe from an island in south Maine or Carolina, in the Atlantic, the Caribbean, somewhere. When I lived in New York City, I used to think that Puerto Rico was off of the city like Staten Island or Long Island. Anyways, Pahbadoe, my daughter's a folk singer, writer, and a published poet like the ones you were just talking about. Elaina conned a friend of hers out of a lot of money. After a while, she felt guilty about it. She donated most of it to the church of Scientology but then, (she laughed) got it all back somehow. She then donated a third to D.A.R.E . . ."

"What's D.A.R.E.?" Alicia interrupted.

"Drug Awareness Resistance Education. Anyways, one third to a small church in the San Joaquin Valley, and the other third, $40,000, she kept. Then, she moved to Nevada and maybe to Arizona to avoid the police. I haven't seen her in years but she calls every week. One time, she said that she just got 'born again'. I thought that she meant reincarnated like . . . from a bug or, uh . . . uh, a cat. She loves cats. Dumb, huh, I mean about me thinking that, huh?

"The menu says a demitasse'. I wonder what that is."

"It's 'espresso' before it was named 'espresso'. I'm going to have another espresso. Want another one or a latté? I'm buying." asked 'Miss' Duck, walking away.

Chapter 2

Ty and Maggie were standing on the London Bridge overlooking Lake Havasu, Arizona on a beautiful Friday afternoon, talking. Ty is the pastor of a church there and Maggie s a member of his congregation.

Maggie was very annoyed. "I mail ordered for some ballet slippers but there was only one slipper in the box."

Maggie, you shouldn't get so upset. Just send them a letter expla . . ."

"That's not the point!" Maggie was almost shouting. "She's the star frog whom the prince kisses in her fourth grade school play. The play is a week and a half away."

"Do you have the company's phone number anywhere?" Maggie nodded 'yes'. "Okay! I'll call them for you this afternoon. Call my wife and leave the number."

"I have to go pick up my daughter from school, Pastor Ty. I'd appreciate your calling and thanks for the latté breve and your advice. I'll think hard about what you said to me."

Pahbadoe, fresh off of the bus from Parker, AZ. walked up to Ty. "Hey, Ty! Howzit? What's with her?" asked, pointed at Maggie.

Ty smiled, "Huh? 'Howzit', Huh? She's a member of my church. We were having a counseling session. I can't discuss it but she's very annoyed about something else. You might say she's 'hopping' mad." (Ty really laughed!)

Pahbadoe looked at Ty puzzled.

Said Ty, "Oh! I guess I should have mentioned the slippers. He tells Pahbadoe the story. What's with the 'Howzit'? You talk different."

"Mama taught and made my sisters and me to talk 'correct English', no slang or even contractions. She always talked that way and then one day, she backslid—talking normal. I got tired talking like she did and being teased so, I learned how to talk colloquial, literally. It was a foreign language

"Ty, I'm so glad that we met again a few months ago in Ely. It was a lucky thing you came into the Wendy's where I worked, huh? If it weren't for that, I don't think that I'd know Jesus now."

"Oh! I think that God had a hand in it. Why did you move here from Nevada?"

"You got my letter didn't you? I got scared that the police were finding me. I thought my boyfriend was going to turn me in. The last thing I told him before I left him was, 'John, I'm going to do my best to make 'John' a household name.' I like Parker and the river. I like small towns, unlike Oakland."

"What I wanted to talk to you about, Pahbadoe, uh, Elaina is baptism, your baptism. In your letter you said that you want to be. If you'd like, I'd like to baptize you here at Havasu, in the Colorado River. Easter is just two days away and I could do it at our sunrise service."

"I'd like that, being we were ex-drinking buddies in Oakland and now Christians in Arizona. You're the only person besides my Mom that I told about me stealing money from Nick."

She paused and then continued, "I was so shocked about you becoming a Christian in prison. From a pimp and smoking opium to being Christian is a strong testimony."

"Yeah! After a while, I found Jesus and soon became involved in the prison ministry. A few months later, my lawyer found a loop hole and I was let out on a technicality. I was holding drugs that I took away from someone. I was arrested before I could turn them over to the police. I still feel that the prison ministry was my calling but just for that time. God has his own timetable.

The sunrise service will be early, six a.m. Have you ever been to a baptism?" Shaking her head, she meant 'no!' "You'll have to bring a change of clothes. I'll explain everything to you and the others this evening when we meet for dinner and Communion, just like Jesus and the disciples. This way, everyone won't have to get there so early on Sunday. You'll of course be staying with Lydia (Ty's wife) and me, okay?"

"Yeah, sure! But won't you have Easter dinner and plans with family or friends?"

"Elaina, you are family."

Thank-you so much for buying me my bus ticket. I'm broke. Nick dropped the charges when I made payment arrangements. I was going to skip the state like I did in California but the Holy Spirit said different. I almost have it paid off, too. Nick said that I didn't have to pay the money back that I donated to the church or to D.A.R.E. He liked that I did that. I'm still scared but I'm not running anymore. I just didn't like the town of Ely.

Are you hungry, Ty? I sure am."

"I just had a big lunch and I'm coffeed out but I'll have a soda while I buy you lunch. Let's go. That shop over there that says 'Fish & Chips' has great fish & chips.

Wait a minute, Elaina. See that old couple dressed alike in Hawaiian shirts and yellow shorts? He's wearing black leather shoes and knee socks, a Gilligan Island hat and sunglasses. He reminds me of a guy at O'Reighly's. He'd come, order a light beer and then bought everyone a 'Milky Way' bar. He was really funny. On his second beer he'd start to stutter and fall asleep. I remember the first time he came in. I think that you were there. He was drunk. You *were* there. Joey was bartending I think that he was afraid to throw the guy out."

"I remember him." They both laughed, not loud, not hard. "What's your wife's name?"

"I just told you a while ago. It's Lydia! Still can't remember names, huh?"

"I remember that mine is Elaina." she smiles and winks. They walked into the restaurant and ordered fish and chips.

"Are you still wanting to have a cat farm? Do you think you'll have as many as Ernest Hemingway did in his home on Key West, or was it Key Largo?

"I don't think anyone will ever have that many or, want that many. A lot of his were strays. He wrote, 'One cat just leads to another.' and 'A cat has emotional honesty: Human beings, for one reason or another, may hide their feelings, but the cat does not.' He loved cats, big game cat and small house cats.

"Quiz time, Elaina! Can cats eat chocolate?"

"Oh, my!" said Elaina. "I do know that dogs can die from eating chocolate. I don't know about cats, though *but, I do know* about milk and cats. At twelve weeks old, a cat can become lactose intolerant. It can be messy, diarrhea or, they can even die."

"We need to get you a Top Cat T-shirt."

"Who's Top Cat?"

"He's an old alley cat cartoon. I guess he's before your time. It's before my time, too but, you can still find him and his gang sometime, somewhere on TV. Hey! There's bristle board dart boards instead of those rinky-dink electronic boards. Want to shoot a game?"

"Of course I don't have any darts, Dumb Dumb."

"Elaina, this is your lucky day. I have mine in the car but we'll have to share." Ty left for the car. Elaina bought another root beer, telling the waiter that Ty would pay for it when he got back.

Two hours later, game after game of dart and a lot of talk, Ty said, "We'd better get going."

Chapter 3

Ty parked his car in a carport in front of a single storied four-plex unit. It was enclosed by apartment four-plexes two and three stories high.

"Well, Elaina, this is where I live. What name do I introduce you as?"

"Elaina! What's your wife's name, again?"

"Lydia! She'll love you. I've told her about you many, many times, how we met in Oakland at O'Reighly's Pub. You, Joey, and I became good drinking friends, didn't we? I quit drinking the day he died—when he was hit by that hit-and-run driver. They were both seriously drunk. That was the day that he quit drinking, too. Oh! I'm sorry that I said that. *He was my best friend of all times*. I really miss him." Ty began to cry.

Elaina hugged Ty and handed him an handkerchief from her purse. "Here, take this, sweetheart. I know he was. I always knew him as Joe. Was his real name really, Joe Kehn?" she giggled. "I don't think Joe liked me much."

"Sure he did! He just was hard to get along with, drinking all the time. Joe Kehn was really his name. He hated it. That's why I always called him Joey. So, let's go in and meet Lydia."

Before they got to the door, Lydia was there waiting. "Hi, Baby! So, this is Elaina. Hi, Elaina. Ty, we're going to have lamb chops and mint jelly, green beans with pearl onions and chopped bacon, scalloped potatoes topped with bacon, and sopapilla with agave honey for supper."

"What's the special occasion?, Ty asked.

"Elaina's here! Plus, that's my favorite supper." she smiled.

"Sweetheart, that sound great but, what day do you think today it is?"

"Thursday, why"

"Nope! It's Friday, Good Friday."

Lydia turned to Elaina, "Oh my! I forgot. Last weekend I was sick. I missed church. I guess I have my days mixed up because of that." Then she turned to Ty. "What time will you both be leaving for the Communion?"

"I have some setting up to do at the restaurant and I have to pick-up the sacraments. Six-fifteen will be good."

Chapter 4

The Good Friday dinner and Communion was held in the upstairs Del Arosa Room at Fisches' Loaf Basket Resteraunt. Including Elaina, there were eleven people with Pastor Ty.

A fellow named Manuel shoved another guy so that he could sit by Elaina. "I hear that you are a 'felinologist'."

"Say what?" she said, puzzled.

"A 'felinologist'. You know, someone who studies cats, an expert."

"I'm not familiar with that term. I'm not an expert. I just know from experience and reading. I just love cats, that's all. I am a 'felinese', though."

"A what?"

"A 'felinese', a person who understands what cats are saying to each other."

"Yeah, right. No one can do that."

"Sure they can. Cats use body language and the sounds that they make express what they're feeling. Cats don't purr just whenever they're happy. Cats can purr when injured, embarrased, or even giving birth. People smile when they're happy but they also smile when they get embarrassed, nervous, or are threated. Cat's basically do the same thing."

"Okay! If you say so."

"I'm a 'mycologist'. I hunt and study mushrooms." someone said from down the table."

"I don't like mushrooms." someone else said.

"What type?" asked the mycologist.

"Mushrooms! They're all the same, aren't they?"

"On the contrary, some are tan, some are red, some are poka-dotted like Christian or magic mushroms." He snickered. "One type is hot like a chile and the Oyster mushroom tastes like oysters, hence their name, to a lot of people but they're not salty." He was pretty much ignored. No one was listening.

Ty stood up at the table. "I realize that some people might actually eat a meal together just like we're about to do, although I've never heard of a church that actually does that. Let's all stand for the blessing." He asks God to bless the food then, "Let's all sit down and let's eat." Elaina didn't sit by the mushroom guy or Manuel. She moved over next to Ty and smiled sheepishly. Ty knew why and smile back.

Dinner was a clam chowder bread bowl and turtle pie. When the dinner was over and the table cleared, Ty stood. "A little while ago, I recieved a phone call. This afternoon Jules' car was hit from behind. He suffered a whiplash in his neck. Let's pray together that he's not seriously hurt and that he can be baptised Sunday. Let's stand and join hands. We'll start from my right. If you don'want to pray either out loud, just squeeze the next hand." They prayed and after Ty prayed, they sat down.

"Now then," Pastor Ty continued, "when being baptized, please put your right foot behind you so that you can balance yourself on it when I dunk you under. This will make it easier, especially for me and I'm not as likley to drop you." Everybody laughed. "I'll be holding your back so you will be secure. Now, the sacrament of Communion.

"I find that passing around the loaf and the wine's Communal Cup and giving it to one another the most powerful act of communion because one, it does the best job of keeping the relationship with others in the church and two, remembering Jesus' components that are the basis of the Communion act. I'll first pass the bread loaf. Tear off a piece and then feed it to the person to your right, then pass the loaf to that person. The same with the wine. Let the person drink from the cup before you pass it to the next. Now, some of you can't or won't drink wine for various reasons. The gold chalace with the brass steam has grape juice.

"We, being Christians, believe that the Communion Supper ordained by our Lord and Savior, Jesus Christ is essentially a New Testament holy sacrament, asserting His sacrificial death, through the merits of which believers have life and salvation and promises of all spiritual blessings in Christ. Let us remember that this is a memorial of the death and passion of our Lord: also a token of his coming again. Communion is only for those who are prepared for respectful Godly understanding of its importance, and by this, they show the Lord's death untill He'll come again. It being the Communion feast, only those who have faith in Christ should be called to participate this evening.

«Also referred to as Eucharist, which means thanksgiving or, 'the breaking of bread', Communion was instituted by Jesus on the night of His betrayal. These sacred symbols of bread and the cup are significant for every believer in Jesus Christ. They go back over two thousand years to the sacrifice Jesus made for our salvation. In looking back, we are reminded of the immeasurable love God had and still has for us, the kind of love that gives Himself completely so that we might know the joy of forgiveness and a restored relationship with Him. The sacrament also points forward, to the wedding supper of the Lamb where we will feast in the very presence of Jesus in Heaven. In looking forward, we affirm that we are a people of hope. And now, in the present, God conveys His grace to us through these tasteable and tangible symbols. We believe that at the Table of the Lord, there is great opportunity for meaningful and memorable encounters with Christ and with one another. His grace comes to us from that Table, grace that forgives, sustains, and strengthens us in the journey."

After sharing the Passover meal with His disciples, Jesus took bread, broke it, and said *'this is my body which is broken for you: do this in remembrance of me.'* The body of our Lord Jesus Christ, which was broken for you, preserves you blameless, unto everlasting life. Take and eat this, in remembrance that Christ died for you."

Ty recites from 1 Corinthians 10:17 "Because there is one loaf, we, who are many are one body, for we all partake of the one loaf." Ty takes and tears off a piece of bread. He feeds it to the person to his right, to Elaina and then he passes the loaf to her. Ty continues, "For whenever you eat this bread and drink from this cup, you proclaim the Lord's death until he comes back.

«Jesus then held up the cup of wine and said, *'This cup is the new covenant in my blood which is poured out for you. Do this, whenever you drink it, in remembrance of me.'* The blood of our Lord Jesus, which was shed for you, preserve you blameless unto everlasting life. Drink this, in rememberence that Jesus Christ' s blood was shed for you, and be thankful. He gave thanks and said, ' *Take this and divide it among you.'* « Ty then takes both cups and passes them to the right.

After Communion, Ty thanked and told the group, "I want everyone to leave silently in a prayerfull temper. I'll see you all early Suday morning at 5:40. Coffee, I'll bring either Kenyan or Costa Rican fresh ground, two of the world's best. I'll bring muffins, too. Actually, Lydia's the baker. I'm the coffee grinder."

]Back at the apartment, they ate banana chocolate cream pie and talked. Lydia looked and sounded very tired. Finally, Lydia told Elaina, "We have two places that you can sleep." She pointed to a futon. This makes into a single bed and the couch, into a double bed. Choose which ever you want."

"I'll start out on the futon and maybe I'll move to the hide-a-bed later on." she chuckled.

Lydia only smiled. It wasn't that funny, maybe because Lydia was so tired. "I'll get you a glass of water." She moved toward the kitchen, turning on a night light. When Lydia came back with the water, they all said 'Goodnight!'"

Chapter 5

About 7:15 Saturday morning, Ty heard Elaina folding up the futon. "Hey Lydia, Elaina's up. Go into the living room and let me know when she's decent." Lydia left the bedroom and came right back in. Ty was getting dressed.

"She's dressed."

"Good! I'll make some coffee. I'd like Costa Rican this morning?" Ty knocked on the bedroom door while opening it. "Good morning, sunshine!" Elaina saw Ty in the wall mirror and then turned around, facing him. "We both want you to stay through Monday and leave Tuesday. Monday's my day off. Want some coffee, Popadue?" Ty smiled.

"Pahbadoe! I'd love some! I can't stay. I have an appointment with my social worker Monday at nine-thirty."

Ty looked at Elaina for a moment and then sighed. "I'll make some coffee."

"I'd like to take you both out for breakfast. It'll have to be fast food."

"Alright! There's a great place that serves great breakfasts. I'm in the mood for eggs Benedict and a side of mushrooms with melted Brie cheese. I'll buy us all breakfast and you buy fast food for lunch, deal? I have to make a private phone call in the bedroom. Excuse me for a minute."

"Did you hear the mushroom guy talking to me last night?"

Ty smiled and nodded, "Yep! I did. Excuse me for a couple of minutes. Lydia will be right out. She's getting dressed."

Soon, they all left for the restaurant, forgetting the ground coffee. Lydia had buckwheat pancakes, eggs over easy (but they weren't) and ham. Elaina and Ty both ordered the eggs Benedict and a side of mushrooms with melted Brie cheese.

"I made a call this morning. My friend Tom Joad has a boat that he's going to let us use at the lake." Ty told the ladies.

"I read a book in high school about a Tom Joad. I don't remember what it was called. It was sad, though." Elaina said.

"Grapes Of Wrath." Said Ty.

"Maybe but I don't really remember."

"Grapes Of Wrath." louder and together from Lydia and Ty. Then Ty added, "Grapes Of Wrath by Steinbeck, John Steinbeck. He wrote it. His home town's Salinas, I think. The book was banned and the town of Salinas planned a book burning but the bookstores didn't have any copies so the town mail ordered some copies from the publisher to burn. I look American Lit."

After breakfast, Ty looked at the two ladies. "Well, I need to get the key to the boat. He's lending us some fishing gear, too. Do you fish, Elaina?"

"I have, from a pier."

"Well, let's go then."

Lydia finished her coffee. "You two go. I'd like another cup. I'll walk over in a little while."

The shop was only a couple of blocks away.

"Hi, Ty!" Tom met them as they walked into his shop, a pet shop. Who 's your friend?"

"This is my good friend, Elaina. Elaina, this is Tom."

"Hi, Elaina. You're the one who love cats, huh? Ty and I have some church business to discuss. Feel free to look around. They're over around the left corner, the cats."

Elaina began walking around. Ty and Tom began talking. Soon, there was an 'O-o-o-h' from Elaina. "I've never seen a Scottish Fold this color before. He's almost a lavender. I can I hold him, I mean, her?"

"Be my guest."

Soon Lydia joined them. A short time later, the duo left.

The lake was unmemorable except that Ty tripped and fell into the lake and Lydia caught four trout. Elaina caught two. They soon left so that Ty could change his wet clothes. After he changed, he said, "I need to work on tomorrow's sermon. Would you both excuse me for a while?"

"You're just embarrassed because you fell into the lake, a distinguished minister, Reverend." Lydia teased. "I'd like to take a nap. Will you be Okay, Elaina?"

"Sure! I brought a book with me to read on the bus. Tell ya what, if you have a sharp boning knife, I could clean and fillet our fish for you."

"Sure, go for it, kid." Said Lydia, encouraging her. What knives we have are in a wooden block there on the kitchen counter."

An hour later, when they both came back into the living room, Elaina was reading. She looked up from her book. "Fish are all cleaned and filleted. I left them wrapped in the fridge. I didn't know what to do with them."

"I'll take care of it. Thanks! What's the book?, Lydia asked.

"Catcher In The Rye. It's kinda boring. Nothing really happens."

"I've never read it. Did you read it, Ty?"

"I started to but couldn't get into it. Other J. D. Salinger books, I really liked reading them."

Elaina continued about books. "My Mom said that she met Jack Kerouac the week before he died. She says a lot of things, though, a lot that aren't true. She may have met him. I only know of him by what Momma has told me and what other people said about him. Momma called him a 'Beat Poet'. I have no idea what that means. She gave me his novel, 'On The Road'. It has a 'Jack Kerouac' signature inside the front cover. That was a book that I couldn't get into. I gave up after a hundred pages or so. She gave me another book that was autographed, too called 'Howl And Other Poems.' On one of the first pages was a quote 'The closet door is open for me, where I left it, since I left it open, it has graciously stayed open.' that reminded me of an O'Reighly's 'legend' when Joey was locked out of his apartment from the outside."

Ty laughed. "Yeah! It's true. Joey met you the morning he got locked in to his cottage and I took him home that night after a pool or a darts tournament when he was locked out. (See *'Just Jokin'*) It was funny. The thing is, no one hated Joey. Everyone liked him. It had to have been someone that knew where he lived. Not many people knew that because he kept that quiet, and thought that he knew Joey good enough to think that Joey had that type of sense of humor. If I remember right, Joey was real drunk and had a real bad night before and a bad day. But we did good in the tournament so, he was happy. I don't know!" Ty chuckled and smiled.

Lydia smiled at Ty "Baby, we're going to have lamb chops and mint jelly, green beans with pearl onions and chopped bacon, scalloped potatoes topped with bacon, and sopapias with honey for supper."

"What's the special occupation?, Ty asked, laughing. He was putting Dave Brubeck into the CD player.

"Elaina's here! Plus, that's my favorite supper." she smiled. "Deja vu." Lydia giggled.

With Elaina's help, they set down at the table in about twenty minutes. Ty turned to Elaina. "Would you thank God for this supper and ask for his blessing?"

"I'd rather you did that, Ty."

After the food was passed "Ty," asked Elaina, "why did you leave Oakland for Arizona?

"When I started to preach, I needed someplace to hold services instead of my studio apartment. We ran about fifteen and that was too crowded for my apartment. Conner O'Conner, the owner of O'Reighly's let me hold church there before they opened on Sunday mornings. Conner sold O'Reighly's when his wife died and the new owner canceled our verbal agreement. I love Lake Havasu and this city so, I moved here and started another church. I met Lydia here. God had two plans in mind for me."

"Ty told me that you know gobs about cats. How did you get so interested in kitty cats, Elaina?" asked Lydia.

"I started telling Ty about that. I was starting a catering business and I had to eat. O-o-o! Bad pun! So sorry about that. Anyways, I had a day job at the humane society. It wasn't that humane. Well, I worked mostly with cats and so I learned about them and read about them, until their endings. I had to put more than my share to sleep. I fell in love with one kitty I named her Trollie because she looked like one of those German troll dolls from the '60's with the round head and the big eyes. She was a very cute Scottish Fold. I'd never seen a kitten like her, very different looking as most breeds go. I'd play with her all the time. Week after week, no one would adopt her. One day, she was in that cramped cage with the others I was to put to sleep. I up and quit my job right then. I would've adopted her but my apartment didn't allow pets. Even after a long time, I still feel extremely sad and dream about that. Please! I need to change the subject." Then, Elaina put on her happy face, sort of. "Lydia, when are you expecting?"

"Eleven weeks! I'll be so happy to sleep on my side again and to quit belching." Lydia started to laugh. "Ty gets morning sickness. He denies it, of course. And lately he craves hot chocolate with Tabasco sauce in it and oyster mushrooms with Limburger cheese. Limburger is quite mild tasting but you can smell it in the next county. Smells like dirty socks. You know, people say that cats are dangerous around babies. Should I be afraid?"

"Babies are dangerous to cats. So many cats find themselves homeless or looking for new homes when a baby comes along. A cat won't smother or suck the breath out from babies. I think that that myth probably came about in the middle ages. Cats are curious and they investigate any new arrival. They might get into the crib and may lick the baby. With the addition of SID's, people put two and two together and blamed the cats. Still, a baby shouldn't be left unattended. Talking about babies, most calicoes are females. One in a thousand are males. The reason for this is that the gene that determines sex is a female gene. It's complicated."

"What's your favorite cat?"

"Yeah! I'm curious, too. Didn't I ask you that at the bridge? You didn't give me an answer."

"Scottish Folds, like Trollie. They are definitely my favorite. They're so cute and very unique looking. The thing about these cat is there ears, folded forward and downward on their heads. That look gives the impression of a pixie or an owl. They have huge eyes full of sweetness, and chubby bodies. They look like a roly-poly stuffed toy. They're very playful and very friendly, not the furniture clawing cats many people have. They take to all family members with a temperament that matches their sweet expression. They adore human company and display that in their own quiet way. They're great with children . . . uh . . . and dogs, the nosier, the better even though *they* have tiny voices and are not extremely vocal. Many live to the age of eighteen or more. There indoor cats so you should never leave them outside. They're as easygoing and loving as they are beautiful. I'd like to have a Fold, a show cat.

"Ty cut in, "Wow, Elaina! I've never heard you talk this way and with such passion."

"Ty, I could talk about kittens, especially folds all day—well, maybe for hours."

"I'll give you another twenty, not hours—minutes." teased Lydia. "How big or small are they?"

"A female will only get to around six or nine pounds. Males, a bit bigger and they're real good company for a single person. Well, I'm done. Oh, wait! There's something more.

"Folds usually sleep on their backs with their legs stretched out and their paws on their belly."

Elaina giggled. "I told a guy last night that I spoke 'felinese', cat's body language and sounds. Folds display a great many different meows and purrs not found in other breeds.

"And, they are *not* finicky eaters like Morris." If anyone caught the reference to the cat food commercial, no one is saying.

"Talking about eating, 'a well-fed cat doesn't hunt' is a myth. The exploits and play of a kitten is really hunting behavior and practicing. Pouncing and leaping at anything that moves, like your finger, a ball, or a leaf shows this."

After dinner, after the table was cleared, and the three of them still sitting at the table, Lydia broke the silence. "How about a quick game of Monopoly? Let's see, we could play Rumi-Kub or bridge."

"I have no idea how to play bridge." pouted Elaina. "I'd been wanting to learn, though."

"Well, I could . . . no, it's much too hard to explain in a short time. How about Gin? Ty likes to play that."

"Sure!" interrupted Elaina. I'm real good at Gin."

"You were real good at bar gin at O'Reighly's." Ty joked.

For the next two-and-a-half hours, they played Gin and ate hot caramel-fudge sundaes with whipped cream/mascarpone cheese topping over the fudge, macadamia nuts, and a cherry on top, with Arizona iced tea. The mascarpone was Elaina's idea. She had seen it in the refrigerator when she put the fish in. Ty won the most games. Elaina didn't win one. Ty stood up to stretch. "There's a 'Taxi' marathon on TV right now. Anyone game to watch some of it? Jeff Conaway, the 'ladies' man' on Taxi', after the show ended became a Christian. He went to Bible school or seminary and became a preacher. His congregation met in a bar like we did in Oakland. I'm sure that somewhere else in this great nation of ours, a church meets in a cocktail lounge, too. I have a friend that has a reverend nephew whose congregation meets in a bar in Hawaii of all places."

"No! I don't think so." Lydia disagreed about TV. "It's late and we have to get up early tomorrow. We need to get to bed." They all agreed.

Behind closed doors, "Boy! She sure can talk." Lydia said about Elaina. "I'm not complaining. I really like her and she is interesting, with a good sense of humor.

I hope that I can get to sleep after taking that nap this afternoon. Goodnight, Sweetheart."

"Goodnight, Lydia. I love you."

"I love you, too!"

Chapter 6

Easter morning came quick after a short night. The weather was clear and nice and a crisp 59°. Ty heard Elaina folding the futon. "Lydia, Elaina's up. Go into the living room and let me know when she's decent." Lydia left the bedroom and came right back in.

"She's dressed and packed, Ty."

"Good! I'll make some coffee. Kenyan or Costa Rican this morning?"

"Okay! Costa Rican!"

Lydia went into the bathroom. Ty knocked on the bedroom door while opening it. "Good morning, sunshine!"

I wish that I could stay. I'm real fond of you, and Lydia, too but I can't. I have an appointment with my social worker tomorrow at nine-thirty."

Ty looked at Elaina for a moment and then sighed. "I'll make some coffee. You know, I'm glad that Joe Kehn came on to you or else we wouldn't have become great friends."

Elaina smiled, "Yeah! Don't get me wrong but, I'm glad that that is all it is but, I still love you dearly, my wonderful, wonderful friend. Lydia's so lucky to have you!"

At 5:50 a.m., everyone being baptized was there but Jules. Strong coffee and muffins and hot water to dilute the coffee was served along with hot chocolate for the kids and non-coffee drinkers. Afterwards, he invited each to be baptized to join him into the river.

He began. "Mathew 3:11, and 13-17 from the NIV Bible. John the Baptist is talking. *'I baptize you with water for repentance. But after me will come one who is more powerful then I, whose sandals I am not fit to carry. He will baptize you with the Holy Spirit and fire.*

Then Jesus came from Galilee to the Jordan to be baptized by John. But John tried to deter him, saying, 'I need to be baptized by you, and do you come to me.

Jesus replied, 'Let it be so, now; it is proper for us to do this to fulfill all righteousness.' Then John consented.

As soon as Jesus was baptized, he went up out of the water. At that moment heaven was opened, and he saw the Spirit of God descending like a dove and lighted on him. And a voice from heaven said 'This is my Son. Whom I love; with him I am well pleased.'

Ty smiled and looked at his congregation. "We believe that Christian baptism… Jules, welcome. We're very happy and proud that you are able to join us." There were several 'Amens' and 'Thank-you, Jesus' from the people. Ty continued, "We believe that Christian baptism, commanded by our Lord, is a sacrament signifying acceptance of the benefits of the atonement of Jesus Christ, to be administered to believers and their declaring their faith in Jesus Christ as their Savior, and full purpose of obedience in holiness and righteousness.

You'll notice that those being baptized range in age from age nine, Jimmy Jentz to Art Simon, who's seventy-two and found the Lord nine weeks ago. Baptism being a symbol of the new covenant, young children can be baptized if they understand what they are doing and have accepted the Lord, upon the request of their parents or guardians who will give testimony that the child has had proper Christian training.

Baptism may be administered by sprinkling, pouring, or immersion, according to the choice of the person being baptized. We're certainly glad that Jules was able to join us today after his car accident. We'll be doing this by immersion except for Jules. Because of his neck injury, I'll do pouring on him.

"The earliest and simplest statement of Christian belief, into which you now come to be baptized, is the Apostles' Creed which reads as follows:

'I believe in God the Father Almighty, Maker of heaven and earth;

'And in Jesus Christ, is only Son, our Lord: who was conceived by the Holy Ghost, born of the Virgin Mary, suffered under Pontius Pilate, was crucified, died, and buried; He descended into hell; the third day He rose again from the dead; He ascended into heaven, and sits at the right hand of God the Father Almighty; from thence He shall come to judge the quick and the dead.

'I believe in the Holy Ghost, the holy Church of Jesus Christ, the communion of saints, the forgiveness of sins, the resurrection of the body, and the life everlasting.'

Then TY addresses the group to be baptized. "Will you be baptized into this Christian faith? If so, answer, 'I will.'"

The group responded, "I will."

"Do you acknowledge Jesus Christ as your personal Savior, and do you realize that He saves you now?"

Someone from the congregation yelled out, "Hallelujah! Praise the Lord."

Each answered, "I will."

"Will you obey God's holy will and keep His commandments, walking in them all the days of your life?"

"I will."

To each one, Ty said, "I bapize you in the name of the Father, in the name of the Son, and in the name of the Holy Spirit. Amen.» before each were immersed.

While Elaina's and then Jules were being baptized, three young men rode by, their music playing very loud. The Edwin Hawkin's Choir's version of 'Oh Happy Day' was playing. Speculation has it that Jules had something to do with that. He could be quite dramatic. Jimmy said, 'Cool!' then his parents were acknowleged.

Ty tells them, "Christian bapisim signifies for this young child God's gracious acceptance on the basis of His prevenient grace in Christ, and points forward to his personal appropriation of the benefits of the Atonement when he reaches the age of moral accountability and exercises conscious saving faith in Jesus Christ.

"In presenting this child for baptism you are hereby witnessing to your own personal Christian faith and to your purpose to guide him early in life to a knowledge of Christ as Savior. To this end, it is to teach him; to watch over his education, that he may not be led astray; to direct his feet to the sanctuary; to restrain him from from evil associates and habits; and as much as in you lies, to bring him up in the nurture and admonition of the Lord.

"Mr. And Mrs. Jentz, will you endeavor to do so by the help of God? If so, say I do." They both say, 'I do'. "Jimmy, I bapize you in the name of the Father, in the name of the Son, and in the name of the Holy Spirit. Amen." Then, Ty askes Jimmy if he'd like to say anything. "I love God and I love Jesus." Then Jimmy got shy.

"That's all, Mr. Pastor Ty." There were several proud giggles and some 'Amens' heard.

Parts of Ty's Baptism sermonette is taken from the Church of the Nazarene's manuel.

"The novelist Henry James wrote in his biography of Nathaniel Hawthorne that 'The best things come, as a general thing, from the talents that are members of a group; every man works better when he has companions working in the same line, and yeilding the stimulus of suggestion, comparison, emulation'

Ty continued, "I commision each one of you to watch over these eleven precious people. To help them so that they may not be led astray; to help direct them to the sanctuary of our Lord; to help restrain them from evil associates and habits; and as to incougage them in there upbringing in their Christian growth and admonition of our Lord. If you promise to do these things, say, 'I do'." They all did."

After the baptisms, Ty told everyone to have another cup of coffee and muffin. Then, he excused himself, changed into dry clothes and then conducted the sunrise service. Ty told the Easter story, combining scripture from each of the Gospels and telling the story in his own words then, preached a short sermon, afterwards giving an invitation to those who wanted to meet Jesus to step forward. Several people did just that.

Chapter 7

After the service, Elaina, Lydia, and Ty had Easter Ham (sandwiches) at the bus station coffee shop. "Ty," said Elaina, "I liked that quote before you told everyone to watch over us. Where did you find it?"

"Joey and I used to throw out quotes to each other at the pub. I don't know where I read or heard it from."

"I liked what you said about helping each other. I didn't understand all of the words in the quote but I got the jist of it. I do remember that you two were always competing with each other. I have one for you: Never play cards with a man named Doc. Never eat at a place called 'Mom's'. Never sleep with a woman whose troubles are greater than your own."

"O-o-o-o! I know that one!' Ty exclaimed quit excitedly and somewhat loudly. I know it was from, 'A Walk On The Wild Side' '57 or '58. O-o-o-o! It was . . . uh . . . um . . . O-o-o-o, shucks! Go ahead and tell me. You don't know!"

"I do, too! Nelson Algreen '56."

"Are you sure? I don't remember that."

"Sure as rain! I win!" she laughed elbowing Ty in his side.

"Ow! That hurt!" said half joking, half serious.

"Elaina, listen to me, sweetheart." Ty stooped down and put her forehead against his and cupped her ears. "I'm sorry that we can't wait here with you until your bus comes. I have a counseling session in thirty minutes."

"That's alright, dear. The bus will be here in just about forty minutes and I have my book. Maybe something interesting will happen in it after all." she smirks. "Thank-you so much for everything, both of you! Goodbye, Lydia. I'll call you when I get home. Put Ty on the phone if you want." They both smiled. Ty and Elaina hugged and kissed each other on the cheek. "I love you, Ty!" Elaina said, hugging him and kissing him on his cheek. Elaina cried as she watched Ty and Lydia drive off, then, she walked to a bench?"

About twenty minutes later, Ty and Lydia were poking Elaina on top of her head. "We forgot to give you something." Ty was holding a small fiberglass cage and Lydia had something bundled up in her sweater. "I have no use for this puppy cage, Elaina. Please give it to someone that can use it. It's just the right size for kittens, too. And Lydia has something for you." Lydia gave the bundle to Elaina who unwrapped the sweater. Elaina let out a huge sigh and grin, "Oh, my! It's a Little Trollie!" she said as tears ran down her cheeks. "Scottish Folds . . . um . . ." still crying, "they're hard to find and they're expensive! That's the one in the pet shop isn't it? And, it's a little girl. Oh, dear! Thank you both so much! Thank-you . . . Wow! . . . Thank-you so much!" She was almost hyperventilating.

Lydia ignored what Elaina said about the cost. "Take it easy, sweetie. Now, breath slowly." She hugged Elaina and gave her a tissue.

"And don't worry about your landlord not letting you keeping her." Ty said. "I'm surprised that you didn't know about our sister church in Parker. Well, they agreed to let you rent a house that they own on their property. They know that you're on welfare and are willing to work with you about the rent. Well *this* counseling session is about over."

"I love you, Ty!", Elaina said, hugging him and kissing him on his ear. She missed his cheek but I don't think that either one noticed. "Good-bye, Lydia." Elaina cried even harder than before as she watched Ty and Lydia drive off. "Ty!," asked Lydia. "That was a sweet thing you did for Elaina. How did you know that you could get that cute little kitten?"

"Tom, the owner of the pet shop called me last week. He wants to start attending our church. I called him yesterday morning about the boat and we made the arrangements about Trollie."

"How expensive was she? No! It doesn't matter. I trust your judgment but, tell me this—will I get a birthday present this year?" Just then, the car sputtered. "Great! Now the gas is being turned off. How much did she cost? No, I don't want to know." Lydia grinned.

As soon as Ty's car was out of eye sight, Elaina took Trollie to a bench? She took her book out of her purse but put it back in. She wasn't in the mood to read. She hugged Little Trollie and just cuddled and stared at her.

A policewoman stood watching Elaina and then walked over to her. "Excuse me, Miss, can I see some ID,

Elaina started to open her purse but then she stopped. "Officer, I think I know what you want. I was wanted for conning a friend out of over $100,00 but Nick Boyer who made the complaint in Oakland, California dropped the charges when I made payment arrangements with him. I was tempted to skip the state when he did that, like I did in California to here, which made things a whole lot worse, but Jesus said 'No!' to me. 'No more hiding, He told me.' I almost have the money paid off, too."

"I'll still need to see some ID and you'll have to come down to the station with me to make a statement and to check out your story." Elaina gives her ID to her. "Is it Miss or Ms Or Mrs Torey?"

"Miss!"

"If it does, I'll bring you back here to catch your bus."

In her soft voice, Baby Trollie 'voiced' her disapproval.

"But my bus leaves in less than fifteen minutes and I can't afford another bus ticket. I'm on welfare."

The policewoman called to the station on her shoulder mike, talked a bit and then asked Elaina, "Why are you leaving town and how did you almost pay back a hundred grand on welfare?"

"I have friends here. I live In Parker. I came to be baptized on Easter by my friend. I got the money from my friends and my church. They gave me very high paying jobs and opened an account that only Nick, the guy that I stole from could draw out the money from but I can't."

"Miss Torey, I'll personally get you home if your story checks, all right?"

STREET FOOD, BE-BOP, AND GEO.
(A 13 HOUR TALE)

Benzedrine

While the drug Benzedrine was initially used for medical purposes, as a bronchodilator, early users of the Benzedrine inhaler discovered that it had a euphoric stimulant effect, resulting in it being one of the earliest synthetic stimulants to be widely used for recreational (i.e., non-medical) purposes. Even though this drug was intended for inhalation, some people used Benzedrine recreationally by cracking the container open and swallowing the paper strip inside, which was covered in Benzedrine. The strips were often rolled into small balls and swallowed, or taken with coffee or alcohol. The drug was often referred to as 'bennies' by users and in literature.

". . . and Jamie, he didn't catch a one."
Suzy & Jamie were talking while riding their bicycles to Miss 'Duck's yard sale. The house sat on four acres in the Senora Desert east of Phoenix, near Coolidge. On it were a kennel of dog houses without dogs; hutches without rabbits; and a dried up duck pond without ducks. Ducks used to fly in and stay for the season but eventually more would fly out than would fly in. Then, one year, the pond dried up. The only birds that would stay were the ones that ate the dead fish.

A man was there looking but, no one was there to 'mind the store'. Miss Duck left out baskets on each table to collect the money and cow bells to let her know when someone was there to buy something. That man, let's call him Jethro, picked up fifty-one souvenir spoons and four spoon racks and then left. There was no money in any of the baskets all day.

"I'm going home." said Suzy. "I don't care for the duck lady much, anyways. She's so weird."

Jamie looked at Suzy. "Really? My daughters love her. She's always giving them cookies or brownies and chocolate milk. The girls say that she'll give them jazz piano lessons someday."

Suzy continued. "She tells people that when she was eighteen, she heard Ginsberg read his poem 'Howl' in '58 and at twenty-one she was at Woodstock in '69. She was twenty-five when Bobby Kennedy was shot and killed in '68. Miss 'Duck' is wack-o!"

Inside 'Miss' Duck sat on her living room recliner with her friend, George sitting in a chair next to her. A mourning dove just flew to her window sill and then flew to her shoulder. She went into the kitchen. The dove stayed with her. 'Miss' Duck fed the bird some Grape Nuts and then, turned on Van Halen's 'Pretty Women'. The dove flew out of the window.

'Miss' Duck hadn't been outside for eight days when she went out to set up for her yard early. On her front door was written, *Requiescat In Peace* in purple. She knew what it meant, 'Rest In Peace'. 'Miss' Duck went back into the house, got some ash and charcoal from her fireplace and some purple paint. Then, she painted and smeared it over the graffiti and her walnut wood front door. Today, she is reading from her journals, smoking her corn-cob pipe. George and she go back a long time, over thirty years.

'Miss' Duck always wears a tan Fedora that she claimed that jazz pianist/ singer Mose Allison gave to her. She always wears two duck feather in its hat band. Her real name was and still is Hannah Torey. She came from the New York 'Beat Generation', which turned hippie culture eight to ten years later.

"It says here, George that my friend Trish and I sat at a side walk café near San Francisco, across the Golden Gate in Tiburon, drinking espresso, reminiscing about the '60's. I always have lemon peel in my espresso. Child, it's a European thing, but I know that you know that. Here in the states, they charge you fifty cents to put lemon peel in. Frisco was nice in the early '60's. All of the coffee houses had music. It might have been just a trumpet but it was music.

"I lived in Times Square. Alan (Ginsburg) called us a 'circle of friends', the poets. The beats didn't live in the Village. At night, my friends and I would usually go into the Village and make the rounds to hear some jazz. Sometimes we'd end up in Harlem to hear more jazz or R&B at some club. Benzedrine[1] was the drug of choice and heroin. I never did heroin—never did."

"Too many people died. Lenny Bruce died from Heroin and maybe Gene Krupa and maybe Jimi Hendrix did, too. Too many talented lives were wasted. They said that Paul McCartney (The Beatles) died in a car crash. 'A Day In The Life' (Sgt. Pepper's Lonely Hearts Club Band) hinted at that. Lots of Beatles' songs and LP covers said that, I mean suggested clues to that. In 'I Am The Walrus' a walrus means death to the Eskimos.

"It all started in '69, in Detroit, MI, when a DJ aired a phone call from a student named Tom. Tom said that when the song 'Revolution 9' is played backwards, that the voice says, 'Turn me on, dead man' at the beginning. He also told the DJ that at the very end of "Strawberry Fields Forever", a muffled voice says, "I buried Paul." The DJ played both songs on the air. The phone lines went crazy. Experts have shown that John is saying "cranberry sauce" at the end of "Strawberry Fields Forever" and not "I buried Paul."

"On the cover of Revolver, near the top is a photo of Paul screaming and Paul is facing to the side on the cover, different from the other Beatles, who are facing front.

"Yellow Submarine, on the cover, someone has their hand over Paul's head, the Eastern blessing for the dead. The Yellow Submarine on the cover is underground, beneath the remaining Beatles. Supposedly, his is Paul's coffin.

"The Abbey Road and Pepper's Lonely Hearts Club Band have the most clues. On the cover of Sgt Pepper's Lonely Hearts Club Band the whole album is a funeral scene. The headstone is the stone statue to the right of the drum. In front of is a yellow floral display which, when looked at carefully, can be read as 'Paul?' or simply the letter "P" for "Paul." Note the younger Ringo is sad, as if he had lost a friend.

"To the right of the stone statue is a statue of a girl who is looking down and to the right at a flaming car. This is 'Lovely Rita the meter maid' who saw Paul's accident and the flaming car. Paul was in the accident because he was looking at 'the meter maid' Paul is seen with a hand over his head, an East Hindu is blessing for the deceased.

"The four-armed doll at the bottom of the cover points with one arm to Paul and is holding some sort of floral bouquet.

"On the record version, the inside photo of the band shows Paul with a patch on his left arm which reads 'O.P.D.' or, 'Officially Pronounced Dead.' Other sources say that it stands for 'Ontario Provincial Police,' where William Campbell was an officer when he won the infamous look-alike contest

"On the back cover of the record version, Paul is facing backwards, symbolizing being dead and George is pointing to the line, 'Wednesday morning at five o'clock,' the day and time of the accident.

"In 'Magical Mystery Tour' the word 'BEATLES' on the cover spelled out in stars becomes a phone number when viewed upside-down is the number 231-7438. It's rumored to be the number to a London mortuary, but some say that when they called the number they heard, 'You're getting closer'. Eerie huh, George?

"In the movie and in a picture book to the record, it shows Paul at a desk with a sticker on it that reads, 'I WAS.' On page twelve, Paul is not wearing any shoes; they are to the left and covered in blood. Tire tracks are seen leading up to Paul.

On Abbey Road's cover might be a funeral procession; John Lennon is dressed as the preacher, Ringo (pause)—I've lost so much weight that my false teeth don't fit anymore—(another Pause) as the pallbearer, Paul as the corpse, and Harrison is the grave digger. Paul is walking with his eyes closed, like a dead man. Paul is walking out of step with the other Beatles. He leads with his right foot, the others with their left. This is a symbol of non-conformity with the living (because he is dead).

"Also, left-handed Paul is walking with a cigarette in his right hand. Cigarettes are known as 'coffin nails.'

"The Volkswagen Bug, on the street has a license plate which reads, '28IF.' Paul would have been 28 when Abbey Road came out, if he lived.

"On the back cover, the word 'Beatles' has a crack running down the letter 'S,' symbolizing a break in the band, (Paul's death). To the left of the 'Beatles' sign are five circles. Four of these are in the light because they represent people who are alive; John, George, Ringo, and William Campbell (Paul's replacement). The fifth circle is in the shade because it represents Paul, who is dead.

"George, I'm remembering all of that from '60's teen magazines. I'm not reading this. (Hannah, smiling, is pointing to a journal.)

"I'm convinced that it was John Lennon who died in a car crash instead of shot. He had a wonderful rock & roll voice like in 'Twist And Shout'. He could shout. Then suddenly, his voice changed. It was really mellow. Listen to 'Imagine' or

'The War Is Over (Happy Christmas)' and you'll see. I think that it's somebody else that looks like John. I'm sure that the guy that wrote 'Catcher In The Rye', J.D. something-Or-Other. . . . uh . . . I hated that book. Nothing happens. No Plot! — killed Lennon. I think that he shot John.

"I had a poet friend, my favorite — poet, poems, and friend. He crashed at our pad quite a bit in the late '50's. He was published in 1950 with a book titled, 'The Town And The City'. Jack also had another book that he wrote in '51 that he didn't think was any good so he didn't send it in to his publisher for many years. In June of '57, he proposed to me. I turned him down because I didn't love him. On Sept. 5th his book 'On The Road' was published. Kerouac made millions.

"I liked the folk music in the sixties, at the coffee houses and the clubs on Bleeker Street and on MacDougal street in the Village, like the Gaslight, Café Wha?, Gerde's Folk City, the Bitter End and I can remember checking out the singers like Phil Ochs, Fred Neil, and Rambling Jack Elliot, the Mugwugs with John Sebastian and Cass Elliot, and, of course, Bob Dylan and the beat poets' like Ferlinghetti. The Gratful Dead were big fans of him — or, Wavy Gravy's and Timothy Leary's Magic Bus trip or whatever they called it. That was in Frisco.

"I remember Washington Park, then' being like Frisco is now, filled with pickers and mimes, bongo and conga players and artists of all kinds and dealers, too — lots of dope dealers. I need some coffee. I'll be right back."

She went into the kitchen and made a cup of microwave espresso and came back to her recliner.

Hannah smiled and took a couple of sips of coffee. "I heard Allen Ginsberg and Ferlinghetti at Ferlinghetti's book store read poetry in a San Franciscan book store / coffee house. He read his famous poem, 'Howl' when I was there. I think that they were there at different times. San Francisco banned that poem for a short time thinking it obscene.

Hannah took another sip of the brew. "I saw Lenny Bruce at the Hungry I in Frisco. He was too vulgar. George Carlin was funny too back then but I saw him recently and he's too vulgar, now. He used to be funny. I saw the Kingston Trio there, too. They were great. They recorded a record there sometime. Maybe I was in the audience but not likely. I was in the audience at Woodstock. I hitched hiked. The traffic to get there was terrible for miles. Worse than L.A.'s.

"Before the ponds outside dried up one spring, a mamma duck had either sixteen or thirteen babies. When it was time, I watched the mamma or the daddy duck take turns teaching the ducklings to swim. After a few days, the animals got all but ten of them.

"The second week that they were out, they began getting their own personalities. Towards the end of the week they were looking for food underwater with their tails sticking straight up. They were so cute. One daring ducky was even brave to dive underwater. That Friday they were near the shore with the mamma duck watching them from about twenty-five feet away by a tree. As I watched them, the ducklings swam closer to me. Their mamma jumped into the water and swam to a spot in the middle of the pond about the same distance she was from them from land. As they moved closer to me, their mamma moved closer to them. I decided to move a good distance from them but I still kept watching them. Eventually, they climbed out of the water and as a group, they started waddling behind a tree and then they were gone. I decided to go home.

"On Saturday, The Momma and Poppa and only two of the duckies were swimming in the pond. It was real sad. Did an animal get the other eight? I cried big tears. I took my walk around the pond like I used to do and there on the other side, in the water were the other eight baby ducks plus one. I was so happy. It really made my day. I thanked God for sparing them. Eventually, and all at once, the whole family left the pond. That summer, the pond started to dry up and they never returned."

For the next five or ten minutes, Hannah finished her espresso without saying a word then, "You know my daughter Elaina. She goes by the name Pahbadoe for some reason. She thinks it's Dutch but it's not. I think that it's American Indian from Arizona or Nevada. Maybe New Mexico, maybe. Did I tell you that she's a folk singer, writer, and a published poet like the ones we were just talking about? She moved to Nevada and maybe here to Arizona. I don't remember. I haven't seen her in years but she calls every week. One time, she said that she just got 'born again'. I thought that she meant reincarnated like . . . from a bug or, uh . . . uh, a cat. She loves cats. Dumb, huh, I mean about me thinking that, huh? I buy first edition books on the Internet and have someone sign them. Then, I send them to Elaina. It makes her happy. She loves to read. Please don't tell her that I do that.

"Oh! Listen, Child, let me tell you about Pepé. He was a wonderful person I knew years ago. He was Latin! (She growled like Roy Orbison). I think that it was in Santa Monaca that his daughter and we went to dinner on the Queen Mary. We had such fun. It was glorious! *We skipped the light fandango, turned cartwheels* 'cross the floor. I was feeling kinda seasick but the crowd called out for more. The room was humming harder as the ceiling flew away. When we called out for another drink and the waiter brought a tray. And so it was that later, as the miller told his tale, that her face, at first just ghostly, turned a whiter shade of pale. She said, 'There is no reason and the truth is plain to see. But I wandered through my playing cards and would not let her be one of sixteen vestal virgins who were leaving for the coast. And although my eyes were open, they might have just as well been closed.

She said, 'I'm home on shore leave' though in truth we were at sea so I took her by the looking glass and forced her to agree saying, 'You must be the mermaid who took Neptune for a ride.'

But she smiled at me so sadly that my anger straightway died. If music be the food of love then laughter is its queen and likewise if behind is in front then dirt in truth is clean. My mouth by then like cardboard seemed to slip straight through my head. So, we crash-dived straightway quickly and attacked the ocean bed.[1]

"I need another cup of coffee." Just like before, she went into the kitchen and made a cup of microwave espresso and came back to the recliner. "I crashed Woodstock in '69. Hippies, maybe it was Abby Hoffman's people tore down a fence and I got in free and stayed the whole three days. They said that three people died there but I didn't hear about it but it sure did rain though. Talking about music, I'm going to put on some records. How about Mose Allison and some Coltrane?" There was no answer but she put on the records anyways. Hannah didn't like CD's. A lot of people don't. They say that the digital takes away the pops of the acoustic guitars and other sounds that you can't hear on digital. Hannah began the Benzedrine stare.

"Let me tell you, George about a fellow that I was dating once. His name was Phil Mickelson. We would play tennis every Saturday morning—early and go to dinner, and a movie, and dancing every Friday night and Bingo every Wednesday night. People said that we were in a boring rut but we enjoyed ourselves. Being together was what it was all about. Phil used to compare me to the Universe. It is so beautiful.

Phil wanted to take me to the Master's golf match one time in Atlanta but—Oh! You probably think I mean Phil Mickelson the golfer. Heavens no! My Phil worked a carnival booth where people would throw Ping-Pong balls into goldfish bowels to win a fish. They'd spend mucho dollars to win a twenty-five cent goldfish.

I just forgot what I was telling you about Phil. Oh, well! It doesn't matter. Anyways, his middle name was Phil. His given name was Mickel after his father, Mickel Mickelson IV. Now, that's funny, right? It's true, though.

"They had some great songs, funny songs in the fifties and sixties — Please! Mister Custer, Along Comes Jones, Its Bitsy Tiny Weeny Yellow polka-dot Bikini, and one I just remembered the words to, They're Coming to Take me Away. Wanna hear it? Sure you do." Hannah got a very serious look on her face and then recited:

Remember when you ran away
And I got on my knees
And begged you not to leave
Because I'd go berserk

Well you left me anyhow
And then the days got worse and worse
And now you see I've gone
Completely out of my mind

And they're coming to take me away ha-haaa (she said that with an eerie smile laugh)
They're coming to take me away ho ho hee hee ha haaa
To the funny farm
Where life is beautiful all the time
And I'll be happy to see those nice young men
In their clean white coats
And they're coming to take me away ha haaa

You thought it was a joke
And so you laughed
You laughed when I said
That losing you would make me flip my lid

Right? You know you laughed
I heard you laugh. You laughed

You laughed and laughed and then you left
But now you know I'm utterly mad

And they're coming to take me away ha haaa
They're coming to take me away ho ho hee hee ha haaa
To the happy home with trees and flowers and chirping birds
And basket weavers who sit and smile and twiddle their thumbs and toes
And they're coming to take me away ha haaa

I cooked your food
I cleaned your house
And this is how you pay me back
For all my kind unselfish, loving deeds
Ha! Well you just wait
They'll find you yet and when they do
They'll put you in the A.S.P.C.A.
You mangy mutt

And they're coming to take me away ha haaa
They're coming to take me away ha haaa ho ho hee hee
To the funny farm where life is beautiful all the time
And I'll be happy to see those nice young men
In their clean white coats

And they're coming to take me away
To the happy home with trees and flowers and chirping birds
And basket weavers who sit and smile and twiddle their thumbs and toes
And they're coming to take me away ha haaa.
They're Coming to Take me Away, Ha-Haaa![2]

George was thinking in his mind, "Sweetheart! 'Miss' Duck! I do love you dearly but they really do need to take you away. That complement about the universe, well, most of the universe doesn't make sense. Most of it is missing according to the Flagstaff Lowell Observatory. We can account for only about 4% of the universe."

Hannah looked a little confused and flustered. "Oh, right! I lost my thought for a second. I was telling you about the golf match. I didn't go. Never cared about golf. Now, hockey and pro wrestling—that's different—and the horses. They're fun. Never made any money off of the horses, though. Phil and I broke up shortly after that when I left town for a of couple months and then went to the Woodstock Festival, upstate New York. No one knew where I was. I met a singer named Boy George (she winked at George) and George and Jimi Hendrix up on the stage and jammed with Pat Boone. This was during Boone's punk rock phase. I played the triangle and sang. Jimi played the Star Spangled Banner a little after that." She began singing 'Da da da ba, ba da da da duh!'

"The talk about New York got me hungry for hot link sandwiches. Maybe later, you can go find some for us. I miss the street food. Did I tell you that the first time I ate piz . . .

The phone rings. "Would you get it? No! Never mind. Stay put. I'll get it. Hello!"

"Hi, Momma! This is Elaina." came a voice on the other end.

"Baby, is everything all right? Where are you?"

"I'm home, Momma. I've tried to call you for over a week. Where were you? Are YOU all right? I wanted to come and see you but I didn't have any way or any money for the bus. I know that you're just half way across the state but I can't get there. I got real worried"

"Yeah! Sure! I'm fine, Baby, really. I guess that I just didn't hear the phone."

"Mother, are you taking those pills again?"

"I don't know what you're talking about. I don't take any pills! What do you mean?"

"Benzedrine, that sent you to detox and rehab over and over again. I worry about you, Mamma. I really do, living so far away across the state. At least you don't drink while you take your 'medicine'—do you? That could be deadly."

Hannah smiled while she took her silver whiskey flask and a paper strip from her pocket, took a swig and put the paper strip in her mouth. "We'll, you should talk—you living all these years in California and Nevada and wherever you are now!"

"Let's not argue, please. I have some wonderful things to tell you. I was baptized Easter Sunday by my really good friend, Ty. I've told you about him. He was in prison for drug possession. Now, he's a preacher."

Hannah interrupted. "I used to be a Christian when you were young. I took you to Sunday school every Sunday. And then, you quit going to church. We both did. But now, you're going again. That's good. When you told me a few months ago that you were born again, I thought you meant reincarnated. That was dumb, huh? I never heard that phrase before or maybe, I just forgot.

"Elaina Baby, at night, when I couldn't sleep or I'd wake up wide awake, I had a chair facing the bed at the head of the bed. I would reach out and it felt like I was holding Jesus' hand and we'd talk—sometimes for hours, sometimes until I fell back to asleep."

"I've always liked that story, Momma. Well, the other good news is that Ty and his wife gave me a kitty I named Trollie and a church put me up in a house, rent free. I'll do some odd jobs for the church."

"I'm glad you're back to church and that you have a fella."

"Mamma, he's not my fells. I told you that he's married, very happily married. He's just a very dear, sweet friend. We're NOT fooling around."

"Darling, I have to go. I need to take my medicine. George is here."

"Please don't take any pills. Is George talking to you now?"

"No! Not really. He's just been sitting in his chair listening to me. I have to go. I love you, Elaina dear." Hannah hung up the phone and then picked up the receiver and put the receiver on to the table.

"That was my daughter. Man, I miss her. You know, George, you would be a wonderful dancer; a tiny dancer. If you were a girl, you'd be a wonderful ballerina. *Blue jean baby, L.A. lady, seamstress for the band, pretty eyed, pirate smile, you'll marry a music man. Ballerina, you must have seen her dancing in the sand and now she's in me, always with me, tiny dancer in my hand.*

Jesus freaks out in the street handing tickets out for God. Turning back she just laughs. The boulevard is not that bad. Piano man he makes his stand in the auditorium. Looking on, she sings the songs, the words she knows, the tune she hums. But, oh how it feels so real, lying here with no one near — only you and you can hear me when I say softly slowly

Hold me closer tiny dancer. Count the headlights on the highway. Lay me down in sheets of linen. You had a busy day today."[3]

"Are you tired, George? Well, when I do go back to New York, the city from time to time, I always eat the street food from the venders. First time I ever ate pizza was from a street vender. I miss the hot dogs. We ate at a lot of automats when I lived there, too. I tell you, street food is a lot better."

Hannah took out her pipe—a tobacco pipe—and filled it with rosemary and Latakia tobacco and lit it. "Excuse me for a minute. I have to take my pill. I'll be right back."

Hannah was gone for over an hour. When she came back into the room with an espresso and a tumbler of spiced rum, she was talking to herself, slurring her words. She had that Benzedrine stare but, she had to have taken it with some other pills or drink. "I found a lemon peel, Georgie." (It was a piece of banana peel from the garbage.) "I think that I'll put on some 'Cream'. I just love old Clapton. She did and then sat down in her recliner. After she finished her rum, she fell asleep.

There was a loud boom—maybe a sonic boom that woke Hannah up after no one knows for how long. Afterwards, the house was very still and quiet and dark except the dim light that filled the room from the kitchen. Hannah called out, "George! George!" She looked around the house. "Oh dear! George!" He was lying on the floor next to his chair. Hannah picked George up—her toy puppy—from the floor and put him back into his chair.

TRAVELS WITH CHUCK

Blessed are the poor in spirit for theirs was the Kingdom of
Heaven; Blessed are the pure in heart for they shall see God

(Mathew 5:3,8)

A Fleming from Flanders, Belgium named Floyd (a Welsh name) became an out of work pastor of a small church almost overnight. One night, the Ku Klux Klan set fire to it, burning it down because the congregation had more blacks than whites. After that, the congregation began to scatter to other churches. Two weeks later, the KKK set fire to Floyd's house. He quit the ministry full time to find work. He couldn't find another church. He couldn't find another job. Employer after employer told him that he had no skills except preaching, which wasn't true. A preacher has leadership, supervisory, counseling, organization, administrative skills among others. Floyd could have done telemarketing or fast food but these jobs never crossed his mind.

After a couple of weeks of living in his car, his wife left him. It was thought that she was a lesbian but there wasn't an ounce of proof.

Over the next few months, Floyd began gaining the respect and dignity and comforts of a homeless man. For a few years, Floyd lived in storefront door ways, and an alley where his home was a refrigerator cardboard carton and he ate at homeless missions or the backdoors of restaurants when they were throwing out the leftover food. One day, another homeless man, Eli took him to a homeless mission where he lived. The mission offered him a job serving meals — in exchange for a place to live. The mission was a big one room warehouse. Each person had a mattress to sleep on. Each mattress had a chest of drawers. The top drawer had a pad lock for 'valuables'. On the east side were the kitchen, dining room (which served as the chapel for the mandatory service before dinners), the offices, and a patio used for the smokers. There were no medical conveniences or meds. The free clinics were for that.

"Say, Eli, What do you think about the food here?"

"You really want to know. I don't use that kind of language. It's terrible! They don't give you enough. Even though I'm always hungry . . ."

"Me, too!" Floyd interrupted.

"I'm glad not to eat very much of it. It's awful! To change the subject, non-swimmer was walking, not too far from here, along the Mississippi River. He fell in and the current carried him a ways, not too far. He started yelling . . ."

"Is this a joke?" asked Floyd.

"No!" answered Eli. "Anyways, he started yelling for help. A swimmer heard him and jumped in and pulled him to shore. By this time, there was a small pack of people. When the first guy caught his breathe, he reached into his pocket, pulled out a big wad of bills and gave his savior five dollars. The pack turned into an angry mob, arguing about the small reward.

"It's o.k.! It's o.k.! The gentleman best knows the value of his life,."

"Is this a true story?"

"I don't know. I just heard or read it once but, I like the story."

Eli and Floyd were fast friends from the third day that they met at the mission. Both were devout Christians.

Today was a day in late October, 8:30 a.m. The temperature was 62° but it seemed quite a bit warmer. Eli walked about two blocks with Floyd, a mate from the Saint Benedict-Joseph Labre Mission *(the patron saint of the homeless was born on March 26, 1748 in Amettes, France & died April 17, 1783)*, Eli and Floyd's home. The two were going to the bus stop where Eli shared a wait with Floyd until Floyd's bus arrived. The Kinks 'Lola' was playing from somewhere. On the way to the stop, Floyd Pan—handled the fare plus some soda money.

Eli told a real tear jerker of a story to Floyd. "I lived with my mother, a single mom in Belleview, Id. (19 mi from Sun Valley, Idaho's most popular ski resort.) One summer, my mom started pushing me to spend a month with my Uncle Frank, here in Memphis. We drove the sixty-six miles to the bus station in Twin Falls. My

Mom gave me my Uncle Frank's phone number and fifty dollars, some in change for vending machines and for the phone.

"In Memphis, I called my Uncle and a Frank answered but it was another Frank. I tried two more times and got the same man who had never heard of me. I was fourteen.

"I lived on the streets and homeless shelters until I moved to this place four years ago."

That's a real sad story. I'm really sad that that happened to you." said Floyd with a hug. Floyd actually was teary eyed.

"Let me tell you a story, Eli." Floyd stopped walking so, Eli did, too. "A long time ago there was a rancher who lived so far east that it was almost west. He had a beard so long that it reached his belly button. His name was Job. Now, Job had seven sons and seven daughters and seven thousand head of fine cattle and sheep, not to mention, a herd of camels. Now, Job was a righteous man and a top dog with the Lord—who bragged about him to the ol' devil, every chance he had about how Job hated evil and temptation and how he never lost his faith in God. Well, that ol' devil sashayed his tail and told God that Job was faithful only because every-thing was going his way. The first sign of trouble and Job would change his ways. The Lord thought about this and bet the devil a hard shekel against a nickel's worth of brimstone that Job would stay a righteous man. Well, the devil agreed. He killed Job's livestock and sent a big wind that blew down Job's house. His sons and daughters died and his wife tried to talk some sense into Job and then turned against him, cursing God. His ranch hands either got scared and left or died—I don't remember. Satin covered Job with sores and boils. Job was as miserable as a man could be. Job sat down in the corral, tearing his clothes and shaking ashes over his head, wondering why the Lord had forsaken him.

"Soon, three of his friends came over and told Job that they had heard about his troubles and that Job must have sinned somewhere down the line. They told him he needed to repent and Job told them that he'd repent when he had something to repent about. He told them that he had been good and righteous and hadn't lost faith in the Lord. 'I know that my redeemer liveth and, he shell stand beside me later on.'

"Well, Eli, the devil was wore out so he cashed in his chips and quit the game. The Lord was so proud of Job that he restored his family and gave him twice as much livestock and land as he had before. And Job lived to be an hundred and forty years old and as happy as a bird dog for the rest of his days."

"I remember that story, Floyd, from Sunday school and church." Eli laughed. "It was told a little bit different if I remember. I guess, compared to Job, our troubles are a mere pittance."

Just like on T.V., the bus came just when the two of them got to the bus stop. "See ya!" said Eli.

"See ya!" said Floyd.

Across the street was a large park, quite different from the city's décor. The park didn't quite fit the downtown buildings and the buildings certainly didn't fit the country look of the park, full of trees and bushes of many kinds.

On the left side, the south side of the park was a grove of yellow buckeye (A great shade tree) and white ash trees—hiding a stream (actually, a drainage ditch flowing from a pipe on the street side, draining into the Mississippi River). On the right side of the park were lawn bowling lanes and a cricket court. On the backside was a softball diamond, a single wall for 'handball' and tennis courts. Sun Records and the Gibson Guitar Factory was within walking distance and the Pyramid Arena can be seen from here. (Read about it on the Internet. It's an interesting story.)

A Frisbee came close to hitting Eli but it kept flying. Eli starting walking towards the grove and then, he sat down under a buckeye tree, watching the children play tag. A little girl fell and began to cry. She didn't skin her knee but when they all heard the ice cream truck music, 'The Farmer In The Dell", she sure got a big smile and they all ran to meet it. Soon, he almost fell asleep but a Frisbee disturbed him. A Labrador ran up so Eli tossed the Frisbee away. The dog chased it, caught it and brought it back. Eli threw the Frisbee again but it boomeranged back into the grove. The dog sat down and then after a minute or so, laid down.

Eli went into the grove and found the Frisbee in the stream—half inside of the pipe and half on a rock. He walked and slid down the muddy bank to the large pipe. Eli looked inside and found a large duffle bag. He picked up the Frisbee, threw it onto the lawn and then picked up the bag and opened it.

"Wow!", he gasped. Inside were many bundles of $20 bills. "I need to call 911 or somebody!", he thought to himself. He carried the heavy bag to the street and then walked to a dentist's office.

"I'm a homeless man and I need to call 911. Could I, please?" The lady at the front desk nodded 'yes', smiled, and dialing 911, handled Eli the cordless phone.

"Excuse me but what is the address here?, he asked. She wrote it down on an orange Post-It along with the phone number.

"Thank-you!, Eli said, walking to a chair on the far side of the room.

"Captain Morgan, can I help you?"

"That's a famous name, Capt. Morgan. He was a famous privateer, sort of a pirate.

"Sort of a pirate. He burned Panama City in the 1700's. Anyways, I found a bag with a bunch of money. I want to do the right thing. I'm a Christian and I want to turn it in but I don't know the procedure."

"How much?"

"How much money?" I don't know—I didn't count it."

"Well, you need to bring it in and we'll check it out if there were any robberies or illegal transactions and if there weren't, you keep the money in nighty days."

Wow! There's a lot of money. I live at Saint Benedict-Joseph Labre Mission. I have no money, no bus fare."

"Well, I know where you are and it's too far for you to walk. Stay there and I'll be out there in a couple of hours or so." And he did. Oh! There was $363,000 in the duffle bag.

Two Days Later

Floyd died from malnutrition, or so they say. He couldn't get the medical care or the nutrition that he needed. This deeply touched and upset Eli greatly. The week that Floyd died, he lost about sixteen lbs., pins and needles pain all of the time, constant chronic constipation, and after he exercised, foaming of the mouth. No one could or would tell Eli about a funeral or any other detail since he wasn't family. Eli mourned for days—memories, for a life time.

Eli's custom, now and before this story was written, was to watch the children's and other games in the park. He never again saw the Labrador Receiver or another Frisbee again in the park. He learned to play bridge and cricket.

[*Cricket is a bat-and-ball team game. Many variations exist, with its most popular form played on an oval-shaped outdoor arena known as a cricket field, at the center of which is a rectangular 22-yard long pitch that is the focus of the game. A game (or match) is contested between two teams of eleven players each. One team bats, trying to score as many runs as* *possible while the other team bowls and fields, trying to dismiss the batsmen and thus limit the runs scored by the batting team. A run is scored by the striking batsman hitting the ball with his bat, running to the opposite end of the pitch and touching the crease (the **crease** is a certain area demarcated by white lines painted or chalked on the field of play. The term crease also refers to any of the lines themselves.) there without being dismissed. The teams switch between batting and fielding at the end of an innings.]*

One day, Eli hit six straight softballs over the fence from a young pitching stranger (of his)—who was wearing brown corduroy knickers, tan long sleeve shirt, and a cap that we used to call a Buster Brown cap. His dog laid at his feet, "He's so cute", said Eli. Then, he asked the stranger. "What's the puppy's name."

"Tige!", he answered.

"Of course it is!" Eli thought with a smile.

The Next Eighty-Seven Days—Condensed

Among others. a new person came to the mission—tall, skinny, and the reddest natural red hair Eli had ever seen. He was dressed in a T-shirt, short pants, one orange and one brown sock and brown and white saddle shoes. This was an odd way to dress because it was very cold outside. His name was Gail Robertson but he said it was 'Red'. I knew two men named 'Red' in my life and two men named Gail—a friends brother and, on the 'Andy Griffith Show', Aunt Bea's best friend' Clara Edwards' son was named 'Gail'. This man had bruises and cuts all over his arms and legs.

Eli said, "Hi! How you doing?" and after that, Red stuck to Eli, following him for days but, not in a weird way. They're friendship only lasted for a short time. Red got angry with everybody real fast and every other word was 'f**k' and 'M/F****r'. Eli would scold him many times during the day. Eli felt like he was Red's Uncle Frank. The guy had no common sense at all. That night, Red asked Eli if there was a free clinic close buy. "I'll show you where it is in the morning. It's on the next block by the bus stop. How about if I meet you outside in the patio after breakfast" Red nodded.

The next day, Red was waiting outside trying to bum cigarettes from the other tenants. "I'll give you my short (an unfinished lit cigarette) in a minute,"

"Thanks, Bro."

Eli came out and as soon as Red finished smoking, Eli walked Red to the clinic. "I fall asleep six times an hour." said Red. Sometimes I'll be watching a commercial and fall asleep and when I wake up, the same commercial is still on. Sometimes I fall asleep before I wake up."

'Paul Revere & The Raiders 'Hungry' was just finishing playing from somewhere. Actually, it was from a speaker hidden outside a used and rare record store. CDs could not be bought here.

"What's your story, Red?" asked Eli.

"Well, I was in prison for a few years. While I was there, I got hooked on heroin for fourteen years. A few days ago I called my Mom and she drove me to a flea-bag hotel, after I bought a fifth of Jack Daniels. I wanted to kick the habit. My Mom really prayed for me hard and cried hard. She's really into Jesus.

I had a friend that did it with Captain Morgan Spiced Rum." He shuddered, "Uck!" "The second day, his arms and face went into contortions. The third day he didn't feel good but he felt like he had kicked it.

"What happened to me was I must have passed out for three days because I don't remember a thing but the JD was almost gone. I felt like—well, you know. I still crave it but I don't want it anymore. I called my Mom and told her about those days and she cried again—hard. Well, that's about it except when I was in prison, I had to have Anger Management counseling."

An hour later, Red came back with gauze bandages taped around his arm, hiding the cuts and bruises. He was also pulling a pole on wheels with an IV hanging on it. He said that they put a pick line on the back of his neck and that he had to go back every day for a fresh IV.

A week and a half later, Red came out with his pole in his stocking feet. "Where's your shoes?" someone asked.

"Too much trouble to put them on!" He cussed and then headed for the free clinic. He disappeared that morning. No one at the mission ever saw him again.

Week ten a group came from a Baptist church to sing and preach. Their keyboard player didn't show up. His keyboard was in a van. Eli overheard the group concerned about what the choir was going to do

"I play! My name is Eli.

"But do you know the songs?"

"I can play by ear and improvise."

Well, okay, we'll give it a try'"

The group and Eli rocked the paint off of the walls. When it was time for the devotional, the residence yelled out for more. They did do more, a lot more and the pastor never did speak. It was a great time.

A week and a few days later, Eli received his money in full from the police and, the duffel bag. He deposited the money into the bank, keeping two twenties (so that a bigger wad of bills wouldn't show in the pocket of his thin slacks), and then applied for a debit card. Eleven days later he was called into the shelter office.

"You have a letter, Eli."

"Thanks!" he said. Eli folded the letter. He felt something flat and hard in the envelope. He put the letter into his pocket and then headed for the grove of trees in the park. Sitting against a tree, he opened the envelope. It was his debit card. Eli put the card into his shoe.

5:30 am the next morning, Eli woke-up, packed his few possessions in his new duffel bag and called a cab from a payphone down the block. Eli had heard from several residents stories about how they caught rides from truckers too far away places. He wanted to go back to Belleview, Id and this would be a new adventure for him. Eli often wondered if his Mother was still alive and living there. He found a truck stop in the phone book, and according to the city map in the book, it was just a few miles away.

The morning was very, very cold. Eli had a heavy winter jacket and a windbreaker donated by a church group and he was darn glad that he had the jacket. "This will be a cold trip." he thought. Inside the truck stop were the coffee shop on the right, and a Burger King and a store on the left. Eli headed for the store where he bought a pair of blue jeans, a brown and blue plaid long-sleeved shirt, socks and underwear, and a pair of dark brown cowboy boots and a brown corduroy 'Buster Brown' cap with a snap. Showers there cost $3 so, that's what he did. There was also a spray cologne machine on the shower wall for 50¢.

After everything was done and groomed, Eli walked into the coffee shop. The counter was full except two seats. Eli sat down at the nearest stool.

"What'll you have, Honey?" asked the waitress'

"Black coffee and, do you have biscuits and gravy? And, do you have an extra newspaper?"

"Sure do!" Darlin'.

"Ok! Oh, also, could you ask around for me if I could catch a ride from someone going west?"

Eli, as always, silently thanked the Lord for his meal and that he was able to afford it. While eating his breakfast and reading the paper, a man, about the same age as the forty-four years old Eli, came up to Eli carrying his coffee mug and breakfast check. His name is Chuck. Chuck is an interesting trucker. He owns his own truck. He never seems to be in a hurry on his runs. He plans them that way. His truck isn't refrigerated so he doesn't carry perishables. When he travels with his wife on runs, it's usually a working vacation. One run with his wife once turned into a four day side trip through Branson, MO. to see some shows.

"Hear your looking for a ride west—where 'bouts?"

"Idaho, north of Twin Falls."

"I can get you as far as Elko, Nevada and then, you're on your own, okay? Name's Chuck. I'm ready to head out."

"Okay, Chuck. Here, let me get your breakfast."

"Much thanks, friend. I didn't catch your name."

"Eli!"

The checks were paid and they headed outside. "That's my rig over there, the blue one with the orange flames."

"Man, that's huge!"

"You haven't seen anything yet. Wait 'til you get into the cab, Eli."

Eli was bugged eyed when he stepped into the cab. "Buckets seats and a bedroom."

"It's called a sleeper. The two seats swivel 280° and tilt back like a recliner with a foot rest. Four people can sleep in here. There's a satellite TV with a built-in VCR/DVD player. I have a microwave and a small fridge with a freezer."

"Man, you must work for a good company."

"No! I own it myself. I work for myself with my wife. She mostly does the bookwork but she travels some, too."

"Well, let's travel! There are a few books, if you feel like reading in the back, 'The Complete Works of Bret Hart' and Steinbeck's, 'Travels With Charlie'."

Eli turned and looked into the sleeper. "I'm not familiar with Steinbeck."

"John Steinbeck? He's my favorite author—'East Of Eden', 'Grapes of Wrath? He's written thirty-three books and I own thirty-two of them. The other one, 'The Sea of Cortez', I can get in e-Bay but it costs $1500."

Eli had a blank look on his face and then he came to. "Did he write, 'Tortilla Flats'?"

"Now you've got it. What kind of music do you like?"

"60's and blues."

"Eli, you're a man after my own heart!"

"We'll stop and get some frozen burritos that I can microwave for lunch."

"Sounds good!"

The day was filled with talk. Eli read some by Brett Hart and took a nap.

Tulsa, OK is about 400 miles from Memphis. Chuck put in a CD and the first track was Eric Clapton's cover of 'Tulsa Time'. They arrived there about 3:15 pm. "I need to unload my load. How 'bout if I drop you off at Tacoma Truck Stop and I'll meet you in a few hours for dinner?" asked Chuck.

"Fine!" said Eli. "Do you own this rig?"

"Me and the bank own it. Most of it, I own. My Grandma died and left me a good chunk of change. I won big in Atlantic City and some in the California lottery. I was lucky except for Grandma dying but she was 103 and she just died old."

The truck stop was on the outskirts of town near trampled down golden pastures. Eli jumped out of the cab and went in.

The counter was empty except one lady about thirty years old. "Is this seat taken?" Eli asked her.

She looked around and then giggled, "No! Have a seat. My name is Jessie."

"I'm Eli." The waitress came by and Eli ordered coffee. The two (not the waitress) hit it off.

After a few hours, Eli asked if they had a barber shop. "Yeah! Two doors before the showers." said the waitress.

"Can I keep my cup here until I come back?" The waitress nodded.

"I can watch it for you or, can I come with you and watch?"

"Sure you can!" Eli liked what she asked.

The barber cut Eli's long ponytail (half way down his back) to collar length, styled it not too much—a shaggy look and gave him a shave for only $16. Eli was surprised and impressed and gave the barber a $5 tip then the couple went back for some more coffee.

Just about then, Chuck came in, passed them and looked around. "Hey, Chuck!" called out Eli.

"Eli? Wow? You look so different. Looks good!"

"Doesn't he?" said Jessie.

"This is Jessie. She'll be joining us for dinner, my treat for all of us."

"Thank-you, sweetheart! You look like George Harrington of the Beatles with a part in your hair with your haircut. You're handsome." Eli smiled and blushed.

"Where you from, Missy?" asked Chuck.

"Athens, a little east of here." Answered Jessie. "I'm heading to Vegas or Reno."

"What are you running from?" again from Chuck.

Eli could tell that Jessie was annoyed by that question. "I'm *not* running. I have a restraining order against my ex-boyfriend but he's ignoring it so, I'm just moving on to a better life. I don't want to talk about it anymore."

"You can join us, if you want to. I'm going to Reno and then to San Jose, CA and Salinas." Eli smiled big and so did she. Chuck took that as a 'yes'. "Well, let's eat. They have *Great* chili cheeseburgers here." They all ordered *Great* chili cheeseburgers — and they were."

On their way back to the truck, Chuck picked up a few brochures near the front door while Eli paid the bill. Eli told Jessie, "His truck is fantastic, Captain Fantastic!" She was very impressed. She had never seen anything like it before.

"I'm very tired. I've had a hard day." Chuck yawned. "I'm going to watch the news and then go to bed. You can watch TV if you want, it won't bother me. Decide where you want to sleep. Here are some brochures. Decide what you want to do tomorrow and I'll drop you two off while I finish my business."

Jessie chose the Tulsa Zoo and then squeezed Eli's hand. Twenty minutes later, Chuck said good-night.

Jessie told Eli that even though it was winter, the zoo opened at nine. "There some shows there but they cost.

"I'm a bit nervous about sleeping in the bed next to Chuck. He seems nice but . . . I'll sleep in the passenger seat." Jessie coyly told Ely with a slight smile.

"It swivels and tilts back like a recliner with a foot rest. It's pretty comfortable." Eli went to the other bed. There was a wooden plaque saying, 'Sebastian slept here!' on the wall by the bed.

In the morning, Jessie found Eli asleep in the driver's seat. She smelled coffee.

"Good morning, Sunshine." said Chuck. "I only have a microwave so is oatmeal alright?" This woke Eli up. "Yeah!" Eli answered.

"I love oatmeal," said Jessie. "We decided to go to the zoo. It opens at nine."

"That's fine! I'll have you there by then and when I finish my business, I'll go in. I'll meet you both outside the gate around three. I'll give you my wife's cell phone so if you need to get in touch with me, just hit *2, She left it the last time she rode with me."

"Who's Sebastian?" asked Eli.

"He's a raccoon that found his way in to here. He stayed for about a couple of three days and just left."

They arrived at the zoo at about 8:30 am. Jessie and Eli got in line and waited for the gate to open.

Chuck came out about 4 pm. Eli and Jessie were sitting at a picnic table holding hands. His arm was around her shoulder.

When Jessie and Eli got into the cab, she was so excited. "Man, the zoo was the highlight of my whole day and a half trip to Oklahoma." she giggled "It was so easy to get lost in there for the whole time Eli and I were in there.

"There was a park surrounding the zoo, with picnic tables. It was so pretty with the flowers and the shrubs and the trees."

"I lived just down the street from a park that it looked like." Eli butted in.

"It only cost me $8 each, minus a dollar off with your AAA card, Chuck. The special exhibits cost extra." Eli continued.

Then, Jessie continued, "We saw the butterfly exhibit, and it only cost a dollar and, it was well worth it. It was worth five." Jessie got the attraction prices wrong. She had no idea what Eli paid.

"When we entered the park, this is where you pay for the special exhibits. We were given tokens for the shows. They cost extra. Eli was so generous." She gave him a kiss on the lips.

They also gave us a map of the zoo with a list and times of the different shows and feeding times but we took a train tour with stops at two of the shows.

"I'm glad that we got there early in this morning, before it opened, because that's when the animals were out. When you met us, the animals were hard to find. The went inside.

"Me and Eli saw two of the shows they had. The first one was the penguin show. It was kind of interesting."

"I enjoyed it!" said Eli.

"Well, yeah! Anyways, the man who was running show gave a lot of info and he got the penguins to swim around the tank for us. The only complaint about the show was that there was very little room for everyone to stand in front of the tank window. The kids need to be up front and the parents need to keep them there. Otherwise, they couldn't see anything and it was probably easy to get pushed out of the way by some of the adults.

"The other show we saw was the seal show. Unlike at the penguin one, there is much more room around the pool, although the best areas did fill up fast.

"My favorite part was the butterfly exhibit. It was amazing. You get to walk around a small enclosed area filled with thousands of butterflies. You can get so close to them that it isn't hard to walk away with several up-close pictures that would probably be almost impossible to take in the wild. There was even a booth with the cocoons hanging in them waiting to hatch."

"It was so much fun, Chuck, Thank you for bringing us here." Jessie smiled.

"It was!" added Eli.

Chuck had seen quite a bit of the zoo but he didn't mind her talking about it.

The trio went the 327 mi., stopping for gas, sandwiches and bathroom breaks at rest stops and, they arrived at Dodge City, KS at 10:30 pm. Jessie and Eli were sound asleep in the beds, Eli in Chuck's. He didn't bother to wake because he knew that they had a fun but a real tiring day. He slept in the driver's recliner.

6:15 the next morning, he went into the truck stop store and bought coffee and cinnamon rolls for everybody. He also got brochures on things to do. Breakfast was at 7:15 am when Eli and Jessie were up.

"I got some literature about Dodge City on what to do. I have nothing to do today or tomorrow so, we can make a day of it. I do need to start out at 4:30 am the next day to make sure that I get to Denver on time. I always allow an hour and a half leeway for emergencies." He handed the brochures to Jessie who read some of the following out loud:

Boot Hill Museum is a non-profit organization dedicated to the preservation of the history of Dodge City and the Old West. Boot Hill Museum's exhibits are organized to explore the rich and diverse history of Dodge City and recreate the atmosphere of Dodge City during the late 1800's. Dodge City had the reputation of the "Wickedest City in the West" and you can find out why when you visit Boot Hill Museum.

Dodge City was founded in 1872 and quickly became the world's largest shipping point Dodge City was a town that persisted and grew, and still honors its western heritage. Dodge was the wildest of the early frontier towns, but law and order was soon established with the help of men such as Bat Masterson, Wyatt Earp, and Bill Tilghman.

The Front Street buildings are reconstructions, exhibiting hundreds of original artifacts. They represent Dodge City in 1876, and were carefully researched through historic photographs and newspapers.

The various exhibits throughout the museum depict life in early Dodge City. There is a collection of over 200 original guns on display, a working print shop, an extensive collection of drug store items, an entire building that was just completely renovated, and many other special exhibits. Each artifact on display is authentic and there are approximately 20,000 artifacts displayed throughout the complex.

Boot Hill Museum is an educational, historical institution with just enough fun added for the whole family to enjoy. We looked forward to seeing you in Dodge City!

People of the Plains

Housed in the original Boot Hill Museum building, this recently completed renovation tells the story of the people who have lived on the plains. Featured exhibits include *The Nomadic Indians of the Great Plains*, *The Railroad*, *The American Buffalo*, *The Era of the Cowboy*, and *Victorian Fashion*. Kids will love "Stan", the talking steer, as he tells about the cattle drives from Texas. Also located in this building is an exhibit dedicated to Dodge City in the movies and on television.

Long Branch Saloon

Walking through the doors of the Long Branch Saloon is like walking into the past. The saloon was purchased by Chalkley Beeson and William Harris in 1878. Through their efforts it became the most popular, refined meeting place of cattlemen

Guns That Won the West

While film and television portray the Old West as a romantic tale, the harsh reality of it was brutal, lawless, and expansive. This is evident as you look upon the firearms that are on display.

Hardesty House

Richard and Margaret Hardesty's House was built in 1879 by A.B. Webster, a mayor of Dodge City, and later sold to the Hardesty's after they were married. A typical home of the 1880's, its interior reflects the middle-class lifestyle of Victorian Kansas. Mrs. Hardesty was the sister-in-law of Fred Harvey, owner of the famed Harvey houses.

Boot Hill Cemetery

The final resting place of buffalo hunters, drifters and others who had no money and no family in the area.

Saratoga Saloon

The Saratoga Saloon, along with the world famous Long Branch Saloon, was owned by Chalkley Beeson and William Harris. It offered billiards, keno, faro and other games. These were two of the 16 saloons in a town where soldiers from Fort Dodge could drink "without fear of attracting the brawling element."

Santa Fe Trail Tracks

Certified by the National Parks Service, The Santa Fe Trail rut site is located nine miles west of town on US Highway 50. It preserves one of the finest remnants of wagon tracks in existence along the entire trail. Interpretive signs are placed along an easily accessible walkway allowing you to experience the Trail first hand.

On his short wave radio, Chuck heard that there was a major snow blizzard in Denver. Chuck was not happy at all to hear this. Chuck never cussed in his life and, he didn't this time. The ride from Denver was 360 mi from Dodge so maybe—the storm would pass by sooner than then. He didn't say anything to Jessie or too Eli. Jessie was microwaving some hot chocolate for the three of them.

Jessie started laughing, "What?" asked Chuck, laughing, too.

Still laughing, "When I was a teenage, me and two of my friends called a number we got out of the book." (Laughing still) "I asked for Chuck Miller. I don't remember what name I used."

"I'm sorry but you have the wrong number."

"Is this 567 something, something?"

"Yes, but there's no Chuck Miller here."

"This is important. Tell him that Mary's in town and want's to meet him."

"You have the wrong number." and she hung up.

Jessie handed Chuck his travel mug of chocolate while continuing her story.

"Ten minutes later, my boyfriend called again and asked for Chuck Miller."

"You have the wrong number!" She sounds upset, Jay told us.

"Is this 567 something, something?" he asked.

"There's no Chuck Miller here!"

"Please tell Chuck that Mary's in town. It's important that he knows."

"I said, you have the wrong number!!!" and she hung up again.

"Twenty minutes later, my girlfriend, Lynn called again and asked for Chuck Miller." The lady hung up.

"An hour later, my boyfriend called back. 'Hello! This is Chuck Miller. Do you have any messages for me?' She was so mad." Everyone laughed and Chuck spilled his hot chocolate.

Chuck smiled, rubbing his left ring finger. "When I was a junior in high school, I had a girlfriend named Lynn. I didn't have a letterman's sweater or a class ring wrapped with yarn . . ."

"Wrapped in yarn?" from Jessie.

"They don't do that anymore? Girls used to wrap the ring in yarn so it would fit their finger. Anyways, I used to live in West Pakistan and I had a real nice fire opal silver ring from there. It was pretty with leaves in graved on the sides. Anyways, I broke up with her in the hall and she threw the ring and broke the opal. Here in the states, it would be too expensive to buy another stone that size, the size of my ring finger fingernail. I walked away to pick up the pieces and she was crying and she grabbed me from behind, a big hug, actually. "Chu-Chu, come back!" I tried to get her away from me and I accidentally flipped her over my shoulder. It was funny, in a sad way.

"What's 'Chu?'" asked Eli.

"Chu-Chu — my nickname, but you don't have to call me that. My baby sister couldn't saw Chuck. The 'K' was hard for her.

"I had a fraternity brother named Dub." Eli raising his hand. "His real name was Walter. We were in Kappa Phi Kappa together. His little brother couldn't say 'Walter' so he was nicknamed 'Dub' for 'Double U.' What, Eli?"

Eli put his hand down. "Reminiscing about when we were kids, I lived in Sacramento when I was three and four. My sister, God rest her soul, a girl next door, and me dug a hole in the backyard and I sat in it. They covered me to my neck and went and got my Mom. She about had a cow."

"That's a cute story, Eli. Why did you say, 'God rest her soul?'"

"She's a preacher's wife and they change churches every so often so I don't know where she is but I was at a Nazarene church once and the pastor was telling the people that she died. Her doctor was out of town and his assistant gave her some medicine that caused blood clots in her lungs and it killed her. I hitched hiked to the memorial. There were over a thousand people there from all over. She was very well known."

"Oooh! That's so sad!" Jessie moaned. "Come here, Darling!" Eli went to the back of the cab and Jessie kissed him and hugged him long and tight. Eli kissed here and then she kissed him again.

"I hate to break this up but I have to take a leak. I just saw a rest stop sign."

They all did what they had to do, and bought some chip. "You seem tired, Jessie." said Eli. "Why don't you take a bunk when we get in to the truck?"

"Yeah! I am tired. I think I will."

Inside the cab, she fell asleep real fast. Eli and Chuck set, listening to Waylon Jennings until Eli fell asleep.

The snow storm came. Chuck struggled to see the road. A few miles outside (No indentation) Straton, CO., Chuck decided to stop. He soon saw a truck stop. Just then, the truck skidded on the ice — not enough to jackknife but enough to move Jessie and Eli around a bit.

Finally at the truck stop, Chuck found a parking spot not too far from the door. "I'm going to see if they have showers." he told Eli and Jessie.

"I need to buy a new shirt and a pair of trousers." Eli added.

"Not without me." Jessie said. "It's too spooky here alone. Man, look at that snow. It's really coming down."

"We're just outside of a small town called Stratton, about 150 miles from Denver. The weather just got too bad to drive. We're stranded for a while. Let's go in." said Chuck.

And they were for two nights and a day.

"The singer formally known as Prince was known as 'Skippy' as a kid"

"Just making conversation!"

Located 150 miles east of Denver along I-70, Stratton is mainly a farming and ranching community rich in pride and progress.

Stratton offers a unique richness to all who live there, protecting a down-to-earth quality of life.

The simple country lifestyle of Stratton begins just beyond the shoulders of 1. Among the rolling wheat and corn fields of Eastern Colorado lies the village *of Stratton. Stratton is in Kit Carson County. The population was 669 at the 2000 census. Stratton was named in honor of the gold miner and philanthropist Winfield Scott Stratton*

There are unlimited recreational pastimes in the community including swimming, tennis, golf, softball, and summer recreation programs for the kids.

Fishing, boating and skiing are less than an hour's drive from Stratton. The Stratton area is renowned throughout the state for its excellent scenery,

"This is info from 'Wikipedia, the free encyclopedia', whatever that is." said Eli. I got it off of my cell Internet.

Eli cleared his throat to read the Internet screen but Chuck cut in, "I've seen the Salt Lake temple many times. I think that it's ugly. In my opinion, the one in the Oakland hills in California is a lot prettier. At night, with the lights, you can see it for miles. It looks like it belongs in Heaven,"

"Well, anyways," continued Eli, "it says here that the Salt Lake Temple is the largest (of more than 130 around the world) and arguably the best-known temple of The Church of Jesus Christ of Latter-day Saints. It is the sixth temple built by the church overall, and the fourth operating temple built since the Mormon exodus from Nauvoo, Illinois.

'The Salt Lake Temple is the centerpiece of the 10 acre (40,000 m²) Temple Square in Salt Lake City, Utah. Although there are no public tours inside the temple (because it is considered sacred by the church and its members, a temple recommend is required), the temple grounds are open to the public and are a popular tourist attraction. Due to its location at LDS Church headquarters and its historical significance, it is patronized much by Latter-day Saints from many parts of the world.

The Salt Lake Temple is also the location of the weekly meetings of the First Presidency and the Quorum of the Twelve Apostles. As such, there are special meeting rooms in the Salt Lake Temple for these purposes, including the Holy of Holies, which are not present in other temples.'

"Should I read on or is this too long?" asked Eli.

"Sure, keep going" replied Jessie,

'The official name of the Salt Lake Temple is also unique. In the early 2000s, as the building of LDS temples accelerated dramatically, the Church announced a formal naming convention for all existing and future temples. For temples located in the United States and Canada, the name of the temple is generally the city or town in which the temple is located, followed by the name of the applicable state or province (with no comma). For temples outside of the U.S. and Canada, the name of the temple is generally the city name (as above) followed by the name of the country. However, for reasons on which the Church did not elaborate (possibly due to the historical significance and worldwide prominence of the temple), the Salt Lake Temple was granted an exception to the new rule and thus avoided being renamed the *Salt Lake City Utah Temple*.

Some think the Temple is intended to look like the Temple of Solomon at Jerusalem. It is oriented towards Jerusalem and the large basin known as Temple Square. The wall is a uniform fifteen feet high but varies in appearance because of the southwest slope of the site.

'The location of the Temple is literally in "The Tops of the Mountains", with several mountain peaks close by, in almost every direction, except to the northwest, where lies the Great Salt Lake. Very nearby, a shallow stream, City Creek, used as a baptismal font is mounted on the backs of twelve oxen as was the brazen sea in Solomon's Temple. However this is only conjecture. At east end of the building, the height of the center pinnacle is 210 feet, or 120 cubits, making this Temple 20 cubits taller than the Temple of Solomon. Splits and flows both to the west and to the south, flowing into the deeper Jordan River, which flows northward into the large Great Salt Lake. There is a wall around the 10 acre Temple site. The surrounding wall became the first permanent structure on what has become known as Temple Square. The wall is a uniform fifteen feet high but varies in appearance because of the southwest slope of the site.'

After the Temple 'tour' the trio went to a deli. A man who was about sixty was in a power wheelchair. All of a sudden, the chair took off and hit a table with two customers sitting there. It seemed as if the joystick got jammed. No one was hurt but the driver and the two customers at the table were startled. The other customers' sure took notice.

The deli was crowded so Eli asked two men if the three could sit at their table. They were two brothers named Colby & Toby. They were twins and roofers, in business for themselves.

"Roofing is terrible in the summer, in the heat — especially on metal roofs." said Toby.

"It sure is!" said Colby. "And on metal, you don't want any water on the roof. You could slip. You don't want to do that three stories up, if you know what I mean." Everybody eventually laughed.

While still at the deli, Chuck dropped his Philly Cheese Steak onto the floor and Jessie spilled her soda twice. Eli bought Chuck one more sandwich. Soda refills were free.

There's a lot not written about Jessie's and Eli's romance which was about to end soon.

Back in the truck, chuck took the wheel and mentioned that he had a Monopoly game. They had played Backgammon and Dominoes in the past few days. "I love Monopoly!" said Eli. "I haven't played it in years, since I was a kid, with my Mom. Want to play, sweetheart? Do we have time, Chuck?"

"Elko's about three-and-a-half, four hours. You have time."

"I play for blood! I play to kill! Let's go, darlin'!"

"I'm scared about seeing my Mom again, if I do see her."

"Darlin', I don't know what to say to you. I can't even empathize with you."

"Jessie, I wish that you'd go with me. I sure will miss you. I sure love you."

"We've been through this before — I can't. I need to be someplace and take care of things. I sure will miss you, too. I sure love you in so many ways."

It was dark when the semi pulled into an Elko truck stop. The hour wasn't late, just dark.

"I hope that we can get a shower." said Jessie.

"You can almost always get a shower at one of these places." from Chuck.

Near the door, Jessie stopped 'dead' near the building's front door. "That is a beautiful bike!" exclaimed an excited Jessie. Against a newspaper rack, a yellow

15-speed bicycle was locked with a 'U' lock through the frame. The front wheel, with another 'U' lock was attached to the rear wheel. "It's expensive—very expensive! I don't recognize the make."

Inside, Jessie was talking about the bike. "Excuse me! Are you talking about the yellow bike outside?" An Asian man, probably in his mid-twenties was sitting at the restraint counter. On the seat next to him were a small sleeping bag and some other gear. "I'm Jan, Jan Culpepper. That's my bike."

"I didn't see a brand name on it. What kind is it?" asked Jessie.

"My friend builds bikes. It was made for my measurements."

"Why do you know so much about bikes?" asked Eli.

"I used to do cross country century bike rides, a hundred miles in a day."

"A hundred miles in a day—you did that?"

"How do you think I got these legs?" Jessie smiled.

"We've never seen them. You've only been in pants."

Jan stood up, looking at Jessie. "Please sit down and join me." The three sat down at the lunch counter. "I'm heading to Frisco. I've never seen it. Its part pleasure trip and also, I need to return something to someone. I'm from Idaho, Ketchum."

"And you're riding your bike all that way in this cold?" asked Chuck.

"I'm enjoying it."

"I'm from Belleview, Idaho. I'm going home in the morning." added Eli. Jessie looked wounded.

The trio ordered dinner. Chuck, looking around, excused himself. Soon, the food came. Everybody else didn't talk, just ate. About twenty minutes later, chuck returned.

"I got on the Internet. There's a bus leaving for Ketchum around 9:00 a.m., in the morning." Chuck told Eli.

After dinner, Eli mentioned showers. Eli and chuck excused themselves while Jessie and Jan kept talking. When they returned, Jan had left, not to return. He had paid the entire bill. Eli handed Jessie a change of clothes and she left to shower. Around ten, they headed for the truck. For a long time, Jessie and Eli just said nothing and held each other. Finally, Eli broke the silence. I can afford to buy you a ticket. I'd wish you'd reconsider . . ."

"Please, don't! I can't!"

That night, Jessie and Eli both had a restless night for obvious reasons, also, Eli was scared about going home — would anybody be there. How would he be received?

The next morning, Eli gave Jessie a green plaid flannel shirt to remember him by. Jessie and Eli went into the coffee shop to take back some French toast and sausage for the three of them. Eli told Jessie, "Chuck won't take any gas money or any money for the trip. I left him some money under a pillow." "Jessie, I've been meaning to ask you, why do you wear an opal earring and a gold stud in the other ear?"

"I lost the partner earrings. Heck, when I was engaged, I lost the ring doing dishes."

Chuck didn't say anything about it but he was soon reaching for his breakfast.

After breakfast, Chuck drove to the Elko bus station. After a handshake and a hug from Chuck and a very long good-bye with Jessie. Chuck handed him his copy of 'Travel's With Charley. "I know that you were reading it. You need to finish it. I've read it twice."

Chuck then had an happy look on his face. "Eli, I wish that you could meet my wife." Chuck said. "Our wedding went without a hitch, like they don't on sitcoms."

After purchasing his ticket and a short wait, Eli boarded the bus. He opened the book and began reading. No one sat by him so he wasn't bothered the entire trip. He just read non-stop and didn't look up until the bus stopped in Ketchum, after stopping in Twin Falls. He may have slept some. Eli finished the paragraph, put the book into his duffle bag, stood up and gasped. "Jessie!" The lady, wearing a green plaid flannel shirt and just exiting the bus door, didn't turn around and Eli watched her from the window. Then, she turned around. It wasn't Jessie.

Eli sat down to collect himself and then exited the bus, walking toward the bus terminal. Two arms wrapped around his waist. He turned around — "Jessie!" He dropped his stuff and then hugged and kissed her hard and long. "How'd you get here? How'd you pay for this?"

"Chuck found the six twenties that you left under the pillow. He convinced me to come. You were reading when I got on and off. I wanted to surprise you. I was really hoping that I wouldn't have to go to the bathroom in the back but when I had too, you were asleep."

"What a minute. I left a hundred, five twenties."

"Well, he had six."

They picked up their bags, put their arms around each other, and went inside.

THE CHAR MS.

Jan had occasional fits of insanity. He was considered by himself, as well as others, a literary genius. People would often attribute the twenty-four year old boy's fits to the fact that he was considered a genius. That was the way a genius was supposed to be. Jan wrote about his Japanese heritage, Zen, and Tea Ceremonies. His last name is Culpepper . . . Jan Culpepper. Jan lived at the Hailey Hotel in Hailey, Idaho, since this Sunday morning because writers either live in Paris, in beach front homes, or in hotels. Indeed, Jan was a writer—a bad writer but, a writer all the same. Except for his writings, his pride was his custom built 15 speed bike. The yellow bike weighed only six pounds, or so he was told.

After he moved in but before he unpacked, Jan went downstairs to enjoy their Sunday champagne brunch, featuring prime rib and trout from the Valley. After drinking too much champagne, Jan went back to his room and fell asleep for the afternoon.

When he awoke, a new layer of snow was on the ground and on everything.

That evening, Jan, still unpacked, went to the desk for some paper to jot down an idea for a story. He opened the top drawer. "Oh my goodness!" he exclaimed. On personalized stationary, he found an eleven page manuscript. Jan went to the love seat and began reading it. After reading it, Jan read it again. "What a talent!" he thought. On the letterhead was the name Thomas Char and a San Francisco address.

Jan put the manuscript back on top of the desk, turned on the T.V. and watched it until he fell asleep. Waking up several times that night, Jan thought about the unfinished story. "What a talent!" he thought again.

Monday morning, Jan reread the manuscript. "What a talent!" he thought again. He looked at the address again—San Francisco. He thought that he had relatives in China Town even though he was Japanese—he didn't and doesn't. "I've never seen China Town or Frisco." He thought out loud (one of his genius things to do). "I could be there in just a couple of days on my bike. It's only two states away and I could return Mr. Thomas Char's valuable manuscript. I'll do it!" Jan had never ridden more than thirty-five or forty miles in one day except to Twin Falls, seventy miles away BUT, that was almost all downhill. After a two day rest, it took him two-and-a-half days to get back to his rented room near Ketchum, eight miles north from Hailey. Frisco is about seven hundred miles away but, he didn't think about that.

Jan started giggling, he was excited. He started planning and packing what he would take for the trip. It didn't take him long. Just two changes of clothes and his shave kit in his Panniers (saddlebags) and his sleeping bag and a one man tent. ♠ Three days later, he had wished that he had planned more carefully ♠ At 7 a.m., still dark in the mountains, Jan set out—not eating the breakfast fuel that he so dearly would need two hours down the road.

Hailey to Twin Falls is about 60 or 70 miles downhill. At a coffee shop in Twin, near the door, Jan locked his yellow 15-speed bicycle with a Kryptonite 'U' lock through the frame. The front wheel, with another 'U' lock was attached to the rear wheel to a bike rack. They were heavy—about five pounds each.

At the counter, Jan met Harlan. They talked about ten minutes. Harlan told Jan that he had just been fired and asked Jan if he could lend him enough money to pay for the cola. Jan said that he'd take care of it.

Hands in the parka pockets, Harlan left, just walking the streets, trying to kill some time. He needed some time to come up with an excuse to tell his Lady. As he walked, he heard a pay phone ring . . . so, he answered it.

"Hello . . . no this is a payphone . . . Harlan, what's your name? . . . Hi, Katie . . . I'm twenty . . ."

He laughed. "How come?" He laughed again. What do you look like, Kathy? (Pause) Katie, oh, I'm sorry. What do you look like, Katie? (Pause) Okay, what's your address? (Pause) Ten minutes, alright? Okay, bye,"

Harlan put his hands back into his pockets. Looking at the sidewalk, he continued to walk. He didn't see the girl walking towards him until she bumped into him, "Sorry!"

Back at the coffee shop, Jan finished his meal, paid and left. He decided to stay the night. It had been a longer ride then he had imagined. Jan found a motel.

Twin to Jackpot, NV is about 50 miles. Jackpot is a unique border town. As of this writing, there are three casinos, a grocery store, and lots and lots of trailers and mobile homes. I don't think that outside of the casinos there are any coffee shops. The forty-seven mile trip from Twin wasn't that hard because like before, it was all slightly downhill.

Jan pulled into Jackpot a little after lunchtime. He first went to a black jack table where he won around $44. His system was to bet the same whether he won or lost and to put his winnings into his shirt pocket so that he's walking away with something.

When he talks about his lunch, he says that it was a trip. He ordered a shrimp salad and iced tea. At one point, a man stood up on his chair and flapped his arms like a chicken, and then he sat down. Almost immediately, the people at his and the surrounding tables clapped and whistled. I guess whatever he did was very good.

A lady sat next to Jan. She was bad company. All she talked about was how at forty-three she looked twenty-five. That's what everybody told her, she said. Jan thought that she was around fifty. That's what he would have told her if she had asked.

In the middle of her sentence, he excused himself, left the counter, and walked out of the coffee shop. It might have been rude but it is a nice thing to be able to do that every once in a while. After a while, Jan returned and paid the check.

Each casino had entertainment during the day and night. For dinner, Jan ate three 50¢ shrimp cocktails. After dinner, Jan went into a lounge that advertised an illusionist, Jan Jhammer. His most amazing illusion in Jan Culpepper's opinion was at the end of the show when Jhammer lifted a cloth in front of him, over his head and instantly dropped it. He was gone. Almost immediately, he yelled 'Back Here!' from a balcony in the back of the room.

After the show, Jan Culpepper went to the coffee shop for one last shrimp cocktail and then to the crap tables for a roll of the dice. There at a table was the illusionist—and his twin. Both were bald and in their white tuxes. Jan soon rode about a mile into the desert by some trees and by the full moonlight, he set up his camp. A dog started barking at him. Jan was afraid of him but soon the dog left,

The morning sun woke him up. The winter morning was very cold. He had lots of French Roast coffee and a banana for breakfast before setting out for Elko. Jackpot to Elko is 130 miles. For some reason, he thought that it was only 50 miles. The odd thing is that he did it with his lack of training.

Twin to Elko is 230 miles. Jan did it in a little over 3 days and he was hungry and tired. It was dusk when he pulled into a truck stop for dinner.

It was dark when a semi with its three passengers, Jessie, Eli, and Chuck pulled into an Elko truck stop. The hour wasn't late, just dark.

"I hope that we can get a shower." said Jessie.

"You can almost always get a shower at one of these places." from Chuck.

Near the door, Jessie stopped 'dead' near the building's front door. "That is a beautiful bike!" exclaimed an excited Jessie. Against a newspaper rack, a yellow 15-speed bicycle was locked with a 'U' lock through the frame. The front wheel, with another 'U' lock was attached to the rear wheel. "It's expensive — very expensive! I don't recognize the make."

Inside, Jessie was talking about the bike. Jan was sitting at the counter. "Excuse me! Are you talking about the yellow bike outside?" I'm Jan, Jan Culpepper. That's my bike."

"I didn't see a brand name on it. What kind is it?" asked Jessie.

"My friend builds bikes. It was made for my measurements."

"Why do you know so much about bikes?" asked Eli to Jessie.

"I used to do cross country century bike rides, a hundred miles in a day."

"A hundred miles in a day — you did that?"

"How do you think I got these legs?" Jessie smiled.

"We've never seen them. You've only been in pants."

Jan stood up, looking at Jessie. "Please sit down and join me." The three sat down at the lunch counter. "I'm heading to Frisco. I've never seen it. Its part pleasure trip and also, I need to return something to someone. I'm from Idaho, Ketchum."

"And you're riding your bike all that way in this cold?" asked Chuck.

"I'm enjoying it."

"I'm from Belleview, Idaho. I'm going home in the morning." added Eli. Jessie looked wounded.

The trio ordered dinner. Chuck, looking around, excused himself. Soon, the food came. Everybody else didn't talk, just ate. About twenty minutes later, chuck returned.

"I got on the Internet. There's a bus leaving for Ketchum around 9:00 a.m., tomorrow." Chuck told Eli.

After dinner, Eli mentioned showers. Eli and Chuck excused themselves while Jessie and Jan kept talking. When they returned, Jan had left, not to return. He had paid the entire bill. Eli handed Jessie a change of clothes from the truck and she left to shower.

The next morning, Jan packed his dome tent and his other belonging onto the bike. Today was his fourth day and he was hurting from the pedaling and from sleeping on the ground but because of his enthusiasm, he really didn't notice. Jan rode to a diner for breakfast. As always, Jan locked his bicycle with the 'U' lock through the frame. The front wheel, with another 'U' lock was attached to the rear wheel to a bike rack.

He ordered a big breakfast of oatmeal, buckwheat pancakes, ham, apple juice, a banana for later and coffee. A couple of hours later, he would regret the coffee. This was before six that morning.

A couple of hours later, he did regret the coffee. Down the road, he saw a big sign of lights reading 'Eats' and Jan rode up to the diner. Jan locked his bicycle to a bike rack. The diner was small and crowded. There were no seats at the counter. Jan had to sit at a table around the corner, in the back. After leaving a book at the table to save his seat, he went to the bathroom. Returning, he ordered a chocolate malt and then read for a while. Besides stopping because of the coffee, his custom was to stop every two hours to stretch and read and refuel.

After paying his bill and one last trip to the bathroom, Jan left. Outside, his bike saddle was gone, stolen.

About an hour later, Chuck saw Jan pushing his bike along the road. He stopped. "What happened?"

"Someone stole my saddle while I was eating back a ways. I couldn't see the window from where I was sitting. Battle Mountain can't be too far from here. I'll buy a new one when I get there."

"Try about forty miles. I'll put your rig in the trailer and give you a ride. It's the least I can do for you since you bought us all dinner last night."

"Thanks!" Jan got into the cab. When Chuck got into the cab, Jan asked, "Where is everyone? I was hoping to see that girl again." He meant Jessie.

"There on their way to Ketchum, Idaho. Anyhow, Jessie is taken, very much so."

In Battle Mountain, they found a bike shop. On the next block across the street was a Wal-Mart. "Listen, Jan, I'll park at the Wal-Mart and get some coffee and you get to the bicycle store. If you want, I have to pick up a load in Reno and I'm heading to Salinas, California so you welcome to tag along. The mountains are steep and I'm sure there's snow up there. It will be dreadfully cold."

"Sure! Thanks! I'll see if I can get a carton to pack my bike in, Thanks!"

Jan got a new seat & a bike carton and packed his bike the way it's supposed to be packed'. "I found a better seat than the one that came with the bike, for cheaper."

"That's great! I'm headed to the Steinbeck Museum in Salinas so I'll drop you off in Frisco. It's just a little out of the way."

Jan took off his parka in the warm cab. "Chuck, I didn't sleep very good last night on the ground. Would you mind if I took a little nap? I'm a little stiff, too. Yesterday I rode over one-hundred and twenty miles to get here. I sure didn't plan very well!" Jan said smiling.

"Sure! Sleep all you want. Want some aspirin?"

Jan slept all of the way to San Francisco.

"Hey, Dude, wake up and we'll get some dinner. We're in Frisco. Let's find that guy's address first."

The panniers were in the cab. Jan took out the Ms. and read Chuck the address and put it into his GPS.

"What are you doing?"

"I'm typing that address into my GPS and getting directions and mileage and you can leave here after a good night's sleep, okay?"

"Okay and what's a GPS?"

"It's a street finder that gives directions and mileage. I can also print it out for you. On second thought, let's eat first."

After dinner, Chuck began driving towards the Char's address.

"Whoops! I just saw a weight limit sign. The truck can't get into this neighborhood. Besides, there may not be any place to park here. Let's find a big parking lot somewhere and then you give me the address again in the morning."

The next morning, in the strip mall where Chuck parked his truck, there was a bagel café.

Jan stood outside a large house in San Francisco to return the lost manuscript to Thomas Char. He put the crossbar of the bike over his shoulder and then started up towards the front door, tripping on some steps. Nobody heard him from inside. Jan brushed himself off and walked up to the door. He rang the bell and then knocked.

Mrs. Char opened the door and stared at the boy for a few seconds. She was dressed in a silk flowered bathrobe and slippers.

"Howdy, I'm Jan Culpepper. This is the house of Thomas Char?"

"Yes . . . yes, it is." She was a little doubtful of the young stranger.

"Great! I just got into town from Idaho and I didn't expect to find this house so easy. Is he in, please?"

"Yes, he is . . . Jan?" Jan nodded, 'Yes!' Look, dear, it's only seven-thirty and Mr. Char is still sleeping. Perhaps you'd better come back later."

"Well, I just got into town and I don't have a place to stay. I'm going back home as soon as I finish my business. I just want to give Mr. Char a manuscript that he lost. It's probably important to him, don't you think?"

"I'll tell you what, Jan, just leave the papers with me and I'll see that Mr. Char gets them."

"I'm a writer, too, Mrs. Char, and I know how important this would be to me. I really want to get this directly to me so I'd better do the same for him. I'll wait outside here until he wakes, if you don't mind."

"Never mind, dear, it is cold outside. I'll get him for you. Won't you come in?" Mrs. Char led him into the living room. "Have a seat, dear, and I'll get Mr. Char for you." She left the room and went upstairs.

Jan looked around the beautiful, old Victorian room. The whole house, inside and out was Victorian. The furniture was antique. This house predated the earthquake of 1908. It was one of the few homes left standing in this area. This particular room, the living room was the room that the Char fortune legend was based around. It seems that several years before the earthquake, Emile Char, Thomas Char's father killed a man and robbed him of 1.4 million dollars. Emile was caught and executed and the whereabouts of the money went with him. It is said that he put the money into the living room wall and then sealed and re-plastered the wall.

In 1963 Mr. Thomas Char's daughter Linda, then seven years old, said that she could find the money. It was thought that she was psychic. The girl, Mr. and Mrs. Char, and several other people went into the living room. Everybody was quiet while Linda walked around the room, chanting her mantra. She seemed to be attracted to one part of the wall in particular. Then, Linda put her hand on the wall.

"This is where the money is, right under my hand."

Immediately, they started cutting a square into the wall. When the hole was cut, Mr. Char looked in. The wall was empty.

"Can I help you, young man?" Jan was facing a very distinguished old man dressed in a man's satin dressing gown and slippers. "It's seven-thirty in the morning!"

"Yes sir! I know how important it is for you to get this manuscript back. I found it in a drawer of my desk in the hotel where I live. I'm a writer, myself." Jan handed the manuscript to Mr. Char.

Mr. Char couldn't believe this. "You came all this way to return *this*? I wrote this and left it in Idaho." And then, he thought to himself, "I must have accidentally left it in a desk drawer."

"Yes sir!"

Mr. Char put his arm around Jan's shoulder and led him towards the door. "Well, thank-you very much, son; I appreciate it very much." He started walking towards Jan, subtly leading him out to the porch and then he shut the door. "What a dumb kid! What a way to spend a Saturday morning, getting up for this." he thought.

Mr. Char walked upstairs to go back to bed. Mrs. Char was sitting up in bed, waiting to hear what had just happened. Mr. Char snickered. "What a dumb kid. He found an unfinished story that I thought that I had thrown away. I thought what I had written was terrible. I must have left it in a desk drawer where we were staying last week. He comes all the way from Idaho, seven hundred miles to return it. Jeez, what a stupid kid!"

Mrs. Char smiled. "I think it was nice, kind of sweet.' You don't see people that concerned every day."

"Thank goodness for that! Anyways, I gave him five dollars for his trouble. Let's get back to sleep."

THE LAST RETURN

(A Tribute To My Sister Sherri From Memories)

Mom and Sherri and I landed at the Honolulu International Airport from San Francisco Oct 31st, '62. We saw the five popular tourist spots of the time, Diamond Head, the Kodak Hula Show, Waikiki, Pearl Harbor, and Paradise Park, a beautiful botanical park of plants, trees, birds, and butterflies of the Islands. I honestly don't remember the beaches. I'm not a beach person. It's hard for me to walk in sand. This is the first time that I remember eating Spam. A popular Hawaiian breakfast is still fried spam and eggs, hash browns, toast, and coffee. On our third day there, we each threw coins from the deck of a boat and then we threw our Leis to the divers, meaning that we'd returnsomeday. The next day, it was off to Tokyo, Hong Kong, and then on to West Pakistan where my Dad had left three months prior

Sherri & Russ' honeymoon 3/72:

I don't have any stories about Sherri's return trip to Hawaii with Russ. It was on their honeymoon and I wasn't invited to go. I continued on the Male Chorale tour.

Beth and my honeymoon '82:

As time went by, we each did return years later with our spouses. On our honeymoon, Beth and I entered our beautiful Waikiki hotel room to two single beds. We had to slide push our beds together since no other rooms were available.

That night, we took a walk, looking for a 'local' restaurant for dinner (plate lunch), getting lost after walking over two miles, and taking a Pedi cab back to the hotel. That night the hotel band played Willie Nelson's 'Angel Flying Too Close To The Ground' in our honor as we danced.

That week, we rented a car and saw the five popular tourist spots of the time, Diamond Head, the Kodak Hula Show, Waikiki Beach, Pearl Harbor, and Paradise Park, a beautiful botanical park of plants, trees, birds, and butterflies of the Islands plus Hanama Bay and The Polynesian Cultural Center, a North Beach park with several small villages, each one representing the major South Pacific Islands and the popular 'memorable' Hawaiian breakfasts of fried spam and eggs, hash browns, toast, and coffee. Our other memorable meal was on a night cruise overlooking the Waikiki and Honolulu lights after a wonderful sunset. We could see as far as the lights of Waielai.

There's a small town over there that isn't much of a town—just a few shop, a grocery store/post office, a restaurant, a shaved ice store and a gas station. In one store, the walls were lined with bags and bags of rock salt. 'You must sell a lot of salt!', I said. 'No, I don't sell much salt', he said. 'Now, the fella that sold me this salt, he sells lots of salt.'

Kailua, HI '88: Russ was called to the Kailua Nazarene Church. A few weeks later, Mom and Dad flew to Hawaii to help Sherri and Russ set up their home. A few days later, a very heavy rain caused a canal to over flow, flooding part of the town and the patronage. Placing things on to shelves, Sherri sighed and crying, said, 'I want to go home.' My Dad sighed and said, 'You are home.' The seven of them (Sherri, Russ, Jenny, Todd, Gabe, Grandpa Gabe, and Grandma Vi) began wading down the street to a couple's house that they knew in college, not knowing that the alley way, twenty feet behind their house (It was dark.) was bone dry. The three kids had to ride piggy-back.

Shortly after returning home, Mom and Dad decided to move to Hawaii to join them. I wanted to return to Ketchum, ID but I was talked out of it by my Sherri and Mom. That June, on my nephew Gabe's birthday, Mom, Dad, & I landed at Honolulu International Airport (Date & Gabe's?) birthday. Our luggage was temporally lost so we wore T-shirts and shorts loaned from Sherri and Russ for (Days). Mine had a large rubber eye on my chest—great for church. It seems that

I wore that shirt for two or three days. They probably had other T-shirts available and I know that Hawaii is terribly expensive but . . .

Sherri was big on spectator sports. She attended almost all of the kid's games, T-ball, soccer, softball and basketball. She also kept the score of the weekly Friday night church softball games. She wanted me to learn how to fill out the sheets (keeping track of runs, bases, etc.) but it was hopeless. Now, I'm as smart as the next person but I get to distracted watching the game.

I gave Gabe a coffee mug when he was still in grade school. More than once, Sherri, Gabe, and I had coffee together. His was always cold with mostly milk and a lot of sugar.

One day, when Gabe was in 10th grade, he and I decided that I would call Castle High School and get him out of class for a while. We both thought that it was funny until Sherri scolded us severely. Actually, we both reminisce and still laugh about it.

Three of my jobs in my seven years in Hawaii were in Honolulu. I often had breakfast before work in China Town, a popular Hawaiian breakfast of fried spam eggs, hash browns, toast, and coffee for $2.95 plus tax. Sometimes I would meet Sherri for lunch near her work, even when work was scarce for me. After a seven year home in Kailua, Russ was called to a church in Lancaster, CA.

Big Bear: In Nov of '05 I had a stroke. The next few months I lived in a rehab hospital and then, as an outpatient, doing physical theropy. My only lasting side effects were (and are) a numb and tingling right hand and lower leg and foot, sometimes so bad that I can't sleep. I progressed from a wheelchair — to a walker — to a cane. I only mention this because I just wanted to mention it — no other reason.

My cousin and his wife invited my Mom, Dad and me to their cabin near Big Bear Lake for the weekend of Aug 25, '06 a few days after Mom and Dad returned from a two week trip. They flew to Lima Peru, to the ancient Inca cities of Cusco and Machu Picchu then flew to Buenos Aires, Argentina to see Iguacu Falls at the corners of Argentina and. Brazil. The watery cascade stretches for 2.5 miles ad plunging 269 feet into the Iguaçu River. They are absolutely gorgeous. Numerous rocky and wooded islands on the edge of the escarpment over which the Iguaçu River plunges divide the falls into some 275 separate waterfalls or cataracts.

During those two weeks I called Sherri often. It was my habit to call Mom and Dad every morning and then to say 'Goodnight!' I asked my sister if I could take the bus over for a visit. She made excuses and finally told me that she had minor surgery and didn't tell Mom and Dad so that she wouldn't ruin their trip. We both knew that they would be worrying about her. Sherri slept downstairs in the family room because it was easier than climbing the stairs to their bedroom. She said that it was easier to roll off of the couch onto the floor and then lift herself using the coffee table or couch. I had to laugh and said, 'Because of my stroke, I do that almost every day from my recliner, using the chair arm and my cane'. She laughed over the phone, I think. After my folks returned home, they called Sherri. She told them about her operation. Dad called me to tell me but I told him that I already knew.

The night before the lake trip, I told my folks that I was having second thoughts of going. I thought that the mountain may be too rough on me and my cane—plus, my leg was really bothering me. Around 1 a.m., I woke up sick and vomiting. I decided not to go. About an hour later, I was able to sleep again. The next morning I awoke early, feeling fine, except the tingling in my hand and leg. I decided to go.

At Bear Lake, we sat outdoors talking and telling family stories. Over one dinner, I enjoyed salmon with pesto sauce that Barbara fixed. I fell in love with Jasmine tea and we ate lunch at my cousin's favorite local eatery which I didn't enjoy that much. Now, as I'm writing this, I'm thinking about Hawaiian breakfasts of fried spam and eggs, hash browns, toast, and coffee.

Sunday after church, on our way back to Bakersfield, we took the long way home through Palmdale, Sherri and Russ' home. Mom and Dad both knocked and then let ourselves in with their key.

"I guess Sherri's feeling better." one of them said but I was skeptical. The blanket was folded on the family room couch. I really feared that something was wrong but my folks were optimistic. Almost immediately, the church youth director walked in without knocking. She told us that a church friend was sitting with Sherri that morning and then suddenly felt led to text Brian, a doctor friend at the church. They doctor told our friend to drive Sherri to emergency immediately. She also said that Sherri was in real good spirits.

Ken Martinez

I've been to my sister's church many times. At the hospital's emergency waiting room, almost as many people were there to wish my sister well as at the Sunday morning service. Although not her doctor, Dr. Brian was scurrying from the waiting room to Sherri's cubicle, to the waiting room — telling each of us that my sister was in good spirits and was joking with the doctor, CNA's and the nurse. About a half an hour later, Brian told the four of us, Sherri's family that we had better go into her cubicle. Two staff members were beating her chest and using the defibrillator paddles for what seemed for more than an hour until they gave up. I was there when Sherri died. I had never seen anybody die before.

We stayed at Russ' that week. By Monday mid-morning, all of the kids — Jen, Dave and their children Josh, Jordan, and Dustin; Todd, Stephanie, and their young daughter Blin; and Gabe, Aiko with their kids, Addy, and Kai Kai were there from Chandler, AZ, Hawaii, and Hanford, CA. On Monday Mom, Dad, and I went back to Bakersfield to get clean clothes. I went to Jack In The Box, my home away from home and told the staff the news. For the last ten years except Sundays, I have ridden my bicycle (a collapsible cane in my backpack) there for iced tea and to read for two or three hours.

Within a few days later, Russ' parents, two brothers, sister and their families were there. I live alone and I was uncomfortable with the crowd and all of the friends dropping by but I knew that I didn't want to be home alone. We tried to do the necessary things to keep from crying, trying to keep busy to try to ease the hurt. We played with Jen, Todd, and Gabe's toddlers and Joshua, age seven. I read much more than usual which is a lot.

Russ' younger brother, Karl gave a wonderful talk about the 60's hippie and there generation's music. I was in high school in the S.F. Bay Area during that time but it was still fun to hear.

Sherri's memorial was held that following Sunday. Eight-hundred plus attended. I saw friends that I hadn't seen in years and others that I didn't know but that remembered me. Sherri was and is very well loved. I wrote this poem on the night before the first memorial. This letter and my poem were read by my Mom at the memorial and Dad at the second memorial in Kailua, HI. Because of my stroke, I couldn't climb the stairs to the podium to read what I had written.

My Mom is known as G.G. — Great Grandma. She wrote and read the following at both of Sherri's Memorials.

A Letter From G.G.

This beautiful lady you all know had a very small beginning. She was born 6 weeks premature, and because we had had to leave our baby Ken in the hospital just 14 months earlier, the Doctor did not have the heart to make us go home alone the second time. Sherri weighed only 4 lbs. 13 ounces and wanted to sleep all the time. We tried everything including tickling her feet to keep her awake long enough to drink a little milk.

But that did not last for long. By the time she was 3 she was given the name "tiny mite". She was so full of energy and curiosity and was the little mother to her brother and any child she met. When she was 3 she attended Vacation Bible School and was made to stand in the corner. We asked the teacher why, and the answer was "Because she would not say her memory verse."

On Sundays both children would "disappear" after church, and we soon learned to just go on home and someone would call and tell us they had the Sherri and Ken and would bring them home after we had had time to rest or visit with our dinner guests. One of the ladies (who was a teenager then) is here today — Verniece Wilcox.

Sherri was very excited about starting to Kindergarten. The first day we saw the little neighbor boy there crying. Being the helpful, caring little Sherri, she told him "Don't worry, if you have to go to the bathroom you come and tell me and I will show you where to go."

I learned quickly that I needed to be very careful what I said to her about school. The first week I explained to her that on Saturday and Sunday she would not go to school, and because Monday was a holiday she would not go on Monday either. The next day the teacher was explaining the schedule to the children, and evidently forgetting that Monday was Labor Day told the class that they would stay home Saturday and Sunday and come back to school on Monday. Sherri raised her hand and said "My Daddy said Monday is a Holiday and we don't have to come to school."

When I questioned her about what she did at school she told me "We play games, we go for walks and we take naps." I said "We send you to school to learn how to read and do math, not to play and take walks." The next day she asked her teacher if they could do some hard work she could take home to her Daddy. That night she brought home a sheet she had colored and at the bottom was a row of 1 +1 = 2, 2+2=4.

When Sherri was 10, Gabe took a job in Pakistan. It was three months before the kids and I could go. At that time 18 shots were required for travel abroad. Sherri dreaded those shots terribly, but after each one she would say to me "That's one shot closer to the time I can see my Daddy."

Since going to Pakistan was to fulfill a dream of traveling around the world, the kids and I took a month to get from San Francisco to Pakistan. I loved pearls and Gabe told me when we got to Japan he wanted me to buy myself some pearls because they were a good price there. But it seemed to me that I was spending so much money on hotels, meals, sightseeing trips, souvenirs, etc. etc. so I decided I didn't need the pearls and didn't buy any. On the plane from Japan to Hong Kong, I decided I had made a mistake and should have bought some pearls and I must have voiced my feelings out loud to the kids. When we got to Hong Kong I hired a guide to take us around to places. Without me knowing it Sherri arranged for him to buy me a pearl and have it put on a chain for me. I had given the children money to spend on the trip, and she used her money to buy me a pearl. She kept it secret until Christmas and then gave it to me. This is my most cherished piece of jewelry, and more precious now than ever.

Sherri made friends in Pakistan very quickly. Soon there were 3-4 boys waiting outside our door every morning to walk her to school and carry her books—a whole block away.

Sherri loved to swim and spent so much time at the swimming pool she soon looked with her tan and her curly hair like a little "Pakistani girl".

Sherri had a beautiful voice and loved music. Don Farrand said in an email "Her beautiful voice certainly qualifies her for a place in the Heavenly Chorus. Her first performance was at age 3 at a Mother-Daughter Luncheon when she stood beside me on the piano bench and sang "Hot Diggitty Dog Diggity Boom What you do to me. She got a standing ovation. When she was 7 she had learned to harmonize and I formed a little girls trio of Sherry, Becky (Flory) Mickelson and Cynthia Martin. All I had to do was play a song and Sherri and Becky would harmonize with Cynthia.

Sherri entered Dad's Club and PTA talent competitions, continuing through High School including Nor Cal District Teen Talent Competition and always came in first place. In Junior High she was singing in the Choir's Christmas program. As soon as the concert was over a man came up to us and said he had watched Sherri sing and said to himself "If that girl has a voice to go with that personality she would make a great contribution to our group." About that time she sang a solo and he was convinced they needed her. He was the Director of the Bay Area teen group comprised of choir, dance and orchestra called Youth of America. Sherri became the youngest teen in the group and performed many solos in outstanding concerts including one hosted by Art Linkletter, one with Andy Williams and one with Bob Hope. They also sang at the Montreal World's Fair.

Sherri was part of the Nor Cal Net team—a group of teens who sang in churches throughout the District. A young man from San Jose named Russ Martin was also on the team. A special attraction soon developed between them and soon he was coming to our house every Friday night to play on the Oakland Church Softball Team. To meet the requirements of attending Oakland First Church he stayed with us until Sunday. We were not sure if it was his love for Sherri or his love for Softball. We soon found out when he asked for Sherri's hand in marriage. A big thing in his favor was that he had many of the same wonderful qualities as Sherri's Dad had.

The wedding took place at Oakland First Church on March 23, 1972. Some of the participants are here today. It was beautiful! At the end of the ceremony Russ and Sherri started singing together "We've only just begun, white lace and promises, a kiss for luck and we're on our way. We've only just begun." At which time the 50-voice Pasadena College Male Chorale who was seated around the auditorium stood and continued the song as the bride and groom kissed and then marched down the aisle. We are still trying to pay for the food those 50 young men ate at the reception.

Our appreciation for Russ has grown over the years and we love him like he is our own son. We have no words to express the joy Sherri and Russ have brought into our lives with the births of Jennifer, Todd and Gabe, and now our six beautiful great grandchildren.

Our lives have been greatly enriched and joy has abounded because of the life of our beautiful, loving, caring daughter. We love you so much Sherri and will see you soon in Heaven.

Sherri's brother, Ken Martinez has written a little poem in tribute to his sister which I will read to you now. "Ken said, 'I wanted to write a short story for the memorial because there is so much to say but, I wouldn't have had the time to read it so, I wrote this poem.'"

My Sister
by Ken Martinez

A light,
   affecting so many lives
passes through a prism.
The colors are bright
   and pretty and vivid.
Some can see the reds…
    others, indigo
    and others, the greens…
    my favorite.
Others can see combinations
    of colors
and others, the whole spectrum.
      This is my Sister

            The mist became a double rainbow…
              something rare and beautiful.
           One day, a dark fog came over me
           and I couldn't see the light
             or the colors
             but they were still there.
           In Heaven,
             the light is brighter
             and the colors, more vivid…
           the reds…
             indigo…
             and the greens…
             my favorite.
           And all can see the whole spectrum…
             still affecting so many lives.
             This is my Sister

Wednesday Sept 14th, we landed at Hawaii International Airport around midnight California time. Mom and Dad stayed with Mits and Louise Uchibori, good friends of ours from the church. Russ stayed at Gabe & Aiko's close to the beach on the other side of the island and I stayed with Rev. Bob Miller, the pastor his wife. (Years ago I was counselor @ church camp. Danny, a punk kid. Now, very mature and dignified.)

During our four day stay, I ate breakfast with ol' friends at Sizzler and then, on other days, my regular breakfast, a Breakfast Jack with tomato and an iced tea at Jack In The Box, alone, reading, waiting for Memorial II.

Other things that we (the family) did were, going to the Pali Lookout overlooking Kailua and the ocean, stopping at a lookout overlooking Kaneohe Bay, and a barbeque (This is not a typo.) at a beautiful beach near Gabe and Aiko's house on the NW side of Oahu.

Memorial II was more intimate than the first Memorial but with the same format. Many friends spoke and G.G.'s letter and my poem were read.

The next morning, a beautiful calm and bright morning, the family drove to a dock on Kaneohe Bay. Sherri, a few years before she died, requested to have her ashes spread in the bay. Russ had chartered a boat for this care, her last return to the island. During the thirty minute boat ride out to sea, Russ recited scripture and a short sermonette. The whole trip was very passionate and still.

When the boat reposed, Russ opened the carved round Koa wood box and spread her ashes over Kaneohe Bay—her last return. We tossed leis, roses, and petals into the Bay. Some cried and others were to numb to cry.

The skipper started the motor, ringing a memorial bell for Sherri.

This short story is, to some degree, a bit of closure for me.

THREE 'n' A HALF DAYS
(The Memphis Airport Story)

Four days earlier:

His name is Augie. He was never called Augie Doggie or Daddy, like the TV cartoons in the late 50's and/or the early 60's. He sat in the gate's waiting room at the Bakersfield, Ca. airport in his airport loaned wheelchair. He usually uses the collapsible cane he carries in his backpack but here, there was a lot of walking. At the end of his trip, he would use it when he turned in his wheelchair. I can only speculate why he was sitting at the airline's gate because he didn't have a scheduled flight. Elevator music was playing Elvis' 'Blue Hawaii.'

"Hi!" he said to the man sitting next to him . . . no response. He smiled at the lady sitting on the other side. She smiled.

"Hi!" she said. "I'm Misty." She looked like a 'Misty', young, tall, bleached blond hair, great figure, lots of make-up.

"Where you headed?" Augie asked.

"Phoenix! I have a brother-in-law, ex-brother-in-law — he's my fourth, through marriage (she giggled). He lives there with his bimbo wife, his second. I'm his first wife.

"Where are you going?" she asked. (There's a short pause!) "His name was, well, is Roger."

Misty began looking at her magazine but she kept talking. "We were married after three month, for three months." She giggled again. "He said I talked too much but, I think that I'm an interesting woman. I'm a part time beautician and waitress and you need to know a lot of interesting topics . . ."

Augie, to be polite, excused himself, got into the wheelchair and then rode to another chair in a group of high schoolers. A group of girls stood up and yelled, "**Give me a P**!"

"**P**!"

"**Give me an R**!"

"**R**!"

"**Give me an O**!"

"**O**!"

"**Give me a T**!"

"**T**!"

"**Give me an E**!"

"**E**!"

"**Give me a G**!"

"**G**!"

"**Give me an E**!"

"What's that spell?"

"**PROTEGE!**"

"What's that spell?"

Augie was getting into the spirit—he was standing and yelling but he had no idea what "**PROTEGE!**" meant.

"What's that spell?"

"**PROTEGE!**" Everyone cheered.

After about fifteen or twenty minutes, he realized that he had left his backpack by the chair next to Misty.

She was still talking. ". . . my puppy, a poodle, a toy—a live toy poodle was digging under the couch and the cushion." She paused.

"I'm going to Memphis. I have a forty minute lay-over in Phoenix. I'm on the buddy plan so I might not get on this flight." (Oh! That's why he was sitting at the Airline gate.), said Augie, finally. He was relieved.

The ceiling speaker was playing the tail end of Charlie Rich's, 'Behind Closed Doors, and announced his flight. Misty seemed startled but then jumped up. "Bye, Honey! Let's get together sometime. I'm in the book."

Augie had to wait about thirty minutes to see if there was a seat available. His name was called just before a man sat in the chair next to him. "Hi! I'm Vern. Where are you headed for?"

"To catch my plane." Augie was the second to board, after a man on stand-by.

When Augie got on board, the stewardess took and folded the wheelchair and put his gym bag in the overhead compartment. He kept his backpack. His seat was an aisle seat. Misty was sitting in the seat behind his. "Hi, Baby! Sorry that this seat is taken." Augie just smiled. He had no intention on sitting next to her. Her seat stayed empty the entire trip.

A "Fat Man" tried to squeeze past Augie to his window seat. "Hold on, sir and I'll move out of your way." said Augie. He was ignored. The "Fat Man", who looked like William Conrad — narrator of The Rocky & Bullwinkle Show and star of the TV 80's/90's show 'Jake & The "Fat Man"' — kept trying to squeeze through.

"Sir, hold on, please and I'll move for you!" said Augie, very annoyed. He 'accidently' kicked the man while getting up from his seat. The man finally got to his seat and said a snobbish, 'Thank-you!'.

"This is not going to be a fun trip!" thought Augie. The "'Fat Man'" placed his arm onto most of the arm rest. As hard as Augie tried, he couldn't put his arm up on the right arm rest.

"Say, Sweetie, up there . . ." Augie pretended to sleep. She kept talking nonsense until the "Fat Man" interrupted her rudely. "Lady, he's sleeping. Shut up, will you?!"

After the 'Fasten Seatbelt' was turned off, a male steward walked by, giving out drinks, honey roasted peanuts, and headphones. Augie took the headphones, plugged them in and, chose a Celine Dion channel. "Is that you, Baby?" called out Misty, meaning Augie.

The Fat Man looked over and putting his index finger to his lips, made a 'Sh-h-h-h-h' sound, softly. "He's asleep, Darlin' and I'm trying to read." said the Bullwinkle guy. (So now, we'll call him 'The Bullwinkle Guy'. Augie wasn't upset anymore.)

She kept talking. "Oh! What're you reading? Who's the writer? Is the book any good?" The Bullwinkle guy didn't answer. He winked at Augie. Augie whispered a 'Thank-you!'

Finally, the hour long flight was over.

Phoenix to Memphis — A 3 hr flight with Augie and the captain, too, Misty and the Bullwinkle guy and the rest here on flight 223.

Augie was the last to get off of the plane in Phoenix. He was wheeled toward the waiting room, stopping at an airport convenience store for a Cheese Danish — he had missed breakfast. At the gate, his 'driver' was stopped. His prior flight from Bakersfield was late and his name was called to board.

After he left the wheelchair, Augie looked around the plane for Misty and the Bullwinkle guy. Neither one was on the plane. Misty said that she was getting off in Phoenix but, you never know.

At his seat, Augie took out his Nook, an electronic reader, and put his backpack under his window seat. A lady was arguing to a man across the aisle from him. She moved to the seat next to him.

"Hi! I'm sorry about that." she said to him.

"I'm Augie." She never introduced herself to him but instead, began to read her book.

Augie turned on his Nook, set it to 'airplane mode' and clicked opened a story, Hans Christian Andersen's 'The Princess and the Pea' and began reading.

After the 'Fasten Seatbelt' was turned off, a stewardess walked by, giving out honey roasted peanuts, and headphones. Augie declined the in-flight movie. He took the headphones, plugged them in and chose a 60's rock channel. About twenty minutes later, she came by with a liquor cart. "I'd like a double dry martini." requested the mystery lady.

I'm sorry Miss, but we don't have vermouth. How would you like a screwdriver?"

"No vermouth! You're kidding! Well then, I'll take that — a double." The stewardess handed her a plastic cup of ice and a carton of orange juice and two one ounce bottles of vodka. That came to eight dollars a drink. She had six in the two hours drinks were served. Twice, she fell asleep on Augie's shoulder. He shrugged and she would wake up. The first time, she said "Hi! I'm Annie. I'm on Spring break. I teach mycology, the study of mushrooms at (she burped the name) University. I'm here for Spring break and for March Madness." Annie kept drinking.

The rest of the flight was quiet, with alcohol in the air. Augie read during the entire trip except to eat the small brunch.

After the flight, Augie went to the front door of the airport but that was as far as they would let him go. He whipped out his collapsible cane and forty minutes later, he boarded the bus heading to the Motel 6 where he had a reservation. The bus trip was an hour and twenty minutes.

This story isn't about Memphis but it is about the Memphis Airport. After a nice three day vacation, Augie is back at the waiting room.

Day 1 6:50 a.m.: This is Augie's sightseeing adventure told to a poor, sleepy passenger at the airport waiting room:

"First, I went to the Memphis Brooks Museum of Art, the oldest art museum in the state. Downtown Memphis is the Peabody Place Museum, with the largest collection of 19th century Chinese art in the nation and there, (a sigh and a smile!) there are the world famous ducks.

"At Graceland I saw two of Presley's private airplanes, and his automobile and motorcycle collection. The guide says that he remembers seeing Elvis riding his bike up and down the driveway. He couldn't go out because of all of the people at the gate. That's sad, huh? Elvis and his mother and father, are buried in a garden there, too.

"I visited Beale Street, where B.B. King used to sing and play his guitar years ago. He occasionally still plays there at his club. There's street musicians playing music, and the club's musicians play the blues around the clock. I heard that Beale Street is the most visited tourist attraction in the state, and considered to be the second busiest street in the southern United States, except for Bourbon Street in New Orleans.

"The Center for Southern Folklore has southern artists and musicians doing performances and exhibitions. They have thousands of photographs, recordings, and films. It's pretty impressive."

The passenger quit listening. The story was getting boring.

Augie didn't notice so he continued, pulling out a brochure. "My favorite, The Pyramid Arena, the official name of the Pyramid is 'The Great American Pyramid' on the Mississippi. It's321 feet tall, or 32 stories—the third largest pyramid in the world behind the Great Pyramid of Giza, 456 ft. and Khafre's Pyramid 448 ft. The Memphis, Tennessee pyramid is a 60 percent replica of the Great Pyramid of Cheops in Egypt. A 20 foot statue of Ramses the Great stands guard at the Pyramid's entrance. The arena seats 21,142. The interior of the Pyramid has more than half a million square feet of usable space. The exterior is clad in stainless steel. It's hosted many concerts, by famous artists of many different genres and in 2002, the arena hosted a concert, commemorating the 25th anniversary to be, of Elvis Presley's death. The Pyramid Arena has not been regularly used as a sports venue since 2004. Bob Seger & the Silver Bullet Band performed, what is reputed the last concert ever in the Pyramid, on February 3rd . . ." The passenger changed seats across the room so, Augie quit reading. (Knowing Augie like I do, after all, he's one of my characters, he's not that insensitive to ramble on—just tired.)

Augie also visited the Gibson Guitar Factory & Showcase a guitar manufacturing plant where visitors can learn how the famous guitars are meticulously crafted, and listen to live showcases of local and world-renowned talent. Famous Gibson musicians include B. B. King, Les Paul, Chuck Berry, Carl Perkins, and Scotty Moore. Also, the Memphis Zoo and, The River Walk, a 2112:1 scale working model showing 1000 mi. of the Lower Mississippi River, from Cairo, Illinois to New Orleans, Louisiana and the Gulf of Mexico.

The Walk stretches roughly 0.5 mi, allowing visitors to walk in the water and see models of cities and bridges along the way. The Gulf of Mexico section was once used as a waterpark named Bud Boogie Beach. The museum offers 18 galleries of regional history and features an indoor life-size replica of a civil war era riverboat.

Victorian Village is a historic district of Memphis featuring a series of fine Victorian-era mansions, some of which are open to the public as museums.

Augie also rode the Mud Island monorail.

His plane was called so he waited the thirty or so minutes till he would hear his name to board but—they didn't call his or anybody's name after the 'space available' passengers were boarded. The next two planes would leave at 12:20 p.m. and at 5 p.m.

The man at the desk told him that there was a bagel shop down the hall (about a half a block on the street). "You'll have to have them take the wheelchair so that someone else can use it. When you're through, just tell someone to call to get you another chair."

"Thanks much!"

5:45 p.m. Augie had to leave the gate by 8 pm, when the last plane arrived. The lady at the gate let him call the motel from her phone. The motel was full. "Sir, this week is March Madness. It's Spring Break at many schools and the NCAA championship college basketball is going on. Good luck, sir." He hung up.

"Augie, I'll get a chair to take you to the front doors. In the morning, just tell them that you need someone to bring you back here." Augie thanked her.

The man that pushed Augie left him at the ticket counter at Augie's request. "Great! Now, what can I do?" Augie thought to himself. Augie took out his cane and went into an airport convenience store to get a Payday candy bar. He found a circular pillow, opened at one end, to put around a person's neck when resting or sleeping. The pillow wasn't really that comfortable but it served its purpose.

After he paid, he went down the hall a ways to Arby's for a roast beef sandwich. He read there for a couple of hours and talked to people. Finally, he decided to find a seat to sleep against. He had to be awake by 5:30 a.m. in time to let the people at the ticket counter that he was here. The seats had arm rests so he couldn't stretch out so, he put the pillow around his neck The seats had arm rests so he couldn't stretch out so, he put the pillow around his neck, put his head against the wall and with much effort, he fell asleep, waking up about each hour—all of the airport lights were on, inside and out. and with much effort, he fell asleep, waking up about each hour—all of the airport lights were on, inside and out. The Mesa Airlines ticket counter was not more than fifty or sixty feet from him.

Day two at the Memphis Airport: Neither the ticket counter nor Arby's was opened yet. Augie sat and waited after he went to the restroom to, you know, and to wash up and change his shirt. When he came out, the ticket counter was opened. After checking in and getting his wheelchair, he was taken to the gate again. "Good morning, Augie. I'm Fred." The ticket agent greeted him after looking at his ticket. "You ready to try again?"

"I remember you from yesterday morning. Yeah, but not really, Fred."

"The plane will be boarding in about two hours. The plane will be late. You have time to get some breakfast at the beagle shop."

"Yeah! Thanks! I will. Want anything?"

"No, I'm set but, thanks anyways. I'll get you a chair."

"That's all right. I feel good enough to walk with my cane for that short distance."

By the time he got back from having coffee, it was slow walking plus rest stops, the plane was boarding. Augie sat and waited for his call. Again, it didn't come. He was frustrated again. He headed for Arby's as soon as he got a wheelchair.

"Hey! Did you miss your flight yesterday?" Augie looked at a pilot or a co-pilot smiling. "I noticed you being wheeled by staff yesterday from the Mesa ticket line."

"I'm on a buddy pass and because of March Madness, I'm still here."

"I'm Cliff. Come on and I'll buy you breakfast."

"Well . . . yeah, O.K.! I'm Augie."

The restaurant was nice, nicer than some up town. Jazz piano music, I think it was Bill Evans, was playing. "Come on, Augie, here's my regular table."

"You come here a lot, huh?"

"Yep, four days a week and then I'm off for three. I fly interstate and then back this afternoon. Today, it's a three hour flight, just like Gilligan's three hour tour but I'll be back in a few hours." Cliff laughed. Augie just smiled. He didn't get it. "Well, let's eat. The rib-eye and eggs is sensational. So is the eggs benedicts, made with Canadian bacon instead of lunch meat ham."

"I love eggs benedict. I'll have that. I'm from Bakersfield. Lived in Wasco my first three years."

Cliff looked up a little bit. "It takes me an hour to get to work and back each way. I guess that's about average for most people but I catch a plane to work — not too smart on the companies part when the have to pay to get me here. I wonder . . ." The waitress stepped up.

"We'll both have the eggs benedict, coffee, and tomato juice with lemon. Do you want tomato juice." he asked Augie. Augie nodded. "Oh! And tobasco, please."

The two talked and ate and drank. Augie mentioned a book titled, 'Everything You've Wanted to Know about Flying but Were Afraid to Ask'. "I learned about the pre-flight stuff and all of the sounds when a plane takes off."

"I met him when I was in flight school. I just blanked out of his name." Cliff seemed embarrassed.

After what seemed a short time but it was a long time, Cliff looked at the clock on the wall. "Oh man! I'm supposed to sign in, in ten minutes ago. I have to go. I'll call and get you a chair. I'm the gate across the hall from yours." He stood up and walked away.

"Great! He stiffed me for the meal!" Augie was thinking.

Cliff turned round and took out a money clip. "Would you pay? The line at the register is a little long. And please, leave a tip." He handed Augie a folded bill.

Augie took another cup of coffee and read his daily devotional from his Nook and then he walked up to the register. He unfolded the bill and saw a $50. "Wow!"

Augie returned to the gate, took out his Nook, and read until his flight was called. He put the Nook back into the case until his name wasn't called again and then he took it out again. He was reading an old book titled 'Lincoln and Alcohol.' Lincoln was a lifelong teetotaler.

Around 10 a.m., Augie called for a wheelchair and went downstairs to Arby's.

11:50 p.m. Augie returned to the gate, took out his Nook, and read until his flight was called at 12:20. He put the Nook back into its case until his name wasn't called again and then he took it out again.

With four pages to go, Augie heard on a TV from the lady sitting next to him, 'The senator, insisting that he wasn't intoxicated, couldn't explain his nudity.' She was watching a 70's rerun of 'WKRP' in Cincinnati on her laptop. Augie chuckled. She chuckled and moved the laptop towards him. He put away his Nook and together they watched an hour-and-a-half worth of reruns—a 'WKRP' and an "Alias Smith and Jones', a Butch & Sundance spoof.

"Hi! I'm Carol." She finally said.

"Hi! I'm Augie. Where're you headed?"

"Cabo San Lucas. How about you?"

"I'm going to Bakersfield, California. My nephew's a pilot for this airline. He got me on free with a buddy pass and I'm having a heck of a time getting home. I've been here for two days so far. The planes are pretty full. I had no trouble getting here."

"Oh, dear, I'm on stand-by!"

"I wouldn't worry. Except for one person, everyone one stand-by has gotten on."

"You know, I'm old enough to remember these when they weren't reruns."

The two talked and watched an episode of McHale's Navy until their flight was called and then, total silence between the two of them.

5:45 p.m.: A loud yell and some profanity from a woman. "Miss, the ticket agent over booked—either the airlines or your travel agent. We have one seat available on stand-by. You're welcome have that seat."

Still **Very** angry, "My husband and I booked this trip five weeks ago. We had to get a connecting flight but our luggage and are two kids are on the direct flight to Cabo San Lucas. Kaitlin is seven and Kyle is only five." This was a very strange thing for her to do with her children.

"Well, Ma'am . . ." The agent looked at her clipboard. "Mrs. Kyle, you or your husband can fly stand-by this evening and the other can fly in the morning. I'll guarantee a morning flight, free of charge."

"What time in the morning?"

"You need to be here by 6 a.m. You can't sleep here. The gate will be closed after our last flight gets in."

"We'll both take that morning flight, free of charge." This was another very strange thing for her to do with her children, if they had children. I hope that they had cell phones if they did.

The Kyles left and Carol got the last seat to Cabo San Lucas, Baja California Sur. Augie stayed a while longer just to see if he got a seat or not. He didn't so, again he headed back downstairs via a wheelchair, bought some iced tea at Arby's and read until he was able to get some sleep.

Day three @ the Memphis Airport: The same thing—neither the ticket counter nor Arby's was opened yet. Augie sat and waited after he went to the restroom to, well—you know, and to wash up. When he came out, the ticket counter was opened. After checking in and getting his wheelchair, he was taken to the gate again. "Good morning, Augie. Are you ready to try again?"

"Good morning, Fred."

Downstairs, he just sat for a while. He's frustrated. "Hey there, Augie!" It was Cliff. "I thought you probably got on a plane yesterday since you didn't show for dinner."

"I got talking with a passenger and lost track of the time. Actually, I forgot about you."

"Was she cute?"

"Actually, yes, she was."

"Then, I'm not offended. Let's get some eggs benedicts."

"I'm hungry for a breakfast burrito and, I'm buying!"

"We'll see!" They ordered and ate and talked and then Cliff said 'good-bye' leaving the check on the table. Augie had another cup of coffee, left a $3 tip, picked up the ticket and walked to the cashier. He handed him the check. "The gentleman that you were sitting with paid. He said that he was in a big hurry and that you'd bring up the ticket, which he forgot to pick it up off the table."

"That son-of-a-gun—dog gone that guy!"

The day went exactly the same as yesterdays. Augie was in a frustrated mood. Cliff had cheered him up a little but not much. He, not being rude, avoided sitting or talking with anyone. Several times a day, he called his folks to tell them what was happened. Each call, they offered to get some money to him but he always declined. Augie took out his cell phone but then put it back into his pocket. "Someday, I'll enjoy talking about these days. It would make for a good story. Someone should write this down." he thought.

That evening, Cliff looked into the gate waiting room and walked up to Augie. "Hey there, Augie!" Augie was startled. "If you're free, let's get some dinner."

"I'm really not hungry. I'm upset but guess that I need to eat something. I haven't eaten since breakfast."

"Arby's and you buy."

"Okay!" Cliff got a wheelchair and pushed Augie downstairs to Arby's. Along the way, they talked.

"I don't follow college basketball. I didn't know about March Madness. I should have planned better."

They got in line and ordered each a roast beef sandwich with 'Horsey' sauce and iced tea. Augie paid.

They each asked God blessing on the meal. "What did you do all day?" asked Augie.

"I flew, worked. What did you do?"

"Pretty much read and slept. I wasn't in a real good mood to talk to anyone." But, for the next hour they did talk.

"My wife wants to meet you. You're coming over for coconut cream pie and a good night's sleep." Cliff said. "I need to be back here at 5 a.m. so no arguments, okay? So, let's go."

"You're flying me to your home?"

"I have a condo here in town by the pyramid. It's a nice convenience that the company lets me use sometimes. My wife flew in with me this morning to shop, you know, the big city."

"It must be nice!" Augie smiled. "Okay! I'll be right back. I have to go to the bathroom. Would you take the chair back?" Augie asked, whipping out his collapsible cane from his backpack.

At Cliff's condo, a beautiful woman, taller than Cliff met them at the door. The sound of the garage door opener was a dead giveaway that they were there. "I'm Cliff's wife, Viv."

"This is Augie. He's a new resident of the airport. I told him about your famous coconut cream pie."

"Cliff, you two have a seat in the den. I'll get the pie."

During pie and coffee, the three did a lot of small talk. Augie held up his plate. "My Mom makes a great coconut cream pie . . ."

"Thank-you, Augie." taking it as a complement.

". . . a lot better than this stuff!" Augie thought to himself.

"I have to apologize. When Cliff called that he was bringing you home, I only had twenty minutes to prepare something. This is from the freezer and a little microwaved."

"Well now, Viv, I'm enjoying it." He looked over at Cliff who looked away. "It's going to be nice to sleep in a bed again instead of a chair against a wall with a doughnut pillow around my neck."

Day four @ the Memphis Airport: The same thing—neither the ticket counter nor Arby's was opened yet. Augie sat and waited, not having go to the restroom to, you know, and to wash up and change his shirt. When Cliff returned with a wheelchair, the ticket counter was opened. After checking in, he and Cliff had coffee and sticky buns and then, he was taken to the gate again. "Good morning, Augie. It was a lady and not Fred." The ticket agent greeted him after looking at his ticket. "I'm Sylvia. I've heard quite a bit about you. Are you ready to try it again?"

Again, Augie couldn't get a seat. When Augie went to the desk to get another wheelchair, Sylvia said, "Augie, we're going to bump you up to employee status so now we're sure that you'll get on the next flight."

Augie smiled. "What's my title? Do I get a raise?" They both laughed.

At 9:30 a.m., Cliff came up to Augie, who was reading, and again, startled him. "How 'bout having one last eggs benedicts, Augie?"

"You're on, Cliffy. It may well be."

Back at the gate, Sylvia smiled with a 'thumbs up'. Augie had a queer feeling and looked at each passenger's face—no Missy but there was the Bullwinkle guy. Augie started unzipping his Nook case when a guy, looking familiar, sat next to Augie. "You look familiar." he said.

"You do, too!" said Augie. "Are you a musician?" He was looking at the guy's guitar case.

"I play bass."

"Maybe I saw you at one of the blues clubs?"

"It's possible. I'm Jaco . . . uh, I'm Nick. Jaco is a nickname that I'm trying to lose. Augie didn't ask. (See, 'An Untitled Memphis Tale'.) "I'm going to start a gospel blues band like Glen Keiser or Darrell Mansfield when I get home. I'm really into blues and fusion jazz."

From somewhere, there was a loud crash. Augie and Nicked looked up along with many people. Someone had dropped their metal luggage. As Augie watched the guy pick them up, he looked around. The Bullwinkle guy was gone. "I'm Augie, headed for California, Bakersfield."

"I have a friend that lives on Norris in Bakersfield named Jim Carman. I'm headed for Oakland. I live in Alameda."

Augie didn't know Jim Carman. Augie and Nick reminisced about their stays in Memphis and Augie's past three days at the airport.

"Augie, would you mind if I prayed that you get on this flight?"

"I'd appreciate that. I believe in prayer, I'm a Christian,"

About noon, the flight was called. Nick boarded. This time, Augie boarded. He and Sylvia smiled with a 'thumbs up'. At the plane's door, Augie stood up and holding onto the first two rows of seats, sat down.

The man sitting next to Augie introduced himself as Cliff. "I'm so glad to finally get on. (He burped—he was drunk, or pretty close to it.) I was bumped off this morning so that a couple could get on. I got reimbursed plus $50 but I sat in the waiting room all morning, for hours, waiting." Augie had his Nook out and, pretending to read, ignored the guy.

Augie contemplated about telling his story but then the man asked, "Did you wait long to get on?" Augie kept reading and had the Nook earphones in his ears. He wasn't listening to anything. After a while and after the man had a few drinks, Augie took out the plane's music earphones (he switched to them), put his Nook into its case and decided to tell Cliff his three-and-a-half adventure but Cliff squeezed past Augie. He went into the bathroom. After a lengthy time, Augie noticed that the new Cliff hadn't come back. He put the headphones back on, took out his Nook and began reading again. After about twenty minutes, (the Nook has a clock) a lady asked if she could sit in the seat next to Augie. "A man came out of the bathroom when I went in. When I came out, he was asleep (Augie started to chuckle) in my seat and we can't wake him up. He's alive but dead drunk."

Augie burst out laughing. "I'm sorry! He was sitting next to me. He got on drunk and kept on drinking. You're much better off sitting here than the person sitting next to Cliff, the drunk."

"Thank-you, kindly! I'm Annie."

"You'll need to sit by the window. I'm handicapped and it's easier if I just stay put. I'm Augie."

"You're sweet, Augie."

The time went by quickly. She was from Fremont, California. They exchanged addresses and phone numbers.

After the plane had landed, after the seatbelt sign went off, after they were told that they could turn on their cell phones, the captain made an announcement that there would be a slight delay but he didn't say why.

Augie's cell phone rang the song 'Zip-a-dee-do-da'. "Hello, this is Augie."

"Well, you finally got out of Memphis, huh?" It was Augie's nephew, Todd, the pilot.

"Where are you, Todd?"

"What side of the plane are you on?"

"My left."

"Look out the window. I'm looking right at you. See that yellow building?"

Augie looked. "No, I can't. Do you know what the delay is?"

"There are two planes blocking the runway, each refusing to budge. Welcome back and I'll see you when you get off."

Augie told the passengers close by, "That was my nephew Toad, I mean Todd. Toad was his nickname when he was little." He told the passengers what Todd had told him. In less than thirty minutes, the plane started moving and then, people began departing the plane. He moved to the door, holding onto the sides of the walls, just like he had done twice before and then, he came face-to-face with Todd.

"Never saw you in your uniform before."

"We need to move." Todd said, helping Augie into the chair and down the terminal halls, lined with shops, even a Ping golf shop and a Barnes & Noble's book store. They zipped down a row of shops, turned the corner, and went passed two more shops. "Because of the delay, you have next to no time to meet your plane." Todd said as they rounded another corner, passing more shops, until they arrived at the planes gate waiting room then, Augie's heart stopped. The Bullwinkle guy was standing in line. "Oh, great!" Augie thought out loud. Then, he saw Misty. "Oh, double great!" Augie thought out loud again. They were sitting towards the back when Augie boarded. His seat was in the front row, sitting next to a Navaho with a 'pirate's' patch over his right eye, named Del and across the aisle from a man watching 'The Bob Newhart Show' on his laptop. The man with the laptop looked like the psychologist, Bob Hartley's Mr. Peterson. (I doubt that Augie had ever heard of the 'Bob Newhart Show', let alone, Mr. Peterson. I used to love that show when it first aired. I still watch reruns of it and of 'Newhart' on Hulu.com but, hey, this isn't about me. This is Augie's story.)

The steward told the Peterson guy that he would have to turn the Internet off until the plane was in the air — after the seat belt sign was off.

"Hi! I'm Augie." said Augie.

"I'm Del."

"What nationality are you."

Del looked at Augie, surprised and then snickered. "I'm Navaho, why?"

"You look like you're part Hawaiian. I lived in Hawaii."

"What part? My sister lives on Oahu, Pearl City, I think."

"I lived on the other side, Kailua. You might not know this but the Army used Navaho as a code in World War two. It was never broken because no one knew the language."

"No foolin'!" Augie was starting on the wrong foot. "My Dad and my Uncles were in W-W-Two, and an Aunt."

Augie looked at Del sheepishly. "Then, I guess you know that."

"Hey, Augie, don't be too eager to impress with your knowledge. You need to relax a little."

271

"I'm sorry! Where are you headed when we land?"

"Springwood, to see my cousin."

"Can you mean, Springwood Court on Norris Avenue?"

"I guess I could,"

"Is he real tall, hair down past the middle of his back with an eagle's feather in it?

"That's him!"

"I live there! I know the guy. My parents live in the Rosedale side of town." Augie was excited. "He's a painter and does maintenance for the apartments. I talk to him all the time. Let's exchange phone numbers and get together." They did! "How long are you going to be here? This is the second time that I met someone today from my street."

Del was looking for a job and didn't know how long he would stay. For the remaining minutes of the hour flight, they talked; Del did most of it, surprisingly.

"Do you work? asked Del.

"I've been in a few bands, too—mostly rock. I played keyboards in a 50's / 60's cover band. I was four, thirty-four years. My Mom taught, still does, piano. One day after a beginning student left, I went to the piano and figured out one of the songs he was playing. My Mom thought, 'My, I have to start Del on piano lessons. That didn't last long. I hated lessons but my Mom had the wisdom not to force them on me. That's the only reason I stuck with it. One time after I was at a Victor Borge concert, I went home and figured out how to play 'Happy Birthday', Beethoven style with 'Moonlight Sonata'. I play by ear, too. I used to play in a 50's/60's cover band called Crusin'. I play a mean Jerry Lee Lewis. We did three sets, classic Rock & Roll, Beach Boys, and Elvis, not Costello." This really tickled Augie but not Del—but Del smiled.

"I was a cook or a chef, depending on the restaurant. To me, they're the same thing but don't tell a chef that. I've cooked but I've never chefed!" answered Augie. "I'm also a writer, poetry and articles. "I'm working on my autobiography, sort of."

Augie's collapsible cane slipped out of his backpack and startled Del. "What is that?"

"My cane—I had a stroke about eight years ago."

"What do you mean, 'working on my autobiography, sort?' Augie"

"I was born with a birth defect called, spina-bifida."

"My niece has it. She's three and she wasn't supposed to live past twelve weeks. You're pretty old."

"I'm fifty-five. I wasn't supposed to live past six weeks. I was told that in my severity, I'm the oldest living person with spina-bifida. Anyways, I've lived an extraordinary life. I've been around the world two-and-a-half times; I have an IQ of 156 and two master degrees, etc. etc. When I try writing my life, I feel like that I'm bragging or boring. I'm writing about me using other characters. My working title right now is, 'The Life Of Me!' — a play on words on the book 'The Life Of Pi!' This trip may end up as a chapter."

"I've read that book, twice. Was this trip that exciting?"

Soon, the plane landed. Again, Augie would be last to get off so, he just sat and waited. As Del walked off, he stopped and turned to Augie, "You're okay! A little excited but, you're okay. I'll see you."

Augie's parents picked him up forty minutes late. They stopped at Denny's for dinner and hot fudge sundaes.

THE IMPORTANCE OF BEING WISCONSON

Once upon a time, a long, long time ago in the decade of our Lord, the 2000's, in a far off land in the Maricopa Valley of Arizona, lived an almost old man of fifty-eight named Kenny Lee (his last name isn't important), of Spanish, Irish, Belgium, Swedish stock. He was soon to receive the self-appointed title of 'The Gaelic Bard. (Bard is Gaelic for 'Poet'.). (See my story, 'The Tale Of The Gaelic Bard'.)

In high school, Kenny Lee was 5'7⅓". Since high school, forty years earlier, he lost 1 inches. This was caused by all of his spinal and leg bone surgeries that he had thru the years.

Because of his handicap, (I don't like the word 'Disabled'. If you disable something like a car battery, it doesn't work — *useless*. A handicap is a hardship.) Kenny Lee needed considerable help in many things, especially after his stroke a few years back. After the stroke, Kenny Lee decided that he had a new normal. What was once normal would never be normal again. His seventy-seven Mom and his eighty year old Dad, as active and nimble as they were, did what he could but it became harder and harder for him to do this. Soon, talk began from his family to have Kenny Lee move into an assistant living facility. Kenny Lee battled this idea for months but then he realized this was for the best. He moved into an assistant living home. Bathing and dressing himself were becoming harder and harder for him.

Greenfields

In June of twenty ten, Kenny Lee moved into an assisted living facility called Greenfields in Mesa, AZ. One thing that he didn't like was that all of the assisted living facilities in Arizona kept all Medicare monies, except $101.10 a month, for room and board. About two weeks later, he met Danté on a group bus ride to Wal-Mart. Danté, his first name, became Kenny Lee's best friend. They both rode power scooters but could also walk with a walker as well as a cane. Danté was sixty-eight years old but looked fifty. One Saturday day, Kenny Lee was riding down the hall and saw Danté sitting on his couch in his studio apartment. "So, this is your place in the country." said Kenny Lee.

"Yep! Come on in." The Barclays golf tournament was on TV.

Kenny Lee rode in. "I used to play golf. I really got my money's worth, too. I'd hit the ball from one side of the fairway to the other, playing and walking further than my partners. I wasn't a very straight hitter." from Kenny Lee, laughing even though it was an old joke, I think.

"Would you look at that!" Danté was really animated. "On a par three from the tee, the ball hit the pin, hit back onto the green about three feet from the hole and then rolled back into the hole for a hole-in-one. He probably used a wedge."

Danté continued. "I was a manager of a golf course so I played a lot. I guess that I was good. My handicap was four when I had to give up playing." He told Kenny Lee that he was Latin, just like his name. He also told Kenny Lee, "Ali-ghieri Dante was considered one of the great poets of all time. He wrote 'The Divine Comedy', important for his graphic description of the medieval version of Hell known as Dante's Inferno.' Kenny Lee knew this. He also owned a copy of the book. Danté continued. 'Dante was actually his nickname; his full name was Durante.' Kenny Lee did not know this.

"Did you ever get a hole in one?" asked Kenny Lee.

"I did twice. I remember it like it was today. On a par four, downhill and a pretty good wind at my back, I hit the ball using my Dad's fifty-five year old driver. I hit the ball into the lake next to the green but, it skipped like a pebble onto the green and into the cup. My second one, a par three, I hit the flag pole and the ball landed about four feet from the hole, on a slope. My ball stopped but then, my ball started rolling back and into the hole, just like I just saw on TV. Did you ever have one?" he asked Kenny Lee.

"Yeah, I hit the ball about six inches from the hole. My friend then hit his shot and his ball hit mine and mine went into the hole."

"Where did his ball end up?"

"Not far. We were at a miniature golf course."

Dante's giggled. "One time, I hit my first shot into the deep rough on a steep hill near the green. I had a ticklish second shot over a mound, over a bunker, next to the green and it went in. I used a 60° wedge.

"Man, you sure lucked out—three times. I was good, well, as good as I could get, with a seven wood. Are you a reader, Danté?

"Yes, I am but when my son put me here, I lost a lot of my things and my books."

"I love to read, too, all types of genre. I had to donate many of my books to the public library. Now when I want to read one of my books, I have to check it out". Kenny Lee smirked. "I had over four hundred volumes and now I have about fifty. What do you read?"

"Westerns mostly. I like Louis L'Amour best and, uh, what's his name? Oh, what a fool I . . . Zane Grey, that's it, Zane Grey. Who's your favorite author?"

"I have several—Steinbeck, Hemmingway, Upton Sinclair, and Saroyan. *The Human Comedy* is one of my favorite novels. I enjoy reading Edward Albee's plays. I also love reading *To Kill A Mockingbird* and *East Of Eden*. Steinbeck is my favorite author. I own all of his books except one, 'The Sea Of Cortez. I found it on eBay once for $1500."

"Ouch!"

"I didn't buy it. Couldn't afford it. I checked it out from the library. Tell me about some of the residents, would you, Danté?"

"Well, if you go out to the patio to smoke, don't give out cigarettes. They'll take advantage of you, especially Gail but she's really a nice lady—a nascence but, a nice lady. She has Alzheimer's. She left here for three months for the hospital. She seemed fine but when she got back her, she had really gone downhill. She will have almost a full pack of cigarettes but she'll ask you for one or she may pick through the ash tray to find a butt big enough to light and then she'll puff on it like mad, not inhaling the smoke. She talks in sevens, especially seventy-seven."

"That's easy. I don't smoke cigarettes, never have. At high school parties, when the kids went out to dance, they'd hand me their lit cigarettes 'cause they knew that I wouldn't smoke it. I'm a writer and writers stereotyping, smoke pipes. I've enjoyed a good cigar a time or two."

Danté's cell phone began ringing. He looked at it. "I have to catch this call. I'll see you later."

Kenny Lee met Gail the next morning in the patio where the smokers and others went to get outside to visit. She was a sweetheart and a minor bother and wheelchair bound; a manual chair. She used her feet to push the chair instead of using the wheels. Sometimes she rode backwards but whichever she did, she could ride fast. Kenny Lee called Gail 'cutie pie' and she blushed. Now he does it all of the time.

Gail told Kenny Lee that she used to teach sophomore high school English. She told him that she didn't smoke but that she enjoyed a good cigar, especially the Cuban cigars that she would buy in Tijuana. Kenny Lee smiled and then, she smiled and then she took a partial smoked cigarette from the ash tray and lit it. She kept puffing it without inhaling. I saw an opened pack, nearly full in her purse. Finishing her cigarette, she wheeled herself back inside and then, back outside. About every twenty minutes, day after day, she'd go through her same smoking ritual.

Gail came back to Kenny Lee's table "What did you do?" Gail asked while searching through the large ashtray.

"I just sat here. You shouldn't do that. You may end up back in the hospital. Suppose the person that smoked that had TB?"

Julie, the self-proclaimed leader of the residents but only had four people in her 'élite' group at her table overheard our conversation. She wheeled over to Gail. "Dear," she said while reaching inside Gail's purse. "You have a whole pack minus four cigarettes." Julie handed the pack to Gail.

"That's two sevens plus two cigarettes. Thank-you."

"Now, don't forget."

"I won't."

Julie looked at Kenny Lee and in the same volume voice said "She will, too." Julie smiled.

One day, Kenny Lee, not knowing her sense of humor, told Gail that Abe Lincoln being shot and killed is a myth. He said that Lincoln is one hundred and forty-seven years old now and that he immigrated to Monrovia, Libya. Kenny Lee didn't for a minute think that Gail would believe the story. It took eight or ten people and about two or three months before she was convinced that the myth was just in fun that backfired. He felt bad but not guilty about the prank. He apologizing to her and her response was always, "Mathew 17:21-23 says in verse 21 'Then Peter came to Jesus and asked, "Lord, how many times shall I forgive my brother or sister who sins against me—up to seven times?"

"²² Jesus answered, "I tell you, not seven times, but seventy-seven times.

"²³ Therefore, the kingdom of heaven is like a king who wanted to settle accounts with his servants."

"That's right!" said Kenny Lee. "The Jews thought that a man was to forgive another three times, but not the fourth. Peter more than doubled this, and asked whether forgiveness was to be used to so great a level."

Kenny Lee continued. "The Bible goes on saying 'I say not to you, until seven times, but, until seventy times seven' "The meaning is, that we are not to limit our forgiveness to any fixed number. You've already apologized."

That same evening at dinner, Kenny Lee met a new person—new to him. His name was Ricky. He had just returned from a month's stay at the hospital. By coincidence, Ricky was a golfer, too and was a manager and part owner of a golf course.

"My son in Ohio, I'm from Ohio, put me here. I like it here but I'm not going to tell him that. Well, I have money, lots of it in the bank. I want to move into a condo and hire someone to come in and take care of me but he won't let me. It was stupid of me to give him total power of attorney over me but I didn't know he'd do what he's doing. He bleeding me dry. Denise the administrator here, that's right, you've met her when you moved in, but I should talk to her to see if she can do anything."

"How long have you lived here, Ricky?"

"About six years, I think."

Gale sat at our table. "Do you have a cigarette?" she asked.

Ricky looked into her purse. "Gale, you have some right here."

She looked into her purse. "Oh, yeah, I do. In certain numerological systems based on the English alphabet, the number 77 is associated with Jesus Christ. CHRIST is, hand me that napkin so I can write this out for you. Thanks!' taking the napkin. "C = 3, H = 8, R = 18, I = 9, S = 19, T = 20, which added together, it equals 77.

"The atomic number of iridium is 77, used in spark plugs.

"Conspiracy theorists often claim that the statistically certainty random appearance of the number 77 in large events such as the terrorist attacks we've had hints of white supremacists or Moslem or Zionist or Christian-based secret societies' like, Flight 77 crashing into the Pentagon on September 11, or the wicked July 7ᵗʰ

2005 London bombings, also known as 7/7." During the 'London Bombings . . .' she rode away.

A month later, in the patio, Danté announced to Kenny Lee that he was moving in with his brother. He said that it was real hard to tell Kenny Lee the news. Kenny Lee was better friends with Ricky so it didn't affect him as much as it did Danté. Being kind and thoughtful, Kenny Lee hugged Danté. "Hey, Man, I'm going to miss you."

"Yeah, me too. We had some good times." he said as he went inside the building.

Gale came out of the building and someone gave her a short (the rest of a cigarette) As she madly puffed on her short she started to talk. "The year 77 . . ." She stopped to put the butt out and to light another cigarette and then began talking again. "The year 77, LXXVII AD was a common year starting on Wednesday in the Julian calendar. Can you name the seven dwarfs, Kenny?"

Kenny Lee looked puzzled. The two sentences didn't belong together as one thought. "Yeah, I can The seven dwarfs are Bashful, Doc, Dopey Grumpy, Happy, Sleepy, and Sneezy."

Gail looked hurt. He thought maybe he should have said 'No' to her. Later in the day Kenny Lee told Ricky about this.

"Yeah, you should've said 'no'. She prides herself on the numbers 7 and 77. Next year when she turns seventy-eight, she'll do the same thing with the number 78."

The next morning there was a new caregiver named Sharon, 4'11" (perfect for Kenny Lee's 5'5" and something frame but she would never agree to go dancing with him. He was in a power scooter.), about fifty, and very pretty. There was no ring on her left ring finger. He went up to Sharon and introduced himself to her.

She smiled and put her hand oon Kenny Lee's arm. "Hi, I'm Sharon. You're on my shower list. What time would you like to take it?" She was very professional and Kenny Lee was very polite. In the coming weeks, they became very good friends. Her son was nineteen; his birthday was eleven days before Kenny Lee's and her live-in boyfriend, Karl was kitchen manager at an assisted living facility in Mesa called Copper Heights.

One day, Kenny Lee's Dad dropped by unexpectedly. Sharon was at the front desk talking to Lena the receptionist. Kenny Lee was waiting on a nearby couch to ask Lena for directions to the library.

"Hi, Ken."

"Hi, Dad. What brings you by?"

"I had to go to the Mesa (Nazarene) church to get some things for the senior retreat."

"Dad, this is Sharon. Sharon, my Dad."

"You have a really sweet son . . ." Sharon led Kenny Lee's Dad to the couch." The couch was only big enough for two people.

"Dad, I'll meet you in my apartment, ok?"

"Oh, well ok."

Kenny Lee's Dad took him to Denny's for lunch. Much of the talk was about Greenfields and Kenny Lee." After lunch, his Dad dropped him at the door. Kenny Lee's Mom gave piano lessons and his Dad was late picking here up.

Kenny Lee went out into the courtyard to talk, if anybody interesting was out there — there was. About an hour later, Sharon came outside to smoke. Kenny Lee walked up to her. "So, your Dad calls you Ken?"

"Yeah, and my Mom does too."

"How come you go by Kenny Lee Martinez?"

"In the mid 70's I played with a 50's 60's cover band. We did three sets, 50's and 60's, the Beach Boys, and an Elvis set. In the 50's 60's set, I played some Little Richard and Jerry Lee Lewis songs, trying to play like they did. My middle name is Leroy so they started calling me Kenny Lee after Jerry lee."

"I'd like to hear you play sometime. Maybe around breakfast time if I'm passing out meds down here on that piano here."

"Sure! I told my Dad that you're the one that gives me my showers and he said that since you've seen me naked, we have to get married."

Sharon giggled some. "I'll have to talk to Karl and see what he says." We both laughed.

In October, four days after Kenny Lee's birthday, a new director was brought in and Denise was demoted, taking on three people's jobs that were let go. During Wayne's reign, he nearly ruined Greenfields. Many residents that had their pets, dogs and cats that residents just paid big money to get them shots, spaded and neutered the month before had to find them new homes or sell them within one week. A resident who was in the hospital had to do the same. There was no way she could do this.

Other unnecessary things that Wayne did were to turn the water machine off from 9 pm - 6 am. Wayne locked the back door 24/7, a fire hazard. The parking lot was in the back and it was a long walk to the front door. This made it very difficult for the elderly or the disabled. He decided that instead of two meal choices, he would offer only one. The headcook and the kitchen manager threatened to quit if this happened. Wayne's idea was scrapped.

One morning, after breakfast, Gail, Rick, and Kenny Lee happened to be at the same table in the patio. Gail was puffing away on a stogie cigar that someone had given to her, while she was looking through the ash trays." During World War II in Sweden at the border with Norway, "77" was used as a password, because the tricky pronunciation in Swedish made it easy to instantly discern whether the speaker was native Swedish, Norwegian, or German." she told Kenny Lee and Rick. They smiled politely. A caregiver came outside telling Kenny Lee to go to the director's office right away.

In the front office were his nurse practitioner, his case worker and, Wayne. He was told that because he had developed severe pressure sores again where his behind reaches the chair, they couldn't take care of him and that he had to move. The sores happened (present & past tense), not weekly or monthly, frequently — sort of a diaper rash although, he didn't wear diapers. he'd been taking care of this situation on his own since he was in grade school.

Authors note: Kenny Lee had other adventures and friends and talked to many people at Greenfield but this romance needs to move on. This is only one chapter or short story and I don't want to make this into a novel. I hope that you understand.

Around 8 p.m., Kenny Lee arrived at his new home. It was an assisted living home with eight other residents. No one except the caregiver spoke to him. He sat in a recliner and fell asleep all night. He was very tired from frustration.

5:45 a.m. the next morning a doorbell woke up Kenny Lee. It was the caregiver for the next twelve hour shift. Kenny Lee asked the caregiver, her name was Lyn, where he was. He didn't recognize the town of Ahwatukee so, he asked her to write it down for him, four or five times during the day. She finally did. He wanted to call his family to tell them where he had moved to.

At 5:50 p.m., a new caregiver came to work, relieving Lynn. Kenny Lee was in the kitchen eating dinner and didn't hear Lynn leave. The graveyard caregiver's mane was Benny, a Filipino who could hardly speak English. This was odd because none of the residents could speak Filipino. Kenny Lee still had no idea as to where he was.

The afternoon, the owners, Elias and his sister Maria came to the home and talked to Kenny Lee. Kenny Lee finally had an idea as to where he was at.

For the next month, nothing much happened of any consequence. The doorbell would ring at 5:45 a.m. Kenny Lee's usual daily schedule would begin. Lynn, who worked 12/7, would make the residents who were awake breakfast which usually consisted of eggs over easy, which were actually almost over hard, and oatmeal. This was a cold December month so Kenny Lee would then bundle up and go out on the front porch and watch the neighborhood rabbits from the adjoining hills, roaming the streets and yards. When he came inside, he would watch TV with the few residents that didn't stay in their rooms. Those few had Alzheimer's disease or could barely speak English. Many there spoke Spanish. After lunch he would turn on his laptop and 60' and 70' TV or music on the Internet. After dinner, after all of the residents went to their rooms to either watch their TV's or turn in for the night, Kenny Lee would turn on the sleep mode to five hours on the TV remote and then watch TV until he fell asleep. Four times a day, he would get his meds.

The week before Christmas, Kenny Lee was told that his folks would pick him up on Christmas Eve morn. They would celebrate his Dad's eighty-third birthday with other family members who lived in Chandler, AZ. Christmas morning, his folks and he would go to his niece's house to open gifts and eat monkey cake and open presents. Christmas dinner would be at two.

Christmas Eve morn while listening to music from his laptop, he began having severe pains in the lower left side of his back. From experience, he knew it was kidney infection but Lynn insisted that it was constipation and refused to call 911. She tried to give him some medicine but he refused it. Kenny Lee's cell phone was in his bedroom so he couldn't get to it because of his pains. After a while, his pain was so intense that he fell to the floor and putting his head on the seat of the recliner, he cried. Lynn was in the bathroom giving a resident a shower while all of this was happened.

In less than twenty minutes, the doorbell rang. It was his parents. "What are you doing on the floor?" his Dad asked. Kenny Lee lifted his head and instantly, they knew something was seriously wrong. While he was telling them his story, Lynn walked out of the bathroom. "We're taking my son to the hospital!" Instantly, they gathered his clothes and other item and wheeled him to their car. Lynn didn't say a word during all of this. The next three days, Kenny Lee stayed in the hospital with kidney infection, often having morphine shots for the pain. Then, the next three days were spent at his folk's home, celebrating his Dad's birthday and Christmas. When they brought him back to the home, Lynn did some serious apologizing from her heart to Kenny Lee's Mom. She said not a word about this to Kenny Lee.

The next day, Kenny Lee called his case worker and she gave him some phone numbers of assisted living facilities in Chandler and Mesa. He made some calls and two days later, sight unseen of his new studio apartment or the location, he moved to Mesa.

Copper Height s, like the nameless home he had just moved from, for the next six month, nothing much happened of any consequence. Most people living there stayed in their apartments except to eat, smoke, play Bingo, going to the Bible studies and the Protestant or Catholic services. Very few people went to the activities that Betty worked so hard on. This was during January. January, like December was a very cold month. The smokers would only go out for five or ten minutes, depending what brand they smoked, and then hurry back inside. Those that did go to the activities would leave when they were done to return to their apartments.

Across the street were a golf course and a restaurant in the club house. Kenny Lee would sit for hours on the sidewalk near the fifth green in his power wheelchair and talk with and watch the golfers. Down the street was a Methodist church. Kenny Lee would attend the church every Sunday morning. A few weeks later, he found out when and where the church service was at Copper Heights — Wednesdays at 7 pm. His friend from the dining room, Frank attended this service as well as a Bible study on Tuesday nights. The leader of the Bible study was more in tuned with Kenny Lee's Nazarene church doctrine then the 'house' service.

One night at the Wednesday night service, the Baptist pastor made the comment that unless one is baptized, he or she could not go to Heaven. Well, let me tell you, Kenny Lee's hand went up fast. Before the pastor acknowledged him, he started talking.

"I have two examples. Suppose a person was in the hospital watching a TV church service and he gave his life to the Lord and he died. #2) There's two soldiers in Afghanistan talking about religion, one is a Christian and the other one is not. The none Christian is converted and accepts the Lord and then is killed moments later. Where would he go?" Kenny Lee's alarm from his cell phone sounds, "I'm sorry but I have an appointment with the nurse. I have to go." As he was leaving, he heard people comment. "Yeah, he has a good point" and other comments agreeing with what Kenny Lee had just said.

The next morning at breakfast, Frank came to Kenny Lee's table. "Man, Kenny Lee, things were sure stirred up after you left last night. Nobody agreed with Pastor Morris. He finally said that we didn't hear him right. He changed his tune." After his devotions (centered on Isaiah 49:8) breakfast of the facility's usual scrambled eggs, toast and coffee, Kenny Lee went outside. The sky was over casted. A caregiver, dressed in bright yellow scrubs came outside to smoke. Kenny Lee called out, "Man, that's a bright outfit. Stand there for a while and let me work on my tan." The caregiver gave a quick smile and smirk laugh,"

In May of that year, Kenny Lee was sent to the hospital and then to a Nursing Home in Phoenix. Why this move happened is anyone's guess. There were two beds per room. Many of the residents were either drug addicts taking methadone to kick heroin or alcoholics trying to dry out. Kenny Lee made some friends and he was very popular because he was very sharp and clever compared to many of the other residents and some staff. He was asked by many who lived there to help or to explain things for them because he was *SO intelligent*. His IQ was 158 but he was embarrassed to mention it. It wasn't that he was *SO intelligent*. Even though he was well-educated, well-read, and cultured, it was because many minds at the home were fried.

Meals were a joke. The meals were served restaurant style. Everything happened in twenties. The meals, the size of snacks might come twenty minutes or more after they were told to go to the dining room. Twenty minutes later, the drinks were brought in and then maybe twenty minutes later, one packet for the whole meal of salt and pepper was passed out. I kid you not. About a month into his stay, Kenny Lee asked why the meals were so small. He was told that if he wanted more, he needed to ask for a large meal. The next morning, instead of one egg over easy, one piece of toast, yogurt, milk, OJ, and coffee, he had two eggs, two pieces of toast, two yogurts, two, milks, two OJs, and two coffees. Sausage and bacon were scarce. Lunch and dinner were the same with two of each.

Kenny Lee spent many hours of his time downloading music and writing on his laptop. He tended to keep to himself for many hours of the day but he did socialize.

Kenny Lee's main friend here was Bradley, not Brad, from Wisconsin. When he first met Bradley, he smiled. I know something about Wisconsin. It's the top producer of horseradish in the world. It's an underground root that is harvested during the winter and, I love the stuff!" Kenny Lee smiled about the fact that he loved horseradish—not by his knowledge.

Bradley seemed bothered. He quickly added, "50% of U.S. dates are grown in Wisconsin and of course, there are the cheeses." Bradley would tell those who would listen and those who wouldn't. He was born and raised in Adrian, WI. When asked, he said that when he moved to Arizona in 2000, the population was a little over 700. Sitting in his power chair, he was short! From the ground up, he was even shorter. Bradley would go to a skate board park there in Phoenix to ride the half pipes, and (Kenny Lee actually witnessed this.) Bradley would do 360° flips (vertical and also horizontal) in his Quickie manual chair and of course, he used a helmet and a seatbelt.

After about a month, Kenny Lee was granted a daily four hour pass. He would ride his power chair to a junior college library to read or to a strip mall with a Target store. On $101.10 a month, he couldn't do or buy much. His monthly cell phone bill was $65+taxes a month. Phone jacks weren't in any of the rooms.

Medical care was poor. The house doctor looked like the younger member of The Manhattan Transfer. He was also the doctor of two assisted living facilities. More than once, Kenny Lee approached him for matters that were important to him. He was told to go to his room and the doctor would be there shortly. An hour and a half later, Kenny Lee went looking for him. "Oh, he left an hour ago." This happened several times. His nurse practitioner gave Kenny Lee a phone number of an assistant living facility, Desert Sky in Glendale.

During an interview with Patty, Desert Sky director, she told him that he was as cute as a button. He made planes to move in. The only drawback was that it was thirty minutes away and over forty plus minutes away from his parent's home.

His stay at the nursing home lasted for seventy-seven days, almost three months.

Desert Sky, joined with Bella Vita, a skilled nursing facility in the same complex, was in a residential neighborhood. Except for a Burger King and a Circle K on one main road two blocks away and a Jack In The Box a block away on Camelback Rd, stores were scarce. Desert Sky was a two story ex-motel. Kenny Lee had a one room studio.

Desert Sky was a blessing and a nightmare. Everyone, staff and residents alike, seemed to like Kenny Lee. In fact, at an assisted living facility that he moved to during the time that this book was done, Patty, the director there, too, and Kenny Lee were talking. He made the comment that he didn't think that Ella the nurse at Desert Sky liked him. Patty looked up from her paper work and said, "Everyone likes you, Kenneth." She smiled. Kenny Lee smiled an embarrassed smile and said, "Thank-you!"

The nightmare came when, after using the pain med Vicodine, off and on for nine years after a stroke, he was cut off cold turkey by his nurse practitioner. He needed it sometimes when his nerve damaged shoulder would flare up causing immense pain. The alternative pill was Tramadol. To Kenny Lee, this med was a joke. He would sometimes drink alcohol for the pain and he would usually 'over-medicated' himself.

Throughout his medical problems, he never forgot God or the church. He tried the 'house' church and a Methodist church a few bloods away but he didn't care for either one. One Saturday morning while visiting a friend at Bella Vita, Kenny Lee read the Activity board and saw that a church group from Phoenix held a service there every Saturday afternoon at 2 pm. He attended there that afternoon and he worshiped there from there on.

About nine months after Kenny Lee moved in, he had to move out—to the hospital. Infections found their way into his bloodstream and he became septic. Reality mixed with fantasy, hallucinations set in. The next week or more became confusing and blurred for this writer.

Rick, a shaggy haired and bearded man that, given a mule, he could fit into any Roy Rogers TV show as the ol' prospector would come out to the courtyard, smoke two cigarettes and leave. When Kenny Lee and Rick happened to be out at the same time, they would say 'Hi'. That was it for Rick. He wasn't much of a talker or a socializer but soon, they two of them became good friends.

"Hey Rick, what's on your mind today?" Kenny Lee asked one day.

"Oh, I just watched a show on the History Channel. I don't watch TV much but this show said that Cleopatra and her two maiden's suicide. I think Marc Anthony murdered them."

"Oh, yeah? I heard on T.V. that it was Octavian."

"Have you been to Michigan, Ken?"

I've been through there but, like the Three Dog Night song says, 'I really don't remember'.

"Huh?"

"Never mind."

"Well, Mr. Lee, on the northern peninsula, there might not be any breezes but there's a tree that is always quivering. That's why they call it, a quaking aspen. It's a big, tall, beautiful tree, especially in autumn when the leaves are golden.

The trees stand strong and tall but when a breeze breezes, they quake. There are a lot of people here that are like that, right?" Kenny Lee just smiled.

The friends that Kenny Lee left behind were Tracy, a caregiver slash med-mech. He used to follow her on her med pass, sharing stories with her. Kenny Lee didn't have a chance to say 'Good-bye!' While he was in the hospital, she took paternity leave; Rick; Neil, a gentle, kind soul with the beginnings of Alzheimer's. He was from Wisconsin where 50% of U.S. dates are grown and of course, there are the cheeses. He wasn't born and raised in Adrian. He had never heard of Adrian; and then, there is Denise. Kenny Lee called her his little sweetheart. She was the girl next door, petite, pretty, blond, and very sweet. Kenny Lee loved and missed them all dearly.

SLEEP WITH THE ANGELS

Bella Vita Skilled Nursing and Rehab (Part 1)

February 2012 I had developed severe pressure sores and pains where my behind reaches the chair. I was sent to the Bella Vita Skilled Nursing side of the facility, across the lobby from Desert Sky, Bella Vita was pretty much like each of the other rehab hospitals that I lived at in the past years, from stroke to sores, except that here, the food was poor and this one had supervised smoking, twenty minutes each, five times a day. Most of the patients stayed in their rooms all day, probably watching TV. The TV at either facility wasn't very good — not many channels. I miss Food TV, Animal Planet, and the Discovery channels. I was in the 300 halls, Rm. 321 — short term care.

Norman, what can I say about Norman? — quite a bit, actually. I met him in the Desert Sky dining room in July of '11, an alcoholic and a pain in the butt but, he was a fairly nice guy. Some days, he would come down in his briefs (Thank goodness he didn't need diapers. Many residents did.) and the Caregivers would escort him back to his room and he'd come back just the same and they'd escort him back and then bring him back, pantsed, being pushed in a wheelchair with a seatbelt.

Most people thought that he was a pest. I thought that he was a pest. Jan of '12 Norman disappeared.

When I arrived here, I was dazed and amazed (Well, maybe this was a bit melodramatic.) when I saw who my roommate was — Norman. This was about lunchtime. Asleep, he slept until about eight o'clock that evening. My anxiety attack (Now, that *IS* a bit melodramatic.) came when I realized that he may stay up all night when I planned to sleep all night. He didn't and I didn't. Norman was a fall risk so he had a mattress pad that let out a very irritating, very penetrating high pitched shrill when he tried to get out of bed on his own. He almost always made it, too—by night, to the bathroom, by day, down the hall. This night, he shrilled four times. He also had one on his wheelchair so, he would shrill by day when he stood up to walk. That week, I decided that he was still a pain in the butt.

He hated following rules, or so it seemed. The med-carts were off limits to us civilians. Norman got the idea that a protein chocolate drink in a large bottle on top of the carts contained alcohol, and quite a bit of alcohol for that matter—which they didn't. On this 'logical' assumption, he would, with the CNA's and RN's usually watching, would slyly walk out, and shrills blaring, to get a shot or two. He almost always got caught. Finally, I told Norman that the next time he broke the rules, I would tell our RN. Soon, very, very soon, Norman was at the door, watching for his chance for a 'chocolate cocktail'. He was caught.

"How did they catch me?" he asked me.

"I told."

"Why did you tell?"

"Because I told you I would!"

The next morning, the first smoke break was at seven-thirty a.m. I slept in. Norman finally quit shrilling around 4 am. I finally got some sleep. The smoke breaks were at 7:30 am, 11 am, 2 pm, 4:30 pm, and 7 pm daily. Ten-fifty a.m. came and I decided to go out to the smoking patio for my first break. The first person that I met was Mike. Mike repeated single sentences three or more times in a row, each sentence getting softer. "Hi! I'm Ken. What's your name?" I asked.

"My name is Mike. My name is Mike. My name is Mike. I'm just here for my eleven o'clock smoke break, my eleven o'clock smoke break, my eleven o'clock smoke break. I used to live in Texas up until a few years ago. I lived on a cattle ranch. I lived on a cattle ranch. I lived on a cattle ranch."

After Lisa Ann fastened on fireproof aprons on some of the patients and had handed out and lit their cigarettes, she came over to me. "I'm Lisa Ann. Who are you?" she asked.

"I'm Ken. Hi!"

Lisa Ann smiled. "Listen, if you need a cigarette, just this once, I'm sure someone will lend you one if you'll pay them back."

"Thanks but I just came out to have some conversation." Also across the table was a small man wearing a red lumberjack jacket, too heavy for this Arizona February heat. His name was San."

Across the table, Mike started chanting "I need another cigarette. I need another cigarette. I need another cigarette."

I guess it's time to get back to work. They each can have two cigarettes." Lisa said as she walked away to the table where the locker box of cigarettes sat.

"Hi! I'm Ken." San didn't say a word and I waited to see if Sam would but he didn't.

At eleven-twenty, Lisa announced to those that hadn't gone inside yet "Ok, smoke brake is over. Finish your cigarettes."

"When is the next one?" I asked.

"2 pm for twenty minutes." answered Lisa. "See you then. Bingo is at two-thirty in the dining room."

Two o'clock came and I went out a bit early. I decided to sit at another table on the other side of the patio. J.D. was sitting in his wheelchair, reading a western. Dottie, if she would dress the part, could be one of Duke Ellington's sophisticated ladies, was sitting beside him. She was mobile. She could walk. A few minutes later, in the corner of my eye, I saw two ladies come to the table. The first lady was walking her wheelchair from behind. The second lady was using a walker. They sat on either side of me.

The lady with the chair walked around it without locking the wheels, and sat in it at the table. I was afraid that the wheelchair would roll out from behind her and she would fall on her butt. It didn't happen. "I'm Elizabeth."

"Hi! I'm Ken." Then, I turned to the other lady and caught my breath. She was the cutest lady that I had seen in a long time. She smiled at me. "Hi, Ken. I'm Maryann." Maryann and I talked for most of the time that it took her to smoke her only cigarette. I honestly have never done this before but as she was standing up from her chair to leave, I said, "I'm going to fall in love with you someday." She smiled and maybe she winked, I don't remember but from that moment on, I made sure that this was my place at the table. Most of the time, it was.

Nothing really came out of knowing Maryann except a friendship. We never had a deep tête-à-têtes ('*Conversation*'. I like the words *Panache* and *Flair*.). We only talked in the smoking patio. The smoking breaks were the only times for me to have someone to really talk too. Four years ago, I promised myself that I wouldn't get close to anyone in places like this or at the assisted living facilities. Too many people leave and I've moved to often and, people do die.

I have no idea why it took so long to notice but the smoking patio lacked class. It looked like a small prison yard. There were three stucco walls with an automatic glass door on both ends. A semi-circular canvas roof covered half of the patio end-to-end. On the fourth side of the patio was a wrought iron fence with a gate with a security alarm. Cactus and other plants were in clay and plastic pots. On the other side of the fence was a green-brown lawn and ragweed, lots of ragweed. The animals were mourning doves, pigeons, and two stray cats. If it weren't for Maryann's beauty or Dottie's sophistication, the patio would be so dreary.

At mealtimes, I sat with Joe and San. San wouldn't talk, but he was a nice guy. Joe would arrive just about the time I was finishing eating so we didn't talk much.

Wed 29-Feb-12, I was back home at Desert Sky. It felt so good to be back in my own apt. I pretty much stayed here, writing and watching classic TV on the internet and twice, visiting my smoking friends. Two weeks later, I was in the hospital. Infected wounds and sores on my right leg got into my blood system and I almost died — twice.

Sleeping With The Angels (Part ll — This is my favorite part.)

31-Mar-12, I'm back at Bella Vita, section 300 again, weak and tired but my medical file said I was 'Alert'. Next door was another Ken, Ken Richardson.

My time was spent watching TV between three meals a day. My new companions were the CNA's who brought me my meals and came in when I pressed the call button. Mariah was my favorite. She would come in at about 3 a.m. to check on me. She was always quiet but I'm a light sleeper so, I would usually wake up and we'd talk for a while.

One early morning, Mariah asked me if I remembered going to the hospital. "Your file said that you were pretty out of it."

"No! I don't. I was septic, having hallucinations. I had nightmares, severe nightmares until the antibiotics took effect. I started having a very pleasant, very colorful, vivid dream over-and-over again. I was a young school kid at a birthday party. All the kids had grown-up faces that I did remember knowing when I woke up. Some were people that I knew years ago and there was a lady named Maryann that was a patient here. We were playing spin-the-bottle and when I spined the bottle, it pointed at Maryann. I woke up before I kissed her. Now that I think about how sick I was, I'm surprised that I didn't wake up with the angles. I was told that I almost died—twice."

Mariah smiled, "I'm glad that you're here and, she's still here." I smiled.

Another early morning around three, Mariah asked if I had lived at a Rehab or Skilled Nursing Hospital before.

"Oh, yes—yes I have! About nine years ago I had a stroke. I was in the hospital for a week or two and then I was moved to Rehab. They gave me speech therapy, among other things. The second day, I could say 'Hippopotamus'. A day or two later, I could say, Rhinoceros'. It took me over a week to say 'Taco'.

"Isn't it amazing how the mind works." She smiled.

They kept asking me how old I was. I was fifty-five. It finally dawned on me that they were seeing how alert I was. I started telling the nurses that I was seventy-eight. One day, I was asked, "Why do you tell people that your seventy-eight?" I answered, "So people will say, 'Man, don't you look good for your age.'" She really laughed.

My other regular visitors were the nurses who would give me my pills, breathing treatments, and changed my IV bags—three by day, two by night. I told my Mom and Dad that they didn't need to come too often since it would take them almost an hour to get here. I think that they appreciated the gesture although they did come to visit once a week.

Two weeks later, I was moved to the 500 hall, for 'long term patients', for a reason I never really understood. My room was 522-A, first bed. As I was riding into the room on my scooter, I saw Maryann, the lady that just a month before, I said, 'I'm going to fall in love with you someday?' across the hall in 521-A. She smiled and waved. My roommate, Howard was asleep. (Do I have this effect on all of my roommates?) He was a model roommate, most of the time—quiet, real quiet. Sometimes I would talk to him and not realize that he wasn't in the room until I asked him a question.

I began going to the dining room instead of having my meals brought to my room. I met Ken Richardson face to face, not just passing by his room. He was sitting where I had been sitting a month ago. We talked in the dining room and out in the smoking patio. Just as soon as he and I were getting to be friends, he went home. A few weeks later, Ken returned to the congregation again. He moved to my table and we picked up where we left off. Ken was good for my ego because he laughed at my jokes—as bad or corny as they sometimes got.

One evening at dinner, Ken sat, laughing at something I said. I chuckled and I told him that I could make him laugh at anything. Still laughing, he nodded, 'No! and then he said, 'No!"

As Ken, almost silently, was catching his breath, I abruptly said "Purple!" He started laughing again, louder. As he became quieter, I turned to Sonny, sitting at the table across the aisle and said to him, "Say Purple"

"Why?"

"Just say it, please, to Ken."

"Purple!" Ken lost it, laughing.

Forty minutes later, we were out in the smoking patio. Ken was sitting at the next table, a little away from me. I held up a piece of typing paper with the word 'PURPLE' on it. In a few seconds, but what seemed like an eternity, Ken looked over and began laughing harder and louder than before, dropping his cigarette. His power chair was too high for him to reach it on the ground and his reacher wasn't agile enough to do the job. Ken was beside himself but still laughing as everyone outside was starring his way.

Bringing up the smoking patio, when I came back, I picked up where I left off by sitting at my old place at the last table, sitting between Elizabeth and Maryann. Maryann was prettier than I had remembered. I remembered that I was going to fall in love with her. After all, she almost kissed me when we were playing spin-the-bottle in my first delightful dream after the nightmares ended. Without a doubt, spin-the bottle with Maryann was delightful even if it was a dream.

Our friendship bloomed into something sensational for me. I began going into her room to watch TV and to talk. About a month later, I began talking about our times gone by.

"Maryann, do you remember February when I told you, 'I'm going to fall in love with you someday?'"

Again, like the first time, she smiled and she winked." I remember".

"If I did or if I do, would you want me to tell you?"

Maryann paused and then she said, "I don't know."

"Will you think about it?"

"Okay, I will."

A week or maybe a couple of weeks later, I did something that took some nerve and a lot of thought. I'm known as being outgoing but when it comes to women, I can be downright shy. About eight-thirty, about the time I go in to say 'Goodnight!' to my Darlin' li'l girl, I asked if I could kiss her 'goodnight'.

"No!" She paused and then said, "It's too soon."

"That's okay. I'm okay with that." Actually, I was scared out of my skin. I told her that sometime later. We said our goodnights, blowing kisses.

27-June-12: On this afternoon, I was told that the next day I was moving to an assisted living facility in Phoenix. Immediately, I went to Maryann's room to break the news. We both struggled to fight the tears. This is all that I remember about that afternoon. That night at the 7 pm smoke break, I gave the news to my friends. Maryann kept her eyes on me with half a sad smile on that lovely, lovely face, knowing that this was a very difficult time for me. This is all that I remember about the break

That night, after I said good-bye to the smoking group, inside, I found Latisha, a very pretty, very happy young lady from activities. She was getting ready for a 'movie and popcorn' activity. I told my good friend about my move. She hugged me hard, saying 'Good-bye'.

I went back to Maryann's room, her in her bed and I was sitting on my scooter. We watched TV for about thirty minutes before the RN came in to give me my meds. "I knew you'd be here." she said as she handed me the pills and a small cup of water.

As I was taking my pills, Maryann sat up on the side of the bed. She took the empty water and pill cups from me, got out of bed, walked over to the wastebasket and threw them away. This was a bit hard for her without using her walker. Then, after she pulled some loose hairs from my shirt, she hugged me long and longer. After this, something incredible happened—she kissed me hard, with love and like.

"I feel like I'm going to cry!" I said misty eyed.

"That was supposed to make you happy."

"That's why I'm going to cry. I'm happy. I'm very happy."

She smiled what could be read as a weeping smile. "I don't want you to leave this place. Now, my Darling Ken, go sleep with the Angels."

I know that I slept but it didn't seem like I did. I was pretty restless. At my usually 5:40 morning wake-up time, my CNA came in. I needed help with my socks and shoes. That being done, I headed down to the 300 day room for coffee and the rest of the five o'clock news. I was still smiling inside from the night before.

After my 7 am pill, I headed out to the smoking patio. I always stopped at Leah's, my social workers' office to say good morning but she hadn't come in yet. Outside, there were many good-byes again.

"What time are you leaving, Ken?"

"Don't know yet."

Back inside, I stopped into see Leah. "You don't seem your happy self. What's wrong?" I told her that it was too fast for me to do this. "Because of your girl, huh? Well. Ken, would tomorrow be better?"

"Can we do this?" I smiled.

"I can."

"Thank-you, so much."

I rushed to Maryann's room to tell her the news. "I'm happy but you're still leaving." she told me. At the 11 o'clock smoking break, I spread the news.

29-June-12: I moved to Rose Court in Phoenix. I was proud to show my picture of my Maryann. One and all said that she was adorable, pretty, or beautiful and I told her that, each of the seven times we talked on the phone over the week-end.

The next day, I saw Harley and Margie of Greenfields Assisted Living fame a few years ago and also Wm. O., a resident that lived across the hall from me at Desert Sky. Harley, like Norman had mellowed out but he still uses 'I', 'I', 'I', 'Me', 'Me, 'Me' quite a bit. Bill does, too. I avoided these two. I avoided Margie then and now.

Sunday night, I couldn't sleep at all. About 3:30 a.m., I e-mailed my former social worker and my friend, Leah. Many hours came and then, more hours came without a response. I called her and I was told that she didn't receive my e-mail. I read the address to her but it wasn't hers. I laughed, "I wrote the address wrong on your e-mail. Someone got my e-mail about Maryann, my sweetie." Leah was laughing, too. "Maybe it's just out there, out there in space."

We said our good-byes and I resent the e-mail.

"Leah, It's only been a couple of days but, I'm doing fine. I'm a bit lonely but, it's only been a couple of days. Many people told me that I'm

a likeable guy and that, I'll make friends but . . . Oh, well, It's only been a couple of days. I miss, really miss Maryann. I almost feel like I've been through another divorce. She and I talk often even though It's only been a couple of days. (Isn't it nice to have 'copy & paste'? ☺) I regret that I never told her that I love her but I think that she feels it. Heck, everybody else figured it out.

The food is better here. This morning I had a cheese & onion omelet that looked like an omelet instead of scrambled eggs w/ cheese.

It's only been a couple of days but, (cut & paste is getting to be a nasty habit, huh?) I'm going to make an effort to come by in a couple of weeks from now. I want to wait a little while because too many people come back to visit too soon for us to know they had gone.

Please say 'Hi!' to the 500 staff, Lisa Ann (Activities), and Ashley (near your door) for me. I really miss you but, it's only been a couple of days. ☺ Thank-you so much for all of your help and friendship and, stay warm

Could I send an e-mail to someone (ie: Maryann or Ashley), in care of you? If so, I wouldn't have a colored font or any background and—staff could e-mail me back with their address but, Maryann or Ken Richardson wouldn't have an e-mail address there. If we can't do this, do you have any suggestions?

Love is like a flower
but, for the life of me
I have no idea why!
Ken Martinez'

!

Nearby on the Rose Court property was a small park surrounded by an iron fence. It was a lovely park with shade trees, a slightly neglected lawn bordered with small lava rocks, and a lot of plants and flowers. Early the next morning, I rode out there for some quiet. Sparrows and mourning doves and a few roadrunners were in the grass looking for their breakfast. A pigeon, walking on the lava, tripped and fell. After a minor struggle, it walked away. I called Ken to tell J.D. "He's right here. Here J.D., Ken Martinez wants to talk with you."

J.D. rarely laughed. He would usually smile a sly smile and point to the joke teller. He said "A drunk pigeon, huh?" and then, he laughed.

I also received Leah's answer. She seemed moved by my affections for Maryann. The rest of the e-mail was . . .

> *As far as the sending of emails through me to other folks in the building: I do not mind if you write one email to each person that you are hoping to reach and make sure to give them all of the contact info they would need to reach you in the future, mailing address, phone #, email. I can print out and deliver one email for each, but beyond that, I can't continue to go back and forth with information/emails. You know how busy it gets around here!*

Leah Greenstein, MSW
Social Services-Long Term Care

To me, what she wrote was just common sense but at Bella Vita, a lot of the patients lacked common sense.

At this point of my story, I want to travel back to Friday afternoon because I want the labor of this story, this labor of love, to close with Maryann and me—especially Maryann. At 1:17 pm, I was in her room talking We were keeping our eyes on each other while listening to the TV when she, out of the corner of her eye, saw a man looking into my room across the hall. 'I think that your ride is here, Sweetie.'

'I'm Ken. Are you here for me?' I grudged. He told me that he was and that it was time to leave for Rose Court. As they were taking me from Maryann's room, she smiled, saying, 'I'm really going to miss you, Sweetie. Sleep with the angels.' She threw me a kiss and I reached up to catch it while I smiled a sadder than blue smile with cloudy, rainy eyes and said, 'Good-bye my Sweetheart and thank-you.' After then, in a very quiet voice, too soft for anyone to hear, I said to my Baby, 'I gave you my 'only-ness'. I love you so much so now, continue sleeping with the angels.'

. . . outside her door, down the hall. 'Wait! Stop! Wait!' The voice became still.

TO BE CONTINUED

THE AFTERWARD

Thank-you for reading my book. I have so much more of my life to write about—past and future stories.

No one from my stories died in real life except Joey. My friend did die while riding his motor scooter from work—drunk, like Joe Kehn did in 'Just Jokin". Also, in one of my favorite stories, you're told on the first page, twice, that Cory died. I used the character of Cory to kill off some bad habits and ideas that I had. Cory was partly me and partly someone else. I was also able to use some of my philosophy and ideas through him and other characters.

Sandy is now director of the orphanage, maybe retired, in Redding, CA. where the story took place.

Until next time, remember those famous first & last words from TV's M*A*S*H psychiatrist," Dr. Sidney Freedman, "Ladies and gentlemen, take my advice—pull down your pants and slide on the ice."

A BLUE LOVE STORY:
The Velveteen Rabbit or How Toys Become Real is a children's novel written by Margery Williams and illustrated by William Nicholson. First © 1922 by Avon Books—All Rights Reserved. Now, it's Public Domain.

STREET FOOD, BE-BOP, AND GEO. (A 13 HOUR TALE):
1   *'Whiter Shade Of Pale'—Written by Keith Reid © 1967.* Used by permission from WikipediA
2   *'There Commin' To Take Me Away'—Written by Napoleon Jerry Samuels A/K/A/ Nepolean XIV (They were the same person.)* © 1966. Used by permission from WikipediA
3   *'Tiny Dancer'—Written by Elton John & Bernie Taupin ©1971 Dick James Music Limited.* Used by permission from WikipediA